JUST IN TIME

JUST IN TIME

Second Edition

David Hutchins

Gower

First edition published 1988 by Gower Technical Press Ltd.

Published by
Gower Publishing Limited
Gower House
Croft Road
Aldershot
Hamphsire GU11 3HR
England

Gower
Old Post Road
Brookfield
Vermont 05036
USA

David Hutchins has asserted his right under the Copyright, Designs
and Patents Act 1988 to be identified as the author of this work.

British Library Cataloguing in Publication Data
Hutchins, David
   Just in time. – 2nd ed.
   1. Inventory control 2. Total productive maintenance
   I. Title
   658.7′87

   ISBN 0 566 07798 1

Library of Congress Cataloging-in-Publication Data
Hutchins, David.
   Just in time / David Hutchins. — 2nd ed.
      p.   cm.
   Includes index.
   ISBN 0-566-07798-1
   1. Just-in-time systems.   I. Title.
TS157.4.H88   1999   98-8748
658.5′6—dc21   CIP

Typeset in Plantin Light by IML Typographers, Chester and
printed in Great Britain by MPG Books Ltd, Bodmin.

CONTENTS

LIST OF FIGURES AND TABLES

Figures

Tables

PREFACE TO SECOND EDITION

The desire to write the first edition of *Just in Time* was prompted by a sudden explosion of interest in the subject in the late 1980s. The motivation was not so much a wish to ride the wave but to attempt to redirect the focus of attention. At that time there were many misperceptions as to both the content and purpose of the concept. The two most highly flawed perceptions were firstly that JIT was something that we forced on to our unwilling suppliers and secondly that JIT was an outcome of MRPII (Materials Resource Planning), a software program designed to improve production efficiency. Unfortunately, despite the passing of several years since that time, both of these misperceptions are still strongly held beliefs in many organizations. Probably for this reason, together with a lack of appreciation of the true power of JIT, the concept has never achieved its full potential in the majority of non-Japanese-influenced organizations.

The motivation to produce this second edition was stimulated by a long lingering desire to make an attempt to bring the realization of the potential benefits of JIT to a wider audience. It was also influenced by the growing use of the European Excellence Model as a reference for self-evaluation of business performance.

JIT impacts on several aspects of the Excellence Model and in particular the section on 'Processes'. In order to assist in the cross-referencing between JIT concepts and the relevant elements of the model, a new chapter has been added.

A further development since the first edition has been a growing awareness of the value of Total Productive Maintenance (TPM) and its relevance to JIT. For this reason, new material has been included to explain this concept. Total Productive Maintenance was developed in Japan in the 1970s. However, its delay in reaching the West was largely due to difficulties in supporting such participative programmes as QC Circles and other forms of self-managing work team activities. The revised work also acknowledges the powerful impact on JIT resulting from the extremely effective 6 Sigma concept developed by Motorola in the USA. This concept, which is really a response to the Taguchi-influenced Japanese goal of eliminating variation from a process, has subsequently spread throughout the Motorola supply chain and into such organizations as IBM. This increases the relevance of the chapter on manufacturing aspects.

In summary the message is this: look after the process and the product will look after itself.

David Hutchins

PREFACE TO FIRST EDITION

The desire to write this book has been building up for some seven to ten years, and has finally been prompted by the recent explosive interest in the topic.

If the book had appeared in 1980, chances are that it would have remained on the shelf. Now, regardless of how popular the book may or may not be, its subject is being discussed and reported more actively than almost any other management topic. The reason for this explosive growth of interest is that during the early 1980s the West has woken up to the fact that its manufacturing industries are in a deep crisis which goes beyond anything experienced in the years since World War II. Unlike previous recessions, that of the early 1980s is not a temporary affair, but represents an irrevocable change in the entire pattern of world trade. Furthermore, the crisis is unlikely to go away in our lifetime (see, for instance, Dr J. M. Juran's Paper *Meeting the Competitive Challenge*).

Part of the reason for the crisis has been the revolution caused by the infamous chip. But at least as important has been the phenomenal economic growth of Japan through the last two decades. In 1952 Japan's Gross National Product was one-third that of either Britain or France: in 1980 it was greater than the combined GNP of those two countries. Japan now has over 50 per cent of world trade in seven of the world's ten leading products.

The only way in which Western industry can survive is to face up to that challenge. It will mean changes for all Western companies whether publicly or privately owned – drastic changes. Like a sick person, some companies may not survive the operation, but without it the prospect may be lingering death.

This book has been written because I do not believe that failure is inevitable. Indeed, with the vigorous application of the techniques and concepts described in the book, any company with the will to do so can face up to any competition. More important than those techniques is the attitude of mind, not just of managers and workers, but primarily presidents, chairpersons, vice-presidents and directors. Only deep and sustained commitment at these levels will give any hope of success. The title of the book, *Just in Time*, refers to a business objective for the reduction and eventual elimination of inventory; an objective whose description really belies its real value, which is far greater. The concepts and techniques involved can be applied in any organization, whether or not inventory is a problem, because, basically, they represent another way of managing a business. It is believed – and proven– to be a better way!

None of the concepts described in the book is theoretical; each has been tried and tested in successful organizations around the world. As an American expert commented recently, 'these concepts have no passport'.

Everything contained in the book is based upon my personal experiences, and examples can be found across a broad spectrum of industries. They are just as applicable to service industries as to manufacturing.

David Hutchins

ACKNOWLEDGEMENTS

The research upon which this book is based spans a twenty-year period. During that time I have met and worked with many people, each of whom has made a contribution to my experience in one way or another. To list them all would take up far too much space, so I hope those not mentioned will forgive me and know that they have not been forgotten.

I should like to make a specific point of thanking three groups of people – my Japanese friends, the Juran Institute and my colleagues in David Hutchins International Limited – not forgetting my wife whose toleration of and support for my obsession with my work make everything possible.

My Japanese friends include the late Mr Noguchi, Executive Director of the Japanese Union of Scientists and Engineers, who was extremely helpful on fact-finding missions; the late Professor Kaoru Ishikawa, who unfortunately passed away after the first edition, introduced me to a better understanding of Japanese concepts, and was always helpful; my very good friend Professor Naoto Sasaki, and Dr Noriaki Kano, the winner of the Deming Prize for literature in 1998, without whose help I would never have gained the insights I have.

I should also like to thank especially Dr J. M. Juran, who has in the past few years provided me with the depth and breadth of knowledge to enable me to put the concept of JIT into effective practice. I must also include the staff of the Juran Institute, and particularly Howland Blackiston, for their generous hospitality and assistance.

Finally, I must thank the clients of the David Hutchins Consulting Group who have provided me with the opportunity to put theory into practice, without which the book would be of little value.

DH

SOME TERMS USED IN THIS BOOK

CONTINUOUS PROCESS IMPROVEMENT   The term used to describe a methodology whereby the JIT objective is achieved. Basically, all improvement is made project by project, and projects are tackled in a systematic manner. A project is a problem scheduled for solution.

5S   A housekeeping concept aimed at improving both the conditions of work and the efficiency of processes.

JUST IN TIME (JIT)   The term used to indicate that a process is capable of instant response to demand without the need for any overstocking, either in expectation of the demand being forthcoming or as a result of inefficiencies in the process.

JUST IN TIME GOAL   The total elimination of inventory at all stages in the process.

MRPII   A computer-based scheduling system based on forecasting. In other words it is a 'push' system.

OVERALL EQUIPMENT EFFECTIVENESS (OEE)   A set of ratios to help monitor continuous improvement to process and equipment performance.

PROBLEM   A problem is a process out of control.

PROCESS   With regard to JIT, the ultimate process is represented by the entire network of events, including both products and services, which results in a response to a given need. The process commences with the initial production of raw materials and ends with the satisfaction of the end users' needs.

   The term process is also used to describe sub-processes within the overall system or process.

TOC   Theory of Constraints developed by Dr E. Goldratt, the process of which is illustrated in *The Goal* (Goldratt, Eliyahu M. and Cox, Jeff, 1986, Gower). In this book, an operations manager discovers that one operations unit is slower than others; he discovers a bottleneck. TOC is a 'push' system at some points and a 'pull' system at others.

TOTAL PRODUCTIVE MAINTENANCE (TPM) A participative approach aimed at making significant reductions to plant and process stoppages and improving the flow of production.

PRELUDE – HOW GOOD ARE YOU NOW?

In the time between the completion of the manuscript for the first edition and the present, both the US National Quality Award (Baldrige Award) and the European Quality Award have been launched. Whilst it is acknowledged that both awards are capable of further development, they remain at this time the best criteria available for an organization to judge its capabilities against. Although the two awards are structured differently, the architects of each have taken into account all of the criteria contained in the other, including the content of the Japanese Deming Prize which preceded both by some three and a half decades.

Whilst the criteria in the self-assessment programme of the awards are clear, they are of course very general and open to interpretation. For this reason, this second edition of *Just in Time* includes a chapter at the end which will enable the reader to evaluate his or her organization in relation to the elements relevant to JIT.

The European Excellence Model

The model contains nine key elements as shown in Figure 11.1 (see page 222). The middle element, 'Processes', is the means by which the organization uses the skills and competencies of its people to achieve success. The processes and the people are the 'enablers' which provide the 'results'.

The model was developed as the framework for the European Quality Award and it is designed to indicate that People Satisfaction, Customer Satisfaction, Impact on Society and Business Results are achieved through concentration on Leadership, People Management, Policy and Strategy, Resources, and Processes.

The elements that are most directly impacted by a serious JIT policy are:

- Leadership – establishment of JIT as a business-wide initiative
- People Management – for total involvement in improvement activities including autonomous maintenance teams
- Policy and Strategy – for the deployment of JIT goals

- Resources – almost all aspects
- Processes – these are at the heart of JIT
- People Satisfaction – from participation in successful results
- Customer Satisfaction – particularly if part of a supply chain
- Business Results – mainly in the area of financial and non-financial measures.

Clearly JIT can be a significant aspect in the process of achieving substantial improvement to business results. The final chapter of the book will enable the reader to reference their own company's JIT performance against the European Excellence Model criteria and to plan how to make good any deficiencies.

1 INTRODUCTION

Imagine a manufacturing plant or continuous process operation of any description similar to your own but with no finished goods inventory, no stock yard, no so-called 'work-in-progress' (if it were progressing it would not be a problem), no unscheduled stoppages or breakdowns, no waiting time, no rework, set-up times almost non-existent and all processes running at full speed all of the scheduled operating time. What would be the costs of running such an operation if it were producing the same goods as your own in the same quantities? How much floor space would be required? How much labour? How much raw material? How much plant? What would be the lead times if every product went from first operation through to finishing with no hold-ups at all? What would be the credit period for payments on such rapid order processing? How much bigger share of market would you be able to take if your customers were able to see this effect?

What are the equivalent costs of running your operation as it is today? What is the difference?

Unless you are already operating according to the principles laid down in this book, the chances are that the differences will be enormous. Of course, you might say: 'The differences are big but that does not mean that they are too big. We employ top professional production and industrial engineers who spend their lives trying to improve processes and to drive down costs. We could probably make some improvements but nothing that would be that dramatic. If this were possible, we would have seen it already and have made the improvements.'

Do not believe it.

There are many companies that thought just that. Until, that is, they visited Japan, or some other place where these principles had been adopted. For example, the managers of a medium-sized electronics company which manufactures small transceivers in the UK made the trip to Toyota. There they saw huge metal forming dies for the shaping of the main body parts being changed in less than two minutes. They were aware that in the West the same operation took approximately one shift to complete.

In their own company, the change of dies for the stamping of the almost microscopic components of their products also took several hours. However, from the Toyota example, they found a way to reduce the time to just one minute forty-five seconds! The effect on production was dramatic. Prior to the improvement, the economic batch sizes for the small parts were in the order of hundreds of thousands of units to justify the long set-up times. Now, due to the improvement, it became possible to make only enough to keep the next downstream operation in good supply. As a result, an entire room was released from being used as a store to being available for an increase in productive capacity. Examples such as this can be found throughout industry today.

Included in this edition of *Just in Time* for the first time are two new chapters. One of these explains the concept of Total Productive Maintenance (TPM); whilst this has existed in Japan since 1971, it has been slow to spread to the West. The reason for this is that it requires the development of Quality Circle-style autonomous workgroup activities before it can be fully effective. Unfortunately, for a variety of reasons that will be explained in the relevant chapter, the West has not found it easy to develop such initiatives. However, some organizations are managing to do so and there is no practical reason why the same should not be possible elsewhere provided the will is there to succeed. The other new chapter shows how JIT can influence the scoring of the European Quality Award and where it fits the criteria. This could be a useful chapter for the would-be JIT-based organization to evaluate its own level of achievement.

Just taking the Total Productive Maintenance aspect of JIT production, the following comments have been made:

> 'Companies that have embraced TPM have good reason to be sold on it: it's one of the surest ways to increase capacity while lowering costs. Process industries should be particularly interested in TPM, because it's easy to rack up huge losses when you're running a continuous, integrated process.' – Raymond Floy, Exxon Chemical Baytown Site Manager, Internet source.

> 'We've set a goal to double shareholder value by our two-hundredth anniversary in 2002. The only way we'll achieve that goal is by improving equipment reliability through focus on the elements of TPM.' – Doug Martin, TPM Manager at Dupont.

> 'Twenty per cent of our machines are very old – 35–40 years old – but with TPM we can still use them very well – as well as our new machines.' – Nissan Yokohama Plant.

In two years from the introduction of TPM the Nissan plant reduced stop-pages to the line from 9 000 per month to 1 284!

Why TPM? It was developed in Japan in the early 1970s as an adaptation of the highly successful Quality Circles concept. With TPM the workers were able to focus their attention on process-related improvement opportunities. It is often said in Japan that if you look after the process, the product will look after itself. Manufacturers such as Toyota were trying to create 'Just in Time' supply chains. With virtually no buffer stocks to fall back on, production personnel were under great pressure to supply a constant stream of high-quality goods. Unexpected breakdowns would snap the supply chain. From being 'inevitable', breakdowns suddenly became 'unacceptable'. The challenge was – how to smooth the ups and downs of the production lines?

Because of the awesome power of the TPM concept, this edition of *Just in Time* devotes a whole chapter to its features.

In the same chapter, reference will be made to the Theory of Constraints developed by Eliyahu Goldratt and expounded in his book *The Goal*, also published by Gower. Under this theory it is suggested that all inventory is created by bottlenecks. If the bottlenecks are removed, the inventory disappears.

In the following chapters it will be shown that JIT is most effective when it is operated throughout the entire supply chain and, in particular, in our own operation. In effect, the JIT supply chain appears as a completely vertically integrated process. This is an important point because many people wrongly believe that JIT is something that we impose on our suppliers but do nothing about ourselves. There should be no imposition on suppliers as such. The truly JIT company treats its suppliers as being part of a mutually dependent chain. This implies long-term relationships with preferred suppliers rather than adversarial relationships through multiple sourcing.

Each chapter in this book is designed to cover a specific aspect of JIT, the only exception being Chapters 4 and 5, which together deal with the totally linked aspects of design and manufacture. Discussion of these topics has been divided into two chapters solely with the aim of making their assimilation simpler. Each chapter begins by outlining its main theme and concludes with a summary of the main considerations related to JIT.

The main object of the book is to provide the reader with, first, a vision of what is currently being achieved with JIT internationally, and then to lead the reader, chapter by chapter, through the philosophy and concepts to a final discussion of the organizational aspects which must be considered by those who decide to implement the processes involved.

Virtually all the case examples are included in this chapter, the object being to provide an insight into the extraordinary potential offered by concepts related to JIT. As the reader progresses through the book, it might prove beneficial to refer back to these case examples from time to time, as their relevance becomes more apparent. Reading the text, it will become apparent that, unlike many other management concepts, JIT is part of a fundamentally different approach to management, which when fully developed will help to create a totally new industrial culture. It is my sincere belief that historians of the future will look back on the 1980s and 1990s as the beginning of a new industrial era, as important in its own way as the growth of the factory system in the eighteenth century, and the dawn of scientific management in the early 1900s.

The book is intended not so much as a reference book, but as a means of conveying an idea or philosophy. However, it is hoped that the chapter summaries will in part satisfy the need for reference material, and help in the use of the book for study purposes. The suggested further reading has been carefully selected, and these texts are well known to me. Serious readers should study that material if the goal of JIT is to be realized.

The goal of JIT is not new. The basic desire for continued reductions in material resource requirements has probably always been in the minds of conscientious business managers. What is new, relatively at least, is the means by which the goal is now being accomplished.

The achievement of JIT may sometimes be a spin-off or by-product of a Company-wide Quality Improvement (CQI) programme, which is itself an expansion of strategy and policy deployment. Alternatively, it may be one of a number of specific goals in such a programme. Either way, CQI is fundamental to the achievement of JIT, and the principles described in this book all form part of that concept.

Company-wide Quality Improvement is the term used to describe an approach to company management which now forms the basis of management in Japan, and is rapidly being adopted by many of the world's leading companies. The concepts are only just beginning to be grasped by most Western organizations. CQI is fundamentally different from Western-style management and is not to be confused with quality assurance or quality control. CQI is applicable to any type of company whether product or service based.

It is worth noting that whilst JIT may or may not be one of the outcomes of CQI-style management, JIT cannot reasonably be achieved without it. CQI itself represents a fundamental realignment of industrial cultural values, and in all but a few companies requires a radically different approach to organizational development. This difference will be made clear through the text of this book.

There is a common misconception that JIT is concerned with such topics as CIM (Computer Integrated Manufacture), MRPII (Materials Resource Planning), and so on. Important though these concepts are to industrial efficiency, they are not in fact integral to the achievement of JIT. For example, in his widely acclaimed book *World Class Manufacturing* (Free Press, 1986), Richard Schonberger states 'The world class manufacturers in Japan have a lot to learn from North Americans about using the computer for management planning; while they learn those lessons, the North Americans have the task of turning off the features of MRP that are made redundant when JIT goes on stream.'

Conversely, JIT must be taken into account if such approaches are being introduced. The authors of works on such topics may judge the relevance of JIT to these concepts – they do not form part of the treatment of JIT offered in this book.

It is worth noting that the same factors which lower the efficiency of MRPII will also affect the achievement of JIT.

The fate of new concepts

Every so often new management concepts are launched into the business world. Conferences are hastily arranged to inform (or sometimes misinform) an eager public. 'Experts' appear from nowhere and for a while the media are filled with accounts from both advocates and sceptics alike.

At one time the source of such concepts was mainly the United States. From that great industrial nation an almost endless stream of new ideas and concepts flowed to occupy the minds of consultants, academics and industrialists alike. More recently Japan has become a more fashionable source and during the past few years industry has been inundated with claims by various students of Japan that a concept they had discovered in that mysterious country contained the secrets of Japan's recent success. Consequently, concepts such as Quality Circles, Statistical Process Control and parts per million defects have all been the subject of much discussion and experiment, and now – more recently – JIT.

Successes have been impressive, but the failures have proved depressing. In the case of Quality Circles, for example, it is my opinion that whilst there are some very dramatic success stories, over 80 per cent of all attempts to introduce the concept have failed. (This is, incidentally, a purely subjective assessment.)

Popular belief is that the failures have been due either to the likelihood that a concept which has produced spectacular results in one culture may not necessarily be appropriate to another or, alternatively, to the possibility that the claims from the advocates are excessive and are therefore bound to lead ultimately to disappointment. More probable is that either the host organization effectively failed to implement the concept correctly or the advice given was either incomplete or inaccurate.

In the case of concepts introduced into the West from Japan, the likelihood is that they were not fully researched prior to introduction. For example, in the case of Quality Circles, Statistical Process Control, and so on, Westerners are usually under the impression that these concepts stand on their own and can be taken off the shelf and introduced without any form of alignment.

They fail to realize that in a Japanese organization no concept stands on its own. Every concept of management forms part of a tightly woven interactive web which provides the whole organization with a high degree of interdependence. That is why it was stated earlier that JIT is just one of the goals of CQI. CQI also embraces the other concepts mentioned such as Quality Circles.

Basically, CQI is the term used to describe, in common language, a concept well established in Japanese organizations from the bottom to the top. The objective is to form an organization where everyone at all levels and in all functions can work together to make their company the best in its field of operation. If one could visualize such an organization in which everyone is totally interactive, where departmental goals are equal to company goals, and each person is being regarded as the expert in his or her own job, an extremely powerful dynamic picture would emerge. It is this *Gestalt* effect, of the whole being the sum of the parts, which forms the basis of Japanese management thinking.

This philosophy of management is not the product solely of Japanese culture, or indeed postwar American intervention. It is a combination of both. Fortunately, the techniques of greatest importance to Western or non-Japanese organizations tend to be those introduced from the United States. It is the philosophy behind the concepts which has largely been influenced by the Japanese.

Disappointment with the results achieved by non-Japanese organizations which have already experimented with those concepts has undoubtedly led to scepticism regarding the validity of others. It is only to be expected therefore that JIT will be cautiously studied by those who have been subjected to such experiences. Not only should the content of this book give confidence to such readers, it should also shed some light on the reasons why other concepts which they may already have attempted could be worth a second attempt using some of the ideas contained in this book.

Overview of JIT

The prime goal of JIT is the achievement of zero inventory, not just within the confines of a single organization, but ultimately throughout the entire supply chain. To achieve even partial success, it is necessary to think far beyond the scope of stock control to virtually all aspects of management control. For example, if the questions 'Why do we keep stocks at all?' or 'Why do we have work-in-progress other than product actually being processed at any one moment?' are considered in depth, a wide range of disassociated causes becomes evident, any one of which may be broken down into broader and broader ranges of sub-causes or detail.

By way of illustration, let us consider the problem of raw material stocks.

These may be held because suppliers' quality is unpredictable. Further analysis may show that many suppliers are used, each of which has its own unique shortcomings. In one case, material specifications may be of dubious quality. In others, difficulties may be evident in the ability to hold tolerances, and so on. These deficiencies will in themselves also lead to further unique undesirable aspects. In addition, deliveries may be erratic or quantities supplied may vary from contract requirements.

Raw materials may also be held for internal reasons such as inaccurate forecasting, machine breakdown, quality-related losses on current products, and a host of other causes all of which are outside the scope of the materials control department and would require considerable collaboration across several functions before improvements can be made.

It is obvious from this that JIT is not an easily achieved objective. In fact, many highly competent managers would be inclined to believe that because stock control is such an obvious target for reducing working capital, there would be little opportunity left for improvement. They might also believe that because there had been several decades of applied scientific management, the point had already been reached where the cost of any further improvement would significantly outweigh the benefits. The chances are that they would be wrong. Experience suggests that few non-Japanese companies will have even scratched the surface of what is ultimately possible from the intensive application of the techniques described in this book.

For most organizations, even those with a history of rigorous application of scientific management techniques by the most competent of specialists, hitherto unprecedented reductions in stock levels, work-in-progress and finished goods stocks become possible. These stock reductions will be accompanied by sufficiently great improvements in quality and production to result in unheard-of cost reductions. Companies which have only recently begun to achieve these results are likely to provide severe competition to others less well advanced.

> Through the diligent application of the techniques and concepts described it is possible eventually to achieve a seemingly impossible reduction in cost equal to 20–60 per cent of sales revenue, and increases in market share beyond those achievable by most other means.

Even if this approach achieves a mere fraction of those claims, the benefit to cost ratio will outperform rival opportunities for investment, often by orders of magnitude.

Consider, for example, a hypothetical company with:

- £100 million sales revenue
- £50 million working capital
- £10 million profit
- £20 million quality-related loss.

A principal cause of high work-in-progress is found to be the scrapping and reworking of a major component. This has effectively held up the production of the product, and caused a pile-up of stock for related components. (These components will still be arriving from the supplier on schedule.)

A study shows that annual quality-related losses due to this problem are:

Scrap	£2 million
Rework or repair	£1 million
Warranty	£2 million
Inspection	£0.5 million
Design modifications	£0.5 million
Total	£6 million

The increase in work-in-progress due to interruptions caused by the deficiency amounts to £2 million.

Therefore in this example the total elimination of the defect will save £6 million in quality-related costs and reduce working capital by £2 million, resulting in a total reduction of £8 million in the first year. If it is assumed that the cost of achieving the improvement was £0.5 million, the benefit outweighed cost by 16–1.

Of course, this is a hypothetical example, but the figures used were not unrealistic.

Companies which have embarked upon approaches similar to those outlined in this book are claiming that the cost of poor quality is being reduced from values which were initially estimated to range from 20–40 per cent of sales revenue to less than half that amount within three to five years of commencing their efforts.

One large international company claimed that, in addition, sales revenue had risen by an adjusted 56 per cent mainly as a result of the improvement gained.

What alternative approach could produce better returns on investment?

Scope of the book

The book is intended to meet the following objectives:

1 to provide a means by which the opportunities offered by JIT-related concepts can be thoroughly evaluated;

2 to provide sufficient guidance to enable an organization to plan, organize and commence its own introductory programme or to enhance existing efforts;

3 to provide a basis for research by students of management science;

4 to link JIT requirements to the criteria of the European Excellence Model.

It may have surprised some readers to read earlier that the concepts underlying the means by which JIT can be achieved have little or nothing to do with computers or computer programs. In fact, the Kanban System (which is more than adequately described in Richard Schonberger's book *Japanese Manufacturing Techniques*, Free Press, 1982), a central element in the Toyota approach to JIT, makes no use at all of computers.

That is not to say that computer-based systems are wrong, or that they cannot produce benefits bearing directly on the achievement of JIT. Without the philosophies, concepts and techniques described in this book, it is unlikely that any really significant moves toward JIT could be achieved with or without computer-aided systems. Even where such means are being used, the concepts of JIT will be necessary to debug and make optimum use of the facilities provided.

Any company which has introduced computerized stock control, MRPII and so on, with the hope that these alone will enable the achievement of JIT, but which has not taken account of the principles described in this book is almost certain to be disappointed. In some cases it will be found that the problems will still persist, notwithstanding that considerable investment has been made.

These are some key points to remember:

1 'Just in Time' is not a jargon term for a new concept. It represents a goal. That goal is the ultimate total elimination of inventory, minimal work-in-progress and is monitored by a constant reduction in

so-called working capital (the paradox being that it is not actually working at all).

2 It is not an 'add on' to the existing style of management. It can be achieved only as a result of a fundamental change in management thinking and industrial cultural values. (The case examples included in this chapter will illustrate the radical changes which might be required in most organizations if JIT is to be achieved.)

3 Companies which are at the cutting edge of JIT have achieved so much that every established norm relating to stock, work-in-progress, quality and reliability must be swept aside before any real move towards closing the gap can be made.

4 Companies at the cutting edge will be aware of the European Excellence Model. JIT can play a major part in the scoring against the relevant criteria. These can be found in a new chapter (Chapter 11) towards the end of this book.

5 JIT is only one element or goal which will be the outcome of a concept which can harness the resources of everyone on the payroll to work towards making their company the best in its business. The concept behind this achievement is known as Company-wide Quality Improvement (CQI).

6 CQI is fundamentally different from previous Western concepts of management and is not to be confused with quality assurance or quality control. These are both part of CQI – but so are many other concepts.

7 While considerable progress can be made towards the achievement of JIT, it nevertheless represents a long-term goal. As with 'zero defects', the end objective is desirable, but it is a goal to be aimed at not in the expectation that it will be achieved but, rather, that all norms will be swept aside and improvement, however small, will always be possible.

Some readers will undoubtedly feel that their companies are already in good shape with regard to JIT.

For industries accustomed to working on tight margins and high stock turnover, the economic effect of even a fraction of a percentage point on stock levels is only too obvious. Even for such industries – perhaps particularly for such industries – very substantial gains may still be possible through the application of JIT-related concepts.

Case examples

To appreciate the key factors which underlie the achievement of JIT, a number of illustrations have been taken from selected Japanese companies well to the front in JIT, and compared with one or two examples of European and US companies which have attempted to equal these achievements. Four

Japanese examples have been selected from a study made by the author on a range of Japanese companies during successive industrial study tours in the early 1980s. Toyota, Matsushita Electric Corporation, NGK Spark Plugs and the Canon Camera factory have been selected, not because they are necessarily superior in any way to other Japanese examples, but because they present good illustrative examples of key points which will become apparent later in this book.

CASE EXAMPLE 1: TOYOTA

The first example is based upon the main body-assembly plant of the Toyota Motor Company near Toyota City. It is a large, modern plant and is designed to produce a variety of small passenger vehicles. The Toyota Company is proud of the plant and many visitors from all over the world are attracted each year.

To avoid interference with production operators, the company has constructed a visitors' cat-walk high above the main assembly track, and running its entire length. From this position the visitor has wide-ranging views of the whole operation.

Apart from the exceptional cleanliness, and brightly lit, well-painted surroundings, first impressions are that this track is little different from others to be found anywhere in the industry. However, it is not long before real differences become apparent. The floor beside the assembly track is carpeted, and the workers wear soft shoes. All plant is freshly painted, the decor is pleasing with pot plants in evidence, all the workers' uniforms appear freshly laundered and look new. The appearance of both male and female workers is impressive and obviously a matter of personal pride. These impressions, together with other aspects to be described, were common to all the other Japanese factories visited, and are believed to typify Japanese factories generally, particularly the larger organizations.

A further feature, which would impress anyone trained in work study techniques, is the extraordinary balance which has been achieved in the work content of successive tasks on the line. Normally, one would expect to find some evidence of imbalance due to one or another task being slightly too lengthy or difficult compared with adjacent tasks, with the effect that one worker must do more than others to keep pace with production. Alternatively, others may be observed with time on their hands because they have completed their task in less time than is allowed or, perhaps, they are working more slowly for the same reason.

In the Toyota assembly plant, each task appears identical in length and the work content such that everyone is working at the same pace. Just as one task is completed, both the upstream and downstream workers will simultaneously have completed theirs. (This infers that there are no bottlenecks.

Under Dr Eliyahu Goldratt's TOC system he claims that with no bottlenecks there will be no inventory.) When things do go wrong, for example an operator encountering some difficulty, the reaction process is also impressive. The operator will activate an alarm system which sets off a siren and a yellow rotating light above the workstation. Circuits are energized to illuminate an electronic panel above the production area to indicate the workstation affected and the time lost in overcoming the difficulty. One or more workers from other workstations pick up toolkits, hurry to the point where the difficulty has occurred, and help their fellow operator to return to normal working.

By the end of the shift, the illuminated board will have totalled each of the events which has occurred, and highlight the causes. These problems subsequently become the focus of improvement projects involving either managers or workers or both, depending upon their nature. The key point of this example is the highly visible nature of the Japanese quest for continuous project by project improvement. Every deviation is examined, the causes identified and remedies applied. Nothing is left to chance, and no deficiency, no matter how rare, is ever regarded as a purely random event which should be ignored. *This mentality is essential to the achievement of real JIT.* All attention is focused on the continued uninterrupted flow of operations. In the calendar year 1986, from a labour force of 60 000 Toyota received 2.6 million(!) improvement proposals, 96 per cent of which were implemented either by management or by the employees themselves.

Equally relevant is the most impressive JIT-related matter obtained from the Toyota experience. In the factory, with the exception of the vehicles actually being worked on the track, there was a total absence of inventory. In the normal way one would expect to find huge stillages of door panels, bumpers, seats, tyres, windscreens, engines, gearboxes, transmission systems, and so on. In the Toyota factory, apart from some low value items, there was none. In their place lorries – or transporters – continually back up to the track and the parts are off-loaded piece by piece into the vehicles being assembled. As one transporter is emptied, another takes its place, the former returning to the supplier for further loads. This may seem incredible enough to those familiar with this type of production, but what is even more staggering is that the vehicles on the track are not all the same. Saloon cars, estate cars with varying engines – all are assembled in mixed sequence on the same track. This sequence is communicated in advance to the parts supplier, and his lorries are loaded accordingly.

For example, at the point where the engines are assembled into the body, an open-topped lorry is backed up to the track. A handling device removes the left-hand corner engine, swings it round, and then lowers it into the body with the operator guiding it into location. The operator will then move along the track with the vehicle to fix the engine into its supports. The handling device then returns to the lorry, removes the next engine from its cradle, swings it round, and locates it in the next vehicle on the track, and so on. The vehicles on the track are not the same, and the appropriate engines are loaded into the lorry at the supplier's factory in whatever sequence is required on the Toyota assembly line.

A Toyota executive stated during the visit that the supplier is told the precise order of manufacture ten days in advance, and is given a further ten days' advance warning, but this sequence could be changed at any time prior to the final ten days. In the previous six years, there had not been a single stoppage because the parts had not arrived on time, neither had there been any serious quality-related problems. In the three years after that visit there had apparently been two stoppages, but of minor importance.

Many Western executives would assume that Toyota had made this remarkable achievement through the use of severe penalties, multiple sourcing and excessive use of techniques for auditing suppliers' quality. In fact the reverse is true. *Japanese companies tend towards single sourcing with long-term contractual co-operative agreements.* Their belief is that by operating in this way the supplier will develop with the customer a common interest in the achievement of market goals. Also, rather than develop an adversarial relationship with the supplier, it is beneficial to help each other. Usually, but not always, the customer has greater resources than the supplier. Therefore, it is common for the customer to offer training and other assistance to the supplier to their mutual benefit. While there is some evidence of this in the West, it is by no means widespread and rarely happens to the same extent as with Japanese organizations.

Typically, in Japanese organizations, the same concepts which are in evidence in the customer's operations will usually be equally well developed in the supplier's organization.

To follow up the Toyota study, a visit was made to a leading supplier at a factory which manufactured water pumps.

Although the product and the plant used for its manufacture were identical to those found elsewhere around the world, the factory is totally nontypical. The entire operation is carried out in a clean environment more normally associated with silicon chip manufacture and pharmaceuticals. In fact it is cleaner than an average food factory, even those which are household names in the West.

Visitors to the plant are required to put on white over-clothes covering shoes, body and hair, before entering the factory. After the complete tour of the works, the white sides of the over-shoes will be hardly marked with dirt!

Inside the factory, the floor is covered in vinyl tiles. While seemingly not new, the plant is all freshly painted, and arranged into cells such as those found in plants operating group technology. In fact, the layout represents the best example of the application of cell manufacture yet seen by the author anywhere in the West, even though the concept developed there. The plant in

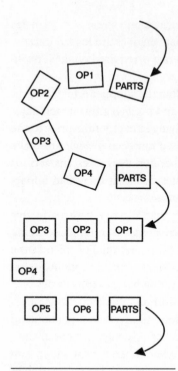

Figure 1.1 'Cell' manufacture for JIT

each cell is painted in a distinctive colour thus enabling each cell to be clearly identified from its neighbours.

A cell comprises approximately six operations which are performed by two or three operators. One operator will take a unit of product and progress that unit through each operation contained in that cell as shown in Figure 1.1. For example, pump bodies arrive from a previous cell to be assembled with the bearing bush. An operator removes one body from a small stillage, and carries out a broaching operation on the bore in which the bush is to be assembled. The same operator then assembles the bush into the body, and presses it home using a hydraulic press (OP2 in Figure 1.1). A further machining operation is then carried out on the completed fixture, followed by the drilling of holes and subsequently a dimensional check. The parts then proceed to the next cell, and so on.

Key points to note are that under this regime each operator carries out a number of different tasks using a variety of equipment. This is to be contrasted with the typical Western approach where one operator would be required to operate a single item of plant. Also, the operator in the Japanese plant checks his or her own work before it is passed to the next cell. *There is no inspector.*

Third, *the batches are extremely small.* The only time an item would be lying idle would be the short time between cells. Because the quantities at this point are deliberately kept to a minimum, the total work-in-progress is extremely low. Within the cell, the only work-in-progress will be product actually being operated on by the worker. This is to be contrasted with the more typical Western approach where work would be stationary, frequently for quite long periods, between each of the operations described above. Additionally, there would be considerably more double handling and space required for 'between process' storage. For example, in the Japanese factory the only time that the work is lying idle would be between cells. In the West, this would happen between every operation, so resulting in something like six times the quantity of work-in-progress in many cases.

At appropriate locations in the factory are a number of well-lit and attractive areas where workers can take a break. Each of these areas is also used by the workers to discuss process-related problems, and on the walls there is much evidence to indicate this. Charts, graphs, slogans and diagrams, all produced by the workers themselves, provide evidence of problem-solving activities such as those conducted by Quality Circles.

The meeting area is specific to a particular group, and they have the opportunity to personalize the area with pictures, plants and so on. This is also common to most of the larger Japanese companies and in many cases there will be internal competitions and awards for the best decorated area. In some cases these areas include imitation brickwork, trailing ivy *and other creative ideas*. This may at first sight seem irrelevant to the uninitiated Western observer but in fact it is extremely relevant to the creation of an appropriate environment for the achievement of a sense of participation and involvement which is essential if the co-operation of direct employees is to be achieved.

A further relevant point worth noting was the almost total lack of automatic assembly operations. It was constantly noted that the Japanese appear to rely far less on numerically or computer-controlled operations than most Westerners would believe. In fact, while most of the plant is kept in extremely good condition and well painted, many Westerners who have visited Japan would agree that plant is on the whole much older than Western equivalents. This usually comes as a surprise to Westerners who have been led to believe that all Japanese factories are manned by robots and other sophisticated machinery.

However, they do appear to use their equipment far more effectively, and it appears to be kept in much better condition than is typical in the West.

CASE EXAMPLE 2: MATSUSHITA ELECTRIC CORPORATION

Matsushita is one of the largest companies in the vicinity of Osaka and one of the largest electronics companies in the world. The factory in this example is engaged in the high-volume manufacture of portable radio/cassette players. The main assembly area contains several production lines. At the beginning of each line blank printed circuit boards begin the assembly process. As each board proceeds along the track components are inserted by hand by female workers.

The workers sit approximately one armspan apart and face the track. Typically in the West, the worker would face upstream along the track, usually with a work bench as illustrated in Figure 1.2.

It is interesting to note that whilst the operations were highly repetitive, and production volume high, there was little evidence of automatic insertion processes, most of this type of work being performed by hand even though this was a very modern factory producing very modern products. An executive explained to us that automatic insertion is uneconomic for all but a few special applications. It is also interesting to note that subsequently this factory featured in a BBC documentary, and the presenters chose to feature at the commencement of the programme the few automatic insertion machines actually being used. Although other scenes shot in the factory indicate that nothing had changed since my visit, and that the majority of the operations were still being performed by hand, the impression given to the viewer was one of highly automated assembly – an erroneous impression!

Following insertion of the components, the product then passes through a

Figure 1.2 (a) Typical Japanese conveyor-based assembly

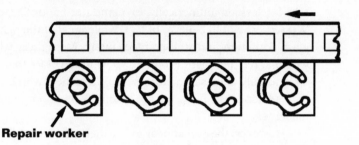

Repair worker

Figure 1.2 (b) More typical Western conveyor-based assembly

wave solder process to be assembled with other components into the case and then to completion. At this point the product passes from the production line on the conveyor into a small, clear plastic-sided cubicle in which a worker carries out final alignment and test operations. Following this, the completed product is passed along the conveyor out of the cubicle to be packed, palleted, loaded on to a transporter and shipped. This happens on a continuous basis. The flow of production was so smooth and steady that it would be easy to gain the impression that this one factory could by itself saturate the world market with these products. In fact, one visitor commented 'What happens when you have saturated the world market?' – the reply was 'Then we will build a better tape recorder!'

Although the party touring the plant was twenty to thirty strong, it was noted that not one worker appeared to look up from his or her work. It was as if the touring group was invisible, and it would be easy to conjecture that our group went totally unnoticed by the workers. By way of contrast, a group of Japanese – or indeed any other nationality – making a similar tour of a Western company would attract considerable attention and curiosity. This point was put to a company executive with the response that the reason for the attention to their work was the fact that the workers were all members of Quality Circles!

Noting that his reply completely mystified his audience, the executive went on to explain that the true situation in the factory is not as it appears to a Westerner. Although the workers were performing a single repetitive task while being observed, they would not be expected to perform just that single task on a continuous basis, as would be typical in a Western factory. In the

Matsushita factory, the workers would normally perform the task observed for approximately one hour, following which they would rotate to another task. 'Otherwise,' we were told, 'they would become awfully bored.' This comment was repeated in almost every factory visited. *This job rotation is not controlled directly by management, but by the workers themselves through Quality Circle activities.*

The workers normally check their own performance both in terms of quality and quantity using all the Statistical Process Control techniques normally in the hands of technicians and engineers in the West. Through the use of these techniques, the workers are able to identify, analyse and solve work-related problems, rotate their own tasks with the object of optimizing overall performance, and achieve maximum flexibility. It is the supervisors' responsibility to help in training new workers to bring them up to the standard of the others.

The real achievement of Matsushita is not simply the organization of work to maximize performance, but to have evolved an approach to employee involvement which, if understood and practised by management elsewhere, could have a profound effect on the attitudes and performance of those who are otherwise forced into repetitive, often meaningless tasks. It is also a way by which it becomes possible to harness the education and creativity of all people irrespective of the repetitive nature of the tasks themselves. It will be seen later that consideration of these concepts is essential if the ultimate goals of JIT are to be achieved.

In the words of Mr Matsushita, the company president, 'First we make people, then we make products.'

To return to the illustration of the two conveyor assembly systems, the Matsushita line contained no slack or buffer stocks at any point. If an operator experiences some difficulty the entire line is stopped. To a Westerner this would appear a disastrous approach, and under conditions familiar to the Westerner it would be easy to imagine that such stoppages would be occurring right through the shift. Hence, in the West it is more usual for the worker to face along the conveyor, and to remove work for processing. If difficulties are experienced, only that worker is affected, and other operations will continue. At a later stage in the process, a special worker will usually inspect the products thus produced, and hope to locate any missing operations. If found they would be completed at this point. Such an operator would probably be more highly skilled than the others, and might in many cases be better paid.

This might at first sight appear more sensible but two points should be noted:

1 A problem experienced by one individual Western operator will not be dramatized in the way it would in the Japanese example; therefore, the problem is less likely to become the subject of an investigation.

2 In the Western organization the inspection/repair operation has become regularized and therefore regarded as a normal and legitimate activity. The cost of the operation has become a permanent and accepted cost element absorbed into standard process costs and is therefore never challenged.

In the Japanese factory, the fact that a fault will stop the entire track means that managers become acutely aware of the reasons for any stoppage, as do the workers themselves, and therefore no assumptions are made regarding the inevitability of such events. Considerable effort is made to locate the causes and find remedies. In the long term the gains from such improvements will far outweigh the costs of the stoppages – even though they will be high in the early days of operating this type of approach.

CASE EXAMPLE 3: NGK SPARK PLUGS

The third example is the NGK Spark Plug factory. It is impressive partly because I visited an equivalent West European factory with similar volume output only a few weeks later. For the same output, the Japanese factory had approximately one-fifth of the total production area of its European counterpart.

In the Japanese factory, everything from raw material to finished product is actually in a state of being processed at any one time. On one single production line the entire product was manufactured from start to finish without a single component leaving the line or being delayed in any way.

Following completion of the assembly of the central electrode, the porcelain stem is moulded, fired and inserted into the component in a single continuous process; the completed assembly is then sprayed with glaze, fired in a continuous through-feed kiln, cooled, top nut attached and the completed product boxed. Completed boxes are then collected into a unit load, palleted, shrink-wrapped and loaded directly into a transporter.

Again, there is no inventory, no part-finished parts stores, no finished goods stock.

The finished product is transported immediately to the customer, such as Toyota, in total harmony with the customer's production needs. On receipt, there would be no need for inspection since the likelihood of defects is so small that the product can be delivered directly to the production line.

In contrast, the European factory visited presents a very different picture. The manufacturing operations did not always follow a clear uninterrupted sequence. Some operations may even be carried out in separate departments, with much evidence of work-in-progress or 'on-line' storage.

It is traditional in Western spark plug factories to store the porcelain stems in containers known as 'saggers'. Saggers are flatbottomed bowl-shaped containers approximately 600 mm in diameter and slightly deeper than the height of a spark plug. Two large bays of this factory were used to store stacks of these saggers each of which was filled with porcelain spark plug stems. There were literally tens of thousands of these units in store.

Because these plugs are of varying length for different vehicles, the stock control problem is horrendous. *In contrast the NGK factory had no such storage and, therefore, no stock control problems.*

CASE EXAMPLE 4: CANON CAMERA FACTORY

The Canon Camera factory has been included to illustrate yet another key point. All the observations made in the previous examples were equally in evidence at Canon as in other Japanese factories visited.

The intricate nature of camera components led to smaller departments than the other companies visited. It was also noted that almost all the operations involved assembly by hand as opposed to machine and the processes were therefore highly labour intensive.

In each working area, wall charts are displayed. Each of these measures approximately 2 metres wide by 1 metre high, and shows a matrix chart. The vertical axis lists the names of all operators in the department and the horizontal axis is divided into columns, each describing a specific skill or task. An example of a similar multi-skill board can be seen in Figure 10.1.

The boxes in the chart were shaded against each employee to show at a glance the skills each has acquired. In the Canon factory it is the supervisor's responsibility to attempt to give each employee the widest possible range of skills. This is achieved both by formal training and through job rotation. Of course there is nothing new about job rotation. Many Western companies also recognize its value, and it makes sense to give operators as wide a range of skills as possible. But what is different is the high visibility given to the approach, the leading role in the achievement of job rotation and skills development on the part of the supervisor as opposed to the personnel department, and the extent to which the approach is used in most leading Japanese factories.

By including this example with the experiences from Matsushita and others elsewhere, a pattern becomes apparent. There can be no doubt whatsoever that Japanese managers attach considerable importance to the direct involvement of employees in process design and process improvement, and the achievement of smooth harmonious production. This attention to detail, together with access to the experience and know-how of the workforce, is essential if real progress towards JIT production is to be achieved.

A Japanese management expert, Professor Sasaki, said 'the involvement of work people in Japan has led mainly to process improvement rather than to product improvement.'

JAPANESE MOTOR TRADES ASSOCIATION DINNER

Yet a further example to elaborate on this last point relates to an unexpected experience during a dinner hosted by the Japanese Motor Trades Association. The president of the Association was also a vice-president of the Toyota Motor Company. During the conversation, he asked each member of the British group of industrialists the name of the company they represented, their products, what did they think of Japan, and so on. Two members of the group were respectively managing director and works manager of a company engaged in the manufacture of small electro-mechanical components such as circuit breakers. The managing director happened to have one or two small items of these products in his pocket and showed them to the president.

The two directors were then subjected to a number of searching quality-related questions concerning the product. What was the fatigue life of the bi-metal strip? How is it tested? How do they know when it will fail? and so on. It was obvious from both the questions and the answers that the Japanese host had considerable technical knowledge relating to this type of product.

There followed searching questions regarding the means of manufacture.

The product was basically an injection moulding produced on a multi-impression tool. The Japanese asked whether other products were made on the same machine. 'Yes,' was the answer. 'How long,' asked the Japanese, 'does it take to change the mould tools?' The two British executives conferred and suggested 'about three hours.' Uncharacteristically the Japanese made no attempt to hide their amazement. At this, the British executives became irritated. 'How long would it have taken you?' they asked. 'About eight minutes,' was the reply. Any Western reader with knowledge of injection moulding would have found this difficult to believe, and two clear points emerge:

1   It is highly likely that the British executives were concealing the truth. In many factories, managers would be relatively pleased with a tool change in three hours. In many cases it could possibly take an entire shift. In extreme cases it could take as long as one week.
2   Eight minutes represents an incredibly quick changeover by any standards and could only be achieved by the most meticulous planning and attention to detail. But such an achievement is not impossible, and neither is it outside Western experience to be so well organized. The disassembly and reassembly of the two gun carriages at the British Royal Tournament each year provides impressive evidence of that fact.

Western attempts to compete with Japan

These Japanese examples are obviously impressive, but what about the West? Some companies claim to be making spectacular progress with JIT. It would be interesting to see how far they have got, and what problems they are facing.

From approximately 1980 Western manufacturers, particularly those in the automobile industry and in consumer electronics, have taken considerable interest in Japanese styles of management and many have been to Japan to see for themselves. Some of their experiences have led to panic reactions, and an article was published in one highly respected technical journal in that decade, claiming that Japan was too far ahead to catch up. Others have reacted differently, and some have seized upon almost anything and attempted to introduce the threads they have gathered into their own organizations, often with disappointing results.

This has been the case with Quality Circles, Statistical Process Control (SPC), Company-wide or Total Quality Control (TQC), and appears to be happening also with JIT.

What all these students of Japan fail to appreciate is that none of these concepts stands on its own. There is no Japanese company operating a Quality Circle programme which does not also have SPC, TQC or JIT. It seems that while the West is spending all its time seeking panaceas, or wonder cures, the Japanese simply get on with the process of sound management. Just about every management concept which has ever been introduced in the West will still be found in some shape or form in almost any Japanese company. What is different is the fact that in the Japanese company the concept will have been moulded into a context compatible with the general philosophy of management. The result is a tightly woven web of interacting and mutually supporting concepts, which collectively are making Japan into the most productive nation on earth.

For the West to succeed in closing the gap with Japan, managers in Western companies must become far more analytical. They must stop being cynical, stop looking for wonder cures because there are none, and start putting all the pieces together. Only then will they find themselves able to make a sustained year-by-year recovery.

The gap is now very wide between Japanese and Western performance, but not so wide that it cannot be closed – but not closed overnight. The West is confronted with a challenge which took three decades to reach current proportions. It may not take three decades to respond but it will take time, and only after a major rethink on industrial cultural values. Companies must start to think in terms of year-on-year improvement. This book has been written to try to make a contribution to that process.

Some Western experiences with JIT

In June 1985 I was fortunate enough to participate in a one-day tour of the General Motors truck plant in Baltimore, USA. The invitation was intended to show visitors what General Motors had done to achieve JIT. Prior to the tour, a senior company executive gave us an account of the progress GM had made, and the difficulties it had to face to achieve its goal.

Before JIT could start GM found that the existing layout of the plant was totally unsuited to its plans. Such was its commitment to JIT that the plant was shut down completely, stripped and all plant relocated, at enormous cost. The time period for this drastic measure was such that all employees were laid off, and those that were required for the new arrangement were then offered new contracts of employment. The executive explained how GM had reduced inventory levels, improved the flow of materials and generally improved the work environment. However, he said that the biggest stumbling block to the ultimate achievement of their goals was found to be the dual problems of poor quality from suppliers and unpredictable deliveries.

While being unspecific as to how GM planned to improve supplier quality, he said that the delivery problem related both to the ability of the supplier to respond to demand, and also to the physical distance between the supplier and the Baltimore plant. To overcome this problem, GM had purchased land in the vicinity of the factory and was encouraging key suppliers to relocate and to take up warehouse space on this land. Other manufacturers in Western automobile industries are following this trend.

The tour of the factory was illuminating. By comparison with Toyota and a previous visit to the Nissan Zama plant near Tokyo, the GM truck plant still had considerable inventory. This is in no way a criticism of GM. It is mentioned only to illustrate how wide the gap has grown between Japanese and Western manufacturing performance, even with all the efforts that the Baltimore plant had made: stillages packed with door panels, wheel hubs, bumpers and so on were stacked to roof height in many parts of the building.

At about the time of my visit to Toyota, I was informed that Toyota inventory was close to zero. At Nissan about ten hours' worth of stock was held. In a typical British plant an executive admitted to about fifteen days' worth of stock of parts but at peak times it could well be a great deal longer. In other cases, stocks may be held for months.

Even in industries where stock rotation and stock turnover are critical, such as the food industry, stock levels are enormous compared with their Japanese counterparts. One well-known West European food manufacturer has two warehouses each of which contains approximately £26 million of stock of finished goods, 0.2 per cent of which is damaged in the warehouses, and which turns over about six times a year. If this stock could be reduced by only a fraction, not only would considerable capital be released for investment, but reductions in stock damage and deterioration would also result in benefits.

Planning for JIT

Clearly the West must react to the dramatic levels of performance of the Japanese or eventually be forced out of business. In some cases this might necessitate massive up-front investments such as that made at the General Motors truck plant. In other cases, the investment is more likely to be in 'time'. Time to conduct research into finding the right approach, or to find the right consultancy or advice. Then, time to plan and introduce new concepts, monitor the results and develop for the future. For most, this will not be easy, particularly when already under pressure, but the time must be found for otherwise there may be no future.

Planning for improvement is the first essential step, and reading this book might be the first stage in the process. At the end of many of the chapters, further reading is suggested. The recommendations have been selected carefully and merit serious consideration. In some cases they are an essential expansion of points covered or referred to in this book. In such cases the material has been left out of this work only because there is little point in simply reiterating the work of others, particularly when it has been well covered and is illustrated. The topic is broad enough to stand many texts on the various aspects.

WHO DOES THE PLANNING?

Planning for JIT is one aspect from which upper management simply cannot abdicate its responsibility.

The successful achievement of anything even remotely approaching JIT will require for most companies a significant change of management style, direction and culture. It will also require considerable commitment and involvement. There is no way in which the decision to make such a change could ever be devolved downwards to lower levels, or that persons at such levels could be left to conduct the research without some involvement from the top.

A second key requirement must be to identify all the major elements of JIT as part of the plan.

The case examples in this chapter were selected to provide a perspective of the scope of JIT.

The real goal can only be achieved when JIT is working throughout the length of the entire supply chain. For this reason, customer/supplier relationships are a key feature in the achievement of JIT but not the only one. There is already an impression that many British and other Western manufacturers believe that JIT is something we do to our suppliers; JIT is *not* something we do to our suppliers, it is something we *involve* them in.

Constant, predictable quality levels hitherto considered impossible are also fundamental to the achievement of JIT. In the past few years the electronic components industry was stunned when Japanese manufacturers began to insist on component defect rates in the order of parts per million (ppm). Such defect rates are simply not possible through traditional methods of manufacture and test. In Western society, acceptable quality levels are usually quoted in terms of parts per hundred. Acceptance sampling techniques based on British Standard 6000, or MIL STD 105D, become obsolete when defect levels in terms of parts per million are called for. Sample sizes become equal to lot sizes and therefore sampling becomes academic. Toyota could not have operated the 'ship to line' system described if it did not have total confidence in the supply quality.

How about the other traditional approaches to quality? What is their relevance to JIT, ppm, etc? For example, ISO 9000, the Defence Standards, Statistical Process Control and so on? Each of them has a role, but the role must be put in context. On its own, none of these approaches stands any chance whatever of even scratching the surface of JIT requirements. That is why, at the beginning of this chapter, it was stated that quality assurance and quality control play only a part in the quest for JIT. Company-wide Quality Improvement holds the key to JIT and this concept is far broader than mere quality control.

JIT-related concepts

1 Just in Time is an objective. To achieve that objective, it is necessary to evolve, develop and integrate many concepts and techniques and to begin changing the culture of the company.

2 These concepts are embraced within the overall concept of Company-wide Quality Improvement (CQI).

3 The object of CQI is to create an organization in which every employee from top to bottom is working towards making that organization the best in its particular field. It is based upon the idea that each person is the expert in his or her own job, and by harnessing the collective thinking power, creativity and job knowledge of everyone in the organization we can compete with any organization on earth.

4 A major aspect of CQI which is essential to the achievement of JIT is the project by project annual improvement process. The underlying philosophy upon which this concept is based is the belief that all improvement, or breakthrough, is made project by project and in no other way.

5 Basically, there are two kinds of problem: sporadic and chronic. Sporadic problems are those which occur spontaneously, generally unexpectedly and at random. For example, a machine may break down or a hose rupture;

for no apparent reason a machine suddenly begins to produce inferior product.

Alternatively, an industrial dispute may flare up with all the ensuing disruption that may cause. Sporadic problems are usually attention getters. They also generate a great deal of excitement, with the result that specialists and other problem-solvers converge on the scene. Eventually the problem is resolved and life returns to normal until the next time – which may not be long.

These sporadic problems vary from trivial to serious and usually consume considerable managerial time on a day-to-day basis. Some managers may find that they spend all their time this way, with the consequence that they have little time for anything else, let alone improvement or JIT.

The chronic problems are different. First, they are not always as readily identifiable on an individual basis as the sporadic problems. For example, one problem which faces most organizations is yield obtained from some source material. Yield is usually quoted in percentage terms, say 90 per cent. It is most likely that while many managers would probably agree that they would prefer yields of 100 per cent with zero buffer stock, they would probably also agree that such goals are unattainable in everyday situations.

In the past, such managers have probably made attempts to improve on the 10 per cent loss, but due to the time they spend dealing with the sporadic problems, and also to the fact that there exists no systematic approach for attacking the 10 per cent loss, the loss remains, year after year. Eventually, after years of having to live with the loss, it becomes accepted as irretrievable, and many theories become held as to why this level can be justified. At this point, rather than find ways to reduce the losses, the managers are more likely to look for ways of preventing things from getting worse. In other words, they look for controls to give early warning of potential sporadic problems. Meanwhile the 10 per cent loss or chronic problem goes on and on year after year.

6 To achieve JIT it becomes necessary to find ways of tackling these chronic problems on a project by project basis. This means that all established norms must be challenged. There can be no 'standard level' of buffer stock, goods inwards stocks, finished goods stock, work-in-progress, machine availability, absenteeism, scrap rework, customer complaint, warranty claim, credit period, invoice error, misdirected phone calls or correspondence, industrial disputes, service complaints, failed product launch, marketing misinformation, design modifications and so on.

The same applies to suppliers; they will not be able to improve unless they know how. Therefore, to achieve the company goals it becomes necessary to help the supplier to do the same. This implies the development of a collaborative relationship with long-term controls rather than an adversarial relationship based upon multiple sourcing.

While the book describes the relevant aspect of CQI, the concept itself is in a continuous state of evolution. Companies at the leading edge of CQI are constantly developing more effective methods to make themselves more and more competitive, but the goals never change. Within CQI there are many objectives. For example:

- elimination of defective product
- reduced waste
- lower cost
- fewer field failures
- eliminate stockholding
- improve market share and reputation
- beat the competitor

and many more.

The concepts, planning and techniques involved include:

- establishment of a top company team
- establishment of functional/regional/plant-based teams
- inter/intra-departmental teams
- small-group activities of direct employees
- techniques for the identification, selection and solution of and remedial action for projects
- cost monitoring
- programme monitoring
- facilitation and support
- system development, audit and period.

These aspects will form the basis of this book.

Recommended further reading

Ishikawa, Professor Kaoru (1985) *What is Total Quality Control?*, Prentice-Hall.

Sasaki, Professor Naoto (1981) *Management and Industrial Structure in Japan*, Pergamon.

2 BASIC PRINCIPLES

In Chapter 1, Just in Time was shown to represent an immediate, continuous and relentless attack on all forms of stockholding. All stock, whether product related or service related, is continuously evaluated and challenged. No 'norms' or standards can be allowed.

This chapter identifies the JIT implications at each stage in a company's operations.

Initially, the process of evaluation would begin at incoming materials stockholding and continue process by process through the entire organization to the ultimate point of stockholding finished product, as illustrated in Figure 2.1. Later, when the principles are thoroughly understood, and the JIT process working, it becomes possible to extend the concept right through the supply chain at one extreme, and into and through the distribution process at the other. Many companies are attracted to the idea of beginning JIT by pressurizing their suppliers. This is unlikely to be a good strategy. Without the benefit of internal experience, it is doubtful whether the most desirable supplier strategy could be developed.

Incoming goods

There is one thing which visibly separates the company with a successful JIT programme from all others. There are *no buffer stocks*! At this point, the reader should attempt to comprehend what this really means in the context of his or her own organization. *No buffer stock of anything*. Think of every point in the organization where buffer stocks normally occur. Then ask why. Why, for example, are there buffer stocks of incoming materials? tools? parts? stationery? fuel? lubricants? and so on.

The reasons are usually obvious and are discussed below.

UNRELIABLE OR UNPREDICTABLE DELIVERIES

The more unreliable the deliveries, the greater the need for the stock. Figure 2.2 illustrates the extreme situation.

For such stocks we have tied our company's capital into safeguarding ourselves against problems which should be the supplier's cost, not ours. Why has capital been tied up this way? Usually, there are two principal reasons:

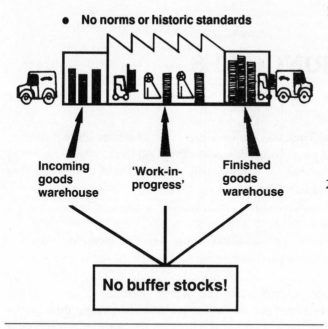

• No norms or historic standards

Incoming goods warehouse

'Work-in-progress'

Finished goods warehouse

No buffer stocks!

Figure 2.1 Principles of JIT

1 Unconsciously it has been accepted as fact that because no supplier can be perfect, because of his or her shortcomings, allowances must be made by building in safeguards. In other words, the costs of his or her weaknesses are being carried for no reason other than that 'things have always been done this way'.

2 Instinctively, because the consequential effect of 'stock out' could be catastrophic, and the responsibility for such an event will usually have been placed on the purchasing officer, it is he or she who will be criticized for not holding safe levels of stock, not the supplier who failed to keep his or her promises.

In reality, the unpredictability of a supplier should be an indictment of the supplier, and of the purchasing policy. More usually, the purchasing officer will be blamed on the basis that 'since the supplier is known to be unpredictable, his or her late delivery becomes a foreseeable event, and therefore buffer stocks should have been adjusted accordingly'.

It can be seen therefore that two mutually exclusive events are possible:

1 excessive buffer stock costs;
2 consequential costs of 'stock out' situations.

The two events differ significantly in the eyes of the purchasing officer. Usually the 'stock out' situation is dramatic. It affects many people, and strong accusations may be made. Sometimes the event may even precipitate a crisis leading to the temporary layoff of many people. In contrast, holding excessive stock is not at all dramatic.

Generally speaking, in times of plenty no one ever questions stockholding levels, partly because they only become an emotional issue when the company is in trouble. Even then, it is rare for detailed studies to be made to ascertain the causes and find systematic remedies. More usually, surgery on buffer stocks is applied in a state of panic with the result that the problem is frequently made worse rather than better. Further, those who could make such a study know that, like the purchasing officer, while they could be

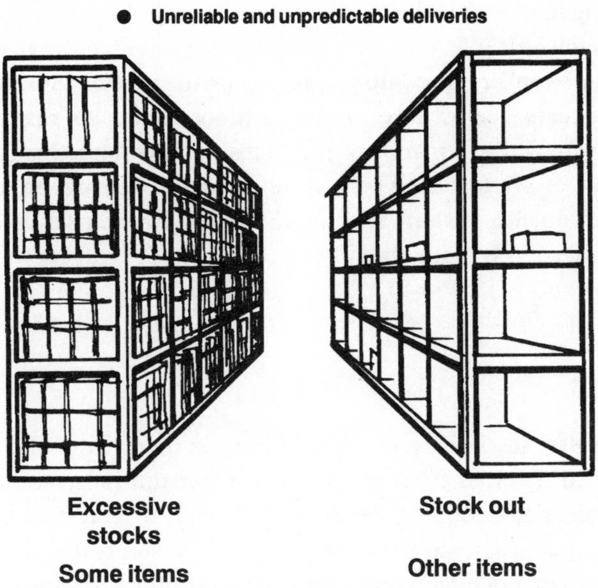

● **Unreliable and unpredictable deliveries**

Excessive stocks

Some items

Stock out

Other items

Figure 2.2 The consequences of unreliable and unpredictable deliveries

successful in making savings, they are just as likely to run the risk of creating a 'stock out' situation with all the implications suggested, but with the added risk of comments like 'I told you so' from those whose previous judgements have been challenged.

This stark difference in the consequences of the two events must inevitably lead to 'safe' strategies by those with direct responsibility for stockholding with the result that buffer stock levels are rarely questioned, and are therefore very likely to be high or excessive.

Of course, 'unpredictable deliveries' are only a symptom. Even for a single product this symptom may house several possible causes, for example supplier quality problems, poor organization, a long distribution chain, problems with the supplier's own suppliers and so on. When this analysis is extended across the entire spectrum of incoming goods, there could appear to be literally hundreds of causes, each requiring its own specific remedy. This is, of course, usually the case. However, strategies can be developed which will greatly reduce the scale of this problem, and there are also techniques which have proven successful for dealing with the specific causes. Both these matters are dealt with in later chapters.

But the lesson is simple. These stockholding levels must be challenged. The causes must be identified and remedies found. The reason for the buffer stock must be identified, not just the mere fact of its existence.

POOR QUALITY FROM SUPPLIERS

The Baltimore truck plant case example given in Chapter 1 indicated that poor quality from suppliers was the principal block to further progress towards JIT. In the West companies have developed adversarial relationships with their suppliers to reduce this problem. In Japan they have adopted another approach. There, it is more normal to establish long-term collaborative relationships with suppliers on the basis that both parties have a mutual interest in the quantity of sales of the ultimate product. Western companies will need to take a long hard look at their policies in this area if they are to make meaningful progress towards JIT.

Simply requiring suppliers to comply with requirements like ISO 9000 will be grossly inadequate. Defect levels must be brought into the realm of parts per million to satisfy the demands of JIT. This requires something like the Sigma approach of Motorola. There is no evidence to suggest that approaches based on quality systems such as ISO 9000 by themselves can even scratch the surface of this requirement.

Factory stocks

In the factory itself buffer stocks exist in several forms. In many cases alternative words are used to describe these stocks, which sometimes make them sound more acceptable. For example, 'live storage' – usually on conveyor belts or temporarily between processes in some other way. These stocks usually ebb and flow continuously, are not documented since no requisitions are involved, and are more difficult to assess than the buffer stocks held in incoming goods stores or at the finished goods warehouse. Sometimes they have simply built up as a result of failure or bottleneck in some downstream process rather like a log jam. Collectively, these stocks are given an air of respectability by being described as 'work-in-progress'. This is usually accounted for in global terms and is rarely broken down on a stage-by-stage basis through the process.

Obviously, at any point in time there are materials, components, chemicals or ingredients being processed, but if these are estimated and the quantity thus determined is subtracted from the total value of 'work-in-progress', the result then represents the opportunity afforded for improvement through JIT. In the ideal JIT factory, this figure would be zero.

Of course, so-called work-in-progress has always been a key industrial measure. The total value forms part of the balance sheet, and industrial managers are under intense pressure to keep the figures as low as possible. Unfortunately, while responsibility for work-in-progress may appear to lie with line management, many of the causes of high work-in-progress lie outside its control. These causes may include:

- machine breakdowns
- absenteeism
- machine setting
- machine capability
- operator capability
- scheduling
- process planning
- product mix

- material variations
- changing product priorities
- product modifications
- shift patterns
- cross-functional organization
- specialist support.

We will first consider the consequential JIT effects of plant and machine breakdowns, then deal with product modifications later in the chapter.

PLANT OR MACHINE BREAKDOWN

Many of these items may be in the line manager's direct control, but many are not, even if they seem so. For example, while machine care might be in the hands of the machine operator, and therefore under the responsibility of the line manager, machine maintenance probably is not. This responsibility

'WORK-IN-PROGRESS'

usually lies with the 'engineering' or maintenance department. The maintenance manager may be responsible for the general level of machine efficiency; it would be unusual if he were held in any way responsible for work-in-progress or even total volume output, except in highly capital-intensive operations such as the chemical industry.

Imagine the following scenario. The scene is set in a management meeting held to discuss and find a culprit for the fact that a delivery promise for a particular line of product has failed yet again.

The manager of the line in question is defending himself:

> I have three machines broken down out there and if the maintenance department got themselves sorted out and fixed my machines, I would have met the schedule requirements.

The maintenance manager responds:

> If your people looked after the equipment better, it wouldn't break down so often, and in any case, I am short of labour. If personnel would let me have another fitter and two more electricians, I could get someone over there to fix your machines.

The personnel officer interjects:

> That's unfair. We would love to provide you with more staff, but for one thing labour turnover is higher in your department than anywhere else in the factory, and for another, finance would not increase the budget to allow you anyone else this year.

This type of debate will go on and on and never get anywhere. It is happening throughout industry all the time. For one thing, such problems can rarely ever be resolved by debate. For another, there are usually many conflicting theories as to the causes. Each manager is likely to have a strong vested interest in his or her own theory, and will often be quite hostile to the theories of others, particularly when these appear to attach blame to that manager or to his or her department.

One effective way of dealing with this problem is through the project approach. If all the managers in the foregoing scene had been members of a project team they would each have identified many theories. These theories often challenge each other and exhibit biases. While the managers might not be the best people to test the theories, due to the biases, they would nevertheless be well placed to identify the theories in the first place. Ideally, the theories should be tested by those who have no vested interest in any of them, have the time to conduct the diagnosis and are trained in diagnostic skills. This often leads to a two-part team structure:

1 the managers who guide the complete project, identify the theories which must be tested, and who will review the results;
2 a diagnostic element which may comprise either key individuals or consultants or a team from the specialist problem-solving department.

Once the true cause has been discovered, the team of managers can identify possible remedies or, alternatively, responsibility for this next stage may be devolved to the department where the skills exist.

For example, the project team comprising the managers in the example given above discovers that the low output happened to be caused by a motor which failed under certain load conditions. An expert from the engineering department will investigate and propose a remedy. This would then be agreed and verified by the project team of managers.

Incidentally, the problem described in the example would invariably not only lead to low output but would almost certainly produce a 'knock on' effect on work-in-progress. The system in operation would be unlikely to be sufficiently sensitive to respond to a sudden, unexpected breakdown. Plant upstream from that point would invariably be kept running, as in the case of production of machine or related components, or the packaging, particularly where the effect of stopping involved layoffs, payment of waiting time, and so on. A buffer stock would then build up behind the offending item of plant. Even if it were possible to stop upstream operations, the components, or raw materials, would probably still be in the possession of the company at the incoming goods store. The only way to prevent a build-up of work-in-progress would have been instantly to freeze supplies to that machine and to parallel processes all the way back to the original source material. A clearly impractical proposition – or is it? In total, yes, but even there we may be able to make some improvement through organizational changes. The aim would be to increase system sensitivity and response to unpredictable events. This is the essence of JIT thinking in a production environment.

Another aspect of sudden unpredictable breakdown would be the measures taken to reduce the after-effect. Typically, workers would be pressed to work harder and faster. Lengthy overtime would be introduced, effectively adding cost, frustration and uncertainty. Perhaps of greater importance but less obvious significance is the use of management time in what is basically a firefighting operation.

Some managers are kept so busy fighting these sporadic 'fires' that they have little time for anything else. In many cases the firefighting is so commonplace that managers mistakenly think that this is what real management is all about. Rolling up one's sleeves and getting down to the shop floor where it is all happening feels exciting, even dramatic. Immediately afterwards comes a feeling of satisfaction, of 'getting the job done' – until the next time, and few such managers have long to wait for that.

The real job of management is to find the causes of these sporadic outbreaks, and provide remedies to avoid them happening in the future. Usually, this requires a better understanding of the relationship between process variables and product results. This work may seem at first sight to be less exciting than firefighting, and makes excessive demands on both time and organization.

Time is the one thing the firefighting manager does not have, but for JIT *it must be found*! It is an up-front investment which cannot be avoided. The amount of time required is debatable: it depends partly on the scale of the problem, partly on the degree of outside pressure from customers, and partly on the rate by which we need to improve. If we intend to change the world overnight, the investment would be large, and beyond the available resources of most organizations. Alternatively, a small-scale tryout, selectively introduced, could if properly managed develop into a large programme, self-funded from the original achievements.

JIT AND PACED PRODUCTION

Hidden buffer stock occurs with conveyor-line manufacture. Consider once again the example from Matsushita.

Apart from the assembly of automobiles, which in the West is usually carried out directly on the track, a high proportion of conveyor- or track-related assembly is carried out immediately adjacent to the track as shown in Figure 1.2. In this case, the work is normally recovered from the track by the operator or worker, the operation is performed and the product is returned to the track. A further operator downstream then performs a subsequent operation and so on through to completion.

At face value this would appear perfectly reasonable and many production lines operate this way. This has been referred to as the 'soft approach'. It makes allowances for unexpected or random interference factors. For example, one operator may experience some difficulty with an operation. This may result in not being able to keep pace with production, and the need for help. The help may be forthcoming, but since there was no apparent interference with production, the event is likely to pass unrecorded, and because it was not sensational probably not remembered.

Sometimes the rate of production and the imbalance of work are such that it is difficult, or even impossible, for some operators to keep pace with production. The operator is frequently unlikely to draw attention to the fact because he or she may feel inferior. Consequently the operator will probably do the best he or she can, with the result that operations may be missed or incorrectly carried out. The movement of operators from task to task and from line to line, together with the fact that these deficiencies are sometimes missed at a subsequent inspection station, usually means that individually these events also pass unrecorded. In such cases, when it is found necessary to record performance in some way or another, the lack of specific data usually results in the production of vague generalized statistics such as 'line defects 2 per cent', which are virtually meaningless and do nothing to help identify the causes.

Also, because the problems cannot be tackled because they have not been specifically highlighted, rather than locate the causes and find remedies, management is more likely to treat the symptom by placing another operator at the end of the line in the hope that that will catch the defectives and repair the damage. Such operators are usually more highly skilled or experienced than others, but they are wasted in this totally non-productive mode.

Eventually this cost will be regarded as a legitimate part of the process, and even a positive operation, rather than the quality-related failure cost it really is.

When all operations are reviewed in the light of this comment, some real opportunities for improvement will soon emerge.

Under the 'hard' approach, operations are carried out in sequence directly on the track or conveyor. The operator faces the track and the product is not removed to an adjacent table or bench as in the 'soft' approach. Under the 'soft' approach there may be many assemblies or parts, either in transit between operations or in 'off-line' storage waiting to be processed. This is unlikely to be the case with the 'hard' approach.

While evidence of 'line storage' can be found in Japanese factories, it is soon obvious to the visitor that every attempt is made to keep this to the minimum. In contrast, a Western factory may sometimes have literally miles of cars or assemblies touring the factory on an overhead conveyor system which often resembles the switchback at a fairground.

The 'hard' conveyor system places high demands on everyone. Normally, operators can stop the track if they have problems, but if they stop it for themselves, they also stop it for everyone else. The effect is to draw immediate attention to the source of the stoppage – unlike the 'soft' conveyor system, where no such attention is given.

It would appear that the 'hard' approach places enormous stress on the operator. This would be true if 'blame' were to be attached to the operator in question. In the JIT factory, this would not be the case. Operator errors are separated into three basic categories (Dr J. M. Juran (1964) *Managerial Breakthrough*, McGraw-Hill):

1 errors due to inattention;
2 technique errors;
3 conscious errors.

Let us first consider errors due to inattention.

On the basis that 'to err is to be human', it must be accepted that all human beings make mistakes. Some perhaps more than others, but at least it is accepted that the errors are unintentional. At the time of making the error, the operator may be unaware of having made it. Such errors occur at random and can be made by any operator at any time, resulting in a random error pattern. The converse is also true. If the errors are random, they are probably of the inadvertent type. The remedy is to provide aids to attentiveness or, alternatively, to make the operation foolproof.

Technique errors occur as a result of a lack of some technique or knack which is necessary to do good work. Workers who possess the technique will constantly do better work than those who lack it. Such errors are consistent both as regards worker and type of error. The 'soft' conveyor system also hides this type of error, particularly if several successive operators perform the same task and their work is subsequently mixed at later operations. Under the 'hard' conveyor approach, such errors would normally be more readily identifiable with the operator who made the error. The correct solution would not be to blame the worker, since the worker is probably ignorant of the cause. The onus rests with management to identify the missing knack, and then to train the workers in the use of the knack. Alternatively, the operation might be changed to compel the use of the knack.

Conscious operator errors can be due to sabotage, but are more usually due to misinterpretation of priorities imposed by management. For example, there may appear to be a conflict between the need for high levels of production and the need for quality. Too much attention to the former may lead some workers to believe that quality is less important. This will result in trade-offs which may be interpreted as wilful errors. This type of error is just as likely whatever type of production flow is used, but with the 'hard' conveyor the pressure really lies with management to design the tasks in such a way that operators are not faced with the need to compromise.

Obviously, the 'hard' conveyor system cannot be achieved simply by turning operators to face the track. The biggest requirement is to design tasks in such a way as to ensure that their work content is identical. Otherwise, some operators may find themselves working excessively hard on some bottleneck operation while others have time on their hands because the work content is too low. The pace of the conveyor must be such that a 'normal' operator can complete the task easily and comfortably within the time available.

Task-related difficulties must be studied with the problem-solving skills available to those faced with overcoming identified shortcomings. Operating such a system, the mere fact that a problem at one workstation will stop the entire track implies that problem-solving must be immediately available if production targets are to be met.

Operation of the 'hard' conveyor system may also create severe stress on the operator who feels trapped into a process which will go on relentlessly without breaks or some form of task rotation. Such systems demand much greater attention to the personal needs of the worker than might otherwise be required with 'soft' systems, where people can ease off or talk to each other from time to time.

For the JIT 'hard' conveyor system to be effective an organization must consider the involvement and use of workers' problem-solving teams such as Quality Circles, together with job rotation and skills development, and provide adequate breaks for relaxation. These considerations will normally be more than rewarded by improved productivity and better working relationships. Figure 2.3 illustrates the systems and summarizes the advantages and disadvantages.

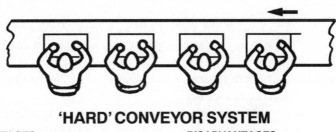

'HARD' CONVEYOR SYSTEM

ADVANTAGES
Less work-in-progress
Fewer undetected faults
Higher production rates
Highlights errors

DISADVANTAGES
One fault stops track
High visible cost per fault

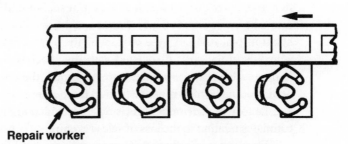

Repair worker

'SOFT' CONVEYOR SYSTEM

ADVANTAGES
Easy to keep track running
Smoother operation

DISADVANTAGES
Faults hidden in process
Costs hidden in process
More work-in-progress
Lower production rates

Figure 2.3 Advantages and disadvantages of the 'hard' and 'soft' conveyor systems

SCRAP AND REWORK

Another aspect of work-in-progress is normally referred to as 'rework'. This term usually refers to product which may be outside specification, but is repairable by reprocessing or off-line repair. In many companies rework levels are so high and have been at constant levels for so long that they are regarded by many as a normal feature of production. Rework should in fact be regarded as a totally unnecessary form of loss, and every item of rework as representing yet another form of excessive inventory.

Occasionally, other words are used to make rework appear respectable, for example 'fitting'. Fitting is usually an excuse to explain why the component elements do not fit together at the first attempt. Historically, imprecise processes may have forced the introduction of a fitting operation. The pressures of everyday work frequently ensure that such operations are not reviewed, with the result that while technology may have long since eliminated the need for 'fitting' the activity remains. This would not be the case in the JIT factory.

One of the more obvious causes of work-in-progress in most factories comes in the form of scrap, a word used to describe product which – like 'reworkable' product – is outside specification but in this case is unfit for use and is not repairable. This is not to be confused with waste, which includes offcuts and the like.

Most companies are very sensitive about scrap. Most keep statistics to show levels of scrap, trends and so on. Surprisingly, considerably fewer organizations convert these quantities into cost figures, and even fewer break them down into specific cost items. Even when the costs are calculated, they are usually expressed in the form of direct added value up to the point where the deficiency was discovered. It is most unusual to find any computations which also take into account the consequential losses. For example, there is the time spent in placating an irate customer; the loss of machine time; the effect on scheduling; the costs associated with the purchase of replacement materials. Where individual components are scrapped, the cost of stockholding associated products which must be held in temporary storage awaiting the arrival of satisfactory replacement parts is never included in the figures. Neither are any estimates relating to the loss of sales revenue.

Even without inflating the costs with these additional considerations, the actual direct cost of scrap and rework is considerably higher than most people would imagine. Typically, figures suggesting 20 per cent of sales revenue are frequently quoted in text material. In fact, these figures, staggering though they may well be, are generally quite conservative estimates. Many cases are quoted from very sophisticated companies which suggest that the true figure can be as high as 40 per cent of sales revenue. When consequential costs are also taken into account, the resulting computation can be horrendous. In most companies these hidden losses are a bigger threat to their survival than any lack of government investment. But then a high proportion of manufacturing companies in the West do have bleak prospects. The fact that Western manufacturing industry has been in a state of decline for two to three decades is a direct consequence of Western inability to face up to the fact of manufacturing inefficiency and do something about it.

These costs or losses represent the real opportunity. Any company which is currently surviving has an opportunity to attack these costs in an effective organized manner, not only to ensure its future survival, but to attain the position of brand leader.

There is nothing that the Japanese can do that others cannot do as well or possibly better.

The 20–40 per cent quality-related loss is not only recoverable, the savings made go straight to the bottom line in the form of profit: possibly not in total but experience suggests that a 50 per cent reduction in three to five years is achievable. This represents a potential gain which is available now. No purchase of sophisticated plant, systems or high flying specialists. Nothing but the simple, down-to-earth application of techniques which have been used by Japanese companies for decades – and which, incredibly, were originally developed in the West.

PRODUCT MODIFICATIONS

Product changes are of two kinds, *planned* and *unplanned*.

Planned product changes normally occur in a predetermined cycle. For example, a television manufacturer or car manufacturer may have a policy to restructure the design completely on a two-yearly or three-yearly cycle, with minor face-lifts every twelve months or so. These changes, assuming that they happen according to plan, should have little effect on stockholding and inventory levels generally. Based on past experience, stocks of replacement parts and tools for customers with obsolete designs can be calculated and held on an economic basis, related to company policy or customer support.

However, it is the unscheduled product changes which cause the biggest nightmare for the 'would-be' JIT factory. Costs associated with these changes usually go far beyond the immediate cost of the changes themselves, and have in some instances been responsible for the demise of the business!

In terms of JIT, the introduction of an unscheduled change will have an immediate effect on the rate of turnover of components or products already in the system. Manufacture of these parts or products would have been planned months, possibly years, ahead of the change which is taking place. Stocks of these items – calculated on the assumption of rapid turnover – will now become slow moving since they will only be required for spares. Sometimes these modifications are forced on a manufacturer by unpredictable changes in customer requirements, by legislation or the actions of competitors. More usually they are caused by lack of design-proving activities prior to full-scale production.

A classic, if dramatic example was that of a large industrial battery manufacturer who introduced a design modification to an existing product but did not adequately prove the new design first. The modification involved the change of specification of the plastic separators between the electrodes. The new plastic was of a higher specification in terms of the materials used, and therefore more expensive. However, the change was made to overcome a production difficulty experienced with the original plastic. On balance the cost saving gained in production outweighed the extra cost of the material.

However, because tests were not carried out, it was not known that the new material had a slow long-term reaction with the battery chemicals. The original battery was known to last well beyond the warranty period under normal conditions of use. The reaction with the chemical changed this and failures began to occur within the warranty period. The result was a sharp rise in warranty costs, accompanied by a loss of reputation in the marketplace. Although a design change was introduced as quickly as possible after the cause had been identified, there were still approximately five years' worth of production of the faulty batteries in the field. The costs of warranty loss and loss of reputation are incalculable.

This example seems dramatic, and many now assume that it was an isolated occurrence. The sad thing is that such experiences are all too common. The rest of this book could easily be devoted to real problems which have arisen across the entire product spectrum, all at least as serious as this example.

In the case of products containing multiple components, such as automobiles, televisions, major domestic products and the like, these changes not only occur to the product itself, but assembly by assembly, component by component and supplier by supplier. Existing components can sometimes be modified. For example, a hole may be increased in size. Even in such cases spares must be held for replacement parts to existing designs already sold. In the other cases, the effect on achievement of JIT is only too obvious.

SUPPLIERS' QUALITY AND DELIVERY – EFFECT ON WORK-IN-PROGRESS

The role of the supplier is critical to the achievement of JIT, as was brought out earlier in this chapter; so much so that many organizations have attempted to tackle this aspect first. In my opinion, this would be a mistake.

It can be seen from the foregoing discussion that even in the aspects of JIT which have already been considered the problems are both numerous and complex. For example, a reduction in the number of unscheduled design modifications can only be achieved by a thorough analysis of why they occur in the first place. To do this successfully would first require an analysis of past modifications to establish common factors and to highlight the root cause. This would probably lead to the identification of weaknesses in the organized relationships between marketing and design, design and production, finance and so on. It is therefore readily evident that the achievement of JIT is not simple. It is not just a case of kicking the supplier on delivery schedules. A great deal of skill and know-how is required, and where better to acquire such skills than in our own organization? Our organization is a laboratory where we can prove the management skills we intend to suggest to our suppliers. Only then should we go to our suppliers, but we would now be going as experts and could help them to achieve success rather than simply exert pressure.

The most obvious place where supplier performance affects JIT is the goods inwards store – a point made at the beginning of this chapter. Frequently less obvious is the effect on work-in-progress when suppliers are late or when there are quality deficiencies. The general manager of the General Motors plant mentioned in Chapter 1 claimed that supplier quality was currently the biggest single obstacle to the further development of JIT.

Parts not to specification, missing components, wrong materials – all these lead to scheduling problems which will affect work-in-progress.

The quality manager of a leading engineering manufacturer once claimed that while the company had a sophisticated on-line computer scheduling system, even real-time could not deal with the unexpected non-arrival of some essential component or other. He said that when the line stopped due either to stock of a particular item being out or the discovery that some component did not fit, production would frequently be diverted to an alternative product for which appropriate stocks were available. There would sometimes be insufficient stocks of all the components for any product. In this case production would continue knowing that the item could not go into the finished goods warehouse until the missing item could be obtained and fitted. He also said that it was not unusual for such products to be subsequently cannibalized to complete the production of other products requiring identical components just to be able to ship some stock before the month-end figures.

The question is, what can be done about it? Are these problems inevitable? The reaction from some companies which identify the problems will be: 'Yes, but you don't understand the peculiar problems we face in our industry.' 'Our market is different.' 'Our suppliers are different.' 'We have special problems with our workforce.' And many more.

These arguments are nothing but roadblocks. There are very few situations which are peculiar to one particular industry. Even when they are, one does not usually have to look very far to find some companies which have found their way around them. These are the challenges which form the essence of JIT thinking, and which must be faced if success or even survival is to be achieved.

The solution, or breakthrough to the solution, to these myriad problems does not normally lie in the organization of a mainframe computer or sophisticated software. These often seem attractive remedies but only because they appear to provide an opportunity to jump straight from symptom to remedy without first establishing the true cause or causes by the necessary data collection and analysis. More usually the assumptions prove wrong with the consequences that more money is spent, or rather wasted, and the original problems remain. Until we can obtain predictability from both our own processes and products and the products of our suppliers, the benefits of JIT will elude us regardless of the sophistication of advanced process-control techniques and scheduling procedures.

SCHEDULING/FORECASTING AND MACHINE LOADING

This book does not contain a detailed discussion of these concepts. As with other computer-aided features of production, such discussion would take the book beyond its objectives.

However, since computerized production control and scheduling are often related to forecasting and forecasting skills, it is necessary at this point to consider an important and relevant concept related to JIT.

PUSH/PULL PRODUCTION

Basically, production can be considered in two categories:

1 produce on demand (pull system);
2 produce to forecasts of demand or make to stock (push system).

Some companies have a policy of not producing anything until a customer is found. At the other extreme, in other companies products may be made in large quantities in the hope that supply and demand can be matched by advertising and by giving high visibility to the product, as in the case of domestic products sold in supermarkets.

Between these extremes, there exists a vast range of products in which the manufacturer may use a combination of both. For example, in the manufacture of wallpaper there are a number of basic materials and operations which are common to all finished products irrespective of the pattern selected by the customer. Usually, literally hundreds of different designs are offered by most leading manufacturers. Clearly, it would not be feasible to manufacture all these in vast quantities to be stocked by retailers in the hope that customers will purchase them proportionately. No one can afford to tie up that amount of money, and the risks relating to the losses from dead or slow-moving products would be inconceivable.

The usual strategy is not to supply the retailer with any stock at all. Only a pattern book. However, it is essential that the manufacturer should be able to respond instantly to demand. People wishing to decorate their houses usually want the materials immediately. Suppliers who can respond most quickly will probably obtain a higher share of the market than their otherwise equal competitors.

The manufacturer normally achieves this by storing product in his or her warehouse at the last possible stage before it becomes dedicated to a specific design. In this way he or she is in the best position to respond to market demand very quickly, and at the same time optimize the capital tied up in stockholding high added value product.

The two systems referred to are generally known as 'push' in the case of production to forecast, but not realized, demand; and 'pull' in the case of making to order.

In the wallpaper example, the process would be regarded as 'push' up to the point of warehousing the part-finished product and 'pull' from that point through to the ultimate customer, assuming that the retailer did not purchase for stockholding.

The JIT company would attempt to use 'pull' as far into the process as it could possibly go. In the case of the wallpaper factory, the virtues of using push/pull in the manner described in the example would appear to be fairly obvious good practice and the concept likely to go unchallenged. In the company where JIT thinking had become established this would not be so. In the JIT factory, the value of these part-finished goods would be regarded as a constant challenge. 'What could we do,' the management would ask, 'to make successive upstream operations sufficiently responsive to demand to render the store unnecessary? Ideally, if we could avoid making anything until it is required, that would be the point of minimum cost.' There are many other examples where push/pull are combined.

In the Toyota factory, for some items the pull system applies almost all the way back through the supply chain. Vehicles on the final assembly line have the customer's name attached to the windscreen.

Advantages and disadvantages of push/pull

The principal advantage of the push system is predictability of scheduling and machine loading. This lends itself to computerization which in turn makes it possible, on paper at least, to produce plans involving the production of products in a variety of mixtures, which could not be easily worked out using manual methods. Also, these plans can be changed easily and options worked out using simulations and literature processes. The disadvantages are that in all but the near perfect plant, the plans rarely work in practice. All the problems identified in the earlier part of this chapter can occur at any time, and frequently do. Some systems allow for this, but the allowances usually generalize based upon past experience. The danger here is accepting these allowances as norms and rarely challenging them. Perhaps the main disadvantage of the push system is inaccuracy of forecasting. Some refer to this as the 'crystal ball gazing' phase. No matter how good the feedback may be from marketing and market research, differences between forecast and actual performances are bound to occur. Sometimes this will result in products moving more slowly than predicted. The result: warehouses full of unsold product; supermarkets stocked with slow-moving items taking up space on the display shelves. At other times it means that demand will outstrip supply. When this happens panic usually sets in, sensitivities relating to lost sales run high, corners are cut and mistakes occur. These will often result in lost sales in the future and a vicious cycle may begin.

With the pull system, things are different. Generally it is less dependent on computers and more on the ability of the system to respond to sudden and unexpected demands. This is the principal advantage of the Kanban System. The principal disadvantage of the pull system is the risk of not being able to respond to unexpected demand. In its ultimate state, there will be no stocks of anything at any point, nothing being made until it is wanted. Any breakdown in this system will result in a failed expectation. In its ultimate state, the pull system has no built-in safety factors. Everything must respond positively when demand materializes. Obviously, compromises must be made, particularly in the later stages of development, but ultimately this is the goal.

The pull system places great demands on those responsible for its maintenance. Machines must be in good working order at all times when demand is expected. Planned maintenance is therefore essential. Process capabilities must be such that inspection of parts becomes totally unnecessary. Everything must be *right the first time*! (Parts per million defects – ppm!) The implications of ppm-level defects for quality assurance and quality control techniques were discussed in Chapter 1. However, the achievement of ppm goes far beyond the application of techniques; it requires a totally new approach to work.

Relationships with the workforce must be such that stoppages are virtually non-existent, motivation levels high and skill levels always at least adequate for the task in hand. It requires professionalism of the highest order. All operators must be skilled in problem-solving both on an individual and a group basis. In fact, the demands of the pull system are identical to those for the 'hard' conveyor system described earlier.

These demands may be hard to achieve in the last stages, but the pay-off comes in the form of zero inventory, virtually zero scrap and rework, no unscheduled plant breakdowns and rapid response to demand.

Where 'push' is required, the aim should be to keep batch quantities at the lowest possible level, frequent small batches being the target. Of course, this puts demands on management to ensure the quickest possible tool changes, and reference has already been made to possibilities in this respect.

Finished goods warehouse

One of the goals of JIT is the total elimination of this facility. Consider the financial implications of such an achievement. Even modest-sized companies often keep huge quantities of finished product in warehouses all over the country. Quite apart from the stock value of products stored in this way, additional costs are incurred through deterioration, heating, maintenance, handling, damage – not to mention 'picking errors', this being the term used to describe the selection of wrong items from stock. Figure 2.4 gives a pictorial example of this.

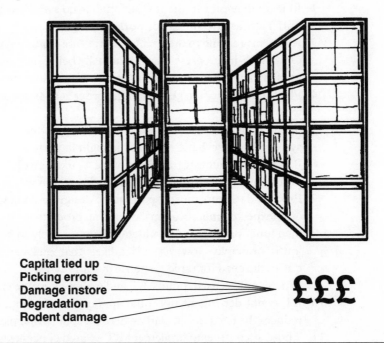

Capital tied up
Picking errors
Damage instore
Degradation
Rodent damage

£££

Figure 2.4   The hidden costs of the finished goods store

In our example in Chapter 1, a large finished goods warehouse containing £26 million of finished product which turns over six times a year, it was found that 2 per cent was damaged by fork-lift trucks, other product by pallet collapse and bad stacking; significant sums were spent to avoid rodent damage. In addition to this, the record system was such that there were frequent instances of the stock records giving inaccurate quantities or even showing the wrong products in some locations. On top of all this is the question of 'shrink-age', a term used to account for 'inexplicable' losses of product from the store.

In the ideal JIT factory operating the pull system, there will be no finished goods warehouse. Following the final operation, the product is loaded on to a pallet, shrink-wrapped and placed into a waiting lorry usually destined for the customer or other point of sale.

The JIT factory is considerably smaller for a given volume of output than its more traditional competitor.

Summary

From all the examples and discussion in this chapter, certain common factors emerge:

1　In its ultimate form, the JIT factory has no safety margins in the form of buffer stocks, live storage or work-in-progress.
2　All norms relating to these safety factors are continually challenged.
3　Only work-in-progress which is actually being processed at any one time goes unchallenged, and even then some operations may be eliminated.
4　Plant must be kept in good working order at all times using planned maintenance routines.
5　'Hard' conveyor assembly is more likely to produce JIT results than 'soft' systems because 'hard' systems highlight faults more dramatically.
6　JIT requires intensive application of worker-involvement programmes, particularly those where problem-solving techniques are incorporated.
7　Product designers must use adequate design proving to minimize the risk of unexpected modifications to existing products.
8　The 'pull' principle of production is more likely to achieve JIT than the 'push' principle. However, it is unlikely that 'pull' can be used exclusively due to the need for rapid response in some cases.
9　Where 'pull' is used, points 3, 5 and 6 above become critically important.
10　JIT is not dependent upon the application of computers. If anything it reduces the need, particularly where the 'pull' principle is being applied.
11　Those attempting to implement JIT-related concepts would be advised to gain success in their own organizations before attempting to put their suppliers' houses in order.
12　JIT cannot be achieved overnight. It is a long-term goal. It involves all personnel at all levels in a continuous year-by-year process. The real questions are when, where and how to get started.

Recommended further reading

Juran, Dr J. M. (1974) *Quality Control Handbook*, 3rd edn, McGraw-Hill – particularly Chapters 4, 'Quality and income', and 5, 'Quality costs'.

Juran, Dr J. M. (1981) *Management of Quality*, Juran Institute – Chapter 5, 'The remedial journey'.

Juran, Dr J. M. and Gryna, Dr F. M. (1980) *Quality Planning and Analysis*, McGraw-Hill – particularly Chapters 1, 'Basic concepts', and 2, 'Quality costs'.

Schonberger, Richard J. (1982) *Japanese Manufacturing Techniques*, Free Press – particularly Chapters 2, 'Just in Time production with total quality control', and 7, 'Just in Time purchasing', and Appendix, 'The Kanban System'.

Recommended further reading

3 THE PROCESS OF IMPROVEMENT

Motivation

The 12 lessons set out in the summary to Chapter 2 require a radical change of thinking in management and can only be achieved by a high level of motivation across the company's workforce.

Motivation is discussed in some detail in Chapter 7. However, since even to start the change process the motivation of upper management is essential, some treatment of the topic is given here. Motivation of managers for JIT comes at three levels:

1 motivation for control;
2 motivation for improvement;
3 motivation for involvement.

All managers accept responsibility for control and most are practised in the techniques for control. They regard their ability to control as a major aspect of the judgement of their performance.

Indeed, a high proportion of management energy is expended fighting to keep the process for which they are responsible within control conditions. The fact that sporadic departures from these conditions occur frequently means that firefighting is regarded as an essential and major part of a manager's everyday life.

Most managers would like to see improvements. However, few managers would generally regard improvement as being a line management responsibility. In these days of specialization of labour and managerial responsibility, improvement would be regarded by most managers as an off-line responsibility. To take an example: in a modern factory the line managers would not typically have been responsible for the design, selection, acquisition and commissioning of the plant in their departments. This would probably have been carried out by an off-line production engineering department. Inevitably the line would have various shortcomings which would affect performance. Because they had not participated in the selection process, they would probably not feel responsible for overcoming these problems. They would regard them as evidence of the shortcomings of the specialist department, and use every opportunity to highlight these when their own overall performance was low, as in the example given in Chapter 2 in the section on 'Plant or machine breakdown'.

The fact that they do not feel responsible for the cause of the problems is likely to lead them to believe that they are not responsible for overcoming them either. In addition, they are probably so busy fighting sporadic 'fires' that they have no time for improvement activities. In this case each manager will inevitably decide 'well, at least I must make sure that things don't get worse'.

The third form of motivation, involvement, is generally accepted by most managers in the sense that they would normally agree to participate in the achievement of the company's goals and plans. Most managers would regard this as being inherent in the role of management. However, there is a problem in as much as many of these goals appear to compete or conflict with one another. For example, the need for volume output might appear to conflict with the need for high quality. Sometimes goals in one department may clash with those of another. For example, design may produce a cheap design to meet cost constraints from marketing or finance, but in so doing conflict with the needs of production, who are primarily concerned with ease of manufacture. This may also conflict with the goals of the quality department which is concerned to establish in the marketplace a reputation for reliability.

These conflicts result in trade-offs, which may or may not be in the company's best interests. Chapter 2, for example, described how fear of the consequences of 'stock out' retribution may lead to holding excessively high stock levels, because these were less likely to be challenged.

The lesson is clear. Since all managers are highly motivated to achieve the company's goals, conflicts arise from apparently competing goals, and from goals where there is an extreme penalty for error in one situation, as in the stockholding case, but not in other, equally important situations. Since upper management is responsible for setting goals, only upper management can provide a remedy for the problem of unclear or conflicting goals.

Managers' preoccupation with 'control' has led precisely to the non-JIT-type organizations with which most of us are familiar.

Added to this, management accounting methods encourage the same type of thinking. Standard costing techniques require budgets to be fixed and standard cost values applied to 'cost centres'. These cost centres do not usually discriminate between productive and non-productive cost centres in a manner which would lead to JIT consciousness.

When standards have been set, 'management by exception' takes over. Only those costs which vary significantly from the standard are highlighted. Even there, it is usually only the adverse variances which are challenged. For example, 'Why has this process got worse?' On the other hand, positive variances are regarded as a bonus, which may sometimes offset some of the negative variances. Rarely do managers find the time to look for the causes of positive variances with the object of holding the gains and reducing the standard cost.

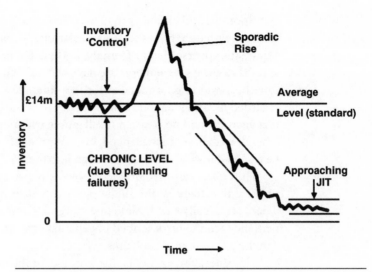

Figure 3.1 Chronic and sporadic inventory problems

Chronic and sporadic problems

Consider Figure 3.1, adapted from Dr J. M. Juran's *Managerial Breakthrough*, which typifies a great many situations. At a given stage in a process, inventory has been running for years at a level of, say, £14 million. At various times managers may have tried unsuccessfully to reduce this level. Eventually they conclude, 'our job is to hold this level'. This would be particularly true if their experience suggested that such a level was typical in the circumstances. In other words, they are now practising 'control'. Suddenly, the situation becomes worse and inventory soars to £20 million. Panic sets in and specialists converge on the scene. The cause of the change becomes known, remedial action is taken, and the inventory levels soon return to £14 million. At this point the problem would be regarded as having been solved. Other sporadic events elsewhere divert managerial attention until a similar event reoccurs. Many managers regard this activity as the core of their responsibility.

In Chapter 2 we saw that in the JIT factory the main concentration would not be directed towards the sporadic problems, because their solution presents no change whatever from past performance. The main effort would be concentrated on the £14 million. If this could be reduced, say, to £7 million or even lower, this would be a big improvement and the savings made could be used for investment elsewhere, or even in the further development of the JIT concept. In 'Juran' terminology, the £14 million represents the 'chronic' level; the sudden rise to £20 million represents a 'sporadic' rise. The achievement of JIT requires a sustained unrelenting attack on the *chronic* level.

Sporadic and chronic problems differ in several ways. Sporadic problems are by their nature both sudden and alarming – mainly because they represent a dramatic adverse change from the normal. On the other hand, chronic problems have always been there. We have become accustomed to them and therefore they tend to go unnoticed for the same reason. These problems are not regarded as being 'anyone's fault'. They have survived successive changes of management and no one can recall a time when these problems did not exist. Therefore they go unchallenged, but it is precisely these problems which must be resolved if we are to break through into the JIT future.

How then can the chronic problems be isolated and tackled? First, it is unlikely that there is one single problem which makes up the chronic level. There are usually a few, sometimes several. Even when they have been identified, they tend to be described in generic terms which in themselves represent a multitude of related problems.

Consider, for example, the chronic problem of £14 million of stock. Analysis may show that this figure represents the average stock level. In practice the stock may fluctuate between £18 million and £10 million between receipt and restocking, as shown in Figure 3.2. This indicates a buffer stock of £10 million.

Ignoring the possibilities for reducing the general level by changing batch sizes and reorder period, the chronic level could be regarded as £10 million. The reasons for this high level could typically be as follows:

1 Following a previous attempt to reduce the base level arbitrarily, a 'stock out' situation arose due to a late delivery. The experimental reduction was abandoned and previous policies were restored.

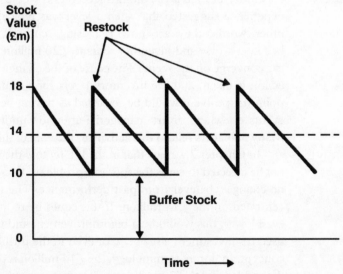

Figure 3.2 Typical stock fluctuations

2 The purchasing officer playing safe.

3 Similar to 1 above, the call on stores was suddenly unexpectedly high and again a 'stock out' situation arose. This time it probably coincided with a crisis situation for other reasons.

Points 1 and 3 above must be resolved on a permanent basis if JIT is to be achieved. Both probably occur frequently. Demand does vary and deliveries are unpredictable.

At this stage, we appear to have only three problems. However, if we study the possible reasons for late delivery, we soon discover a multitude of possibilities. For example:

- supplier quality problems
- distribution
- poor communication
- inadequate documentation
- too many small suppliers
- supplier too far away
- supplier given wrong information
- supplier took risk
- sub-supplier.

This complexity in the specific causes of chronic problems is another key reason why such problems are not often tackled. No one has the time to identify the symptoms, and then to establish the causes, find remedies, implement them, and then hold the gains. So, the problems go on and on.

How then can the JIT improvement concept be put to work? Usually on a teamwork basis.

The first step is to establish an organization team or steering team to guide the development of the process throughout the company as a whole. Usually a team is formed comprising high-level managers. In most companies, the team comprises directors or vice-presidents of the company. In large organizations, sub-teams are formed in the larger sectors of the organization. In multi-site organizations, separate teams are formed at each location. A more detailed discussion of this type of team appears in Chapter 9.

These teams formulate the general policy, set priorities and monitor the programme. They also identify team leaders to form specific JIT action teams. The JIT team leader will usually work with the steering team to agree terms of reference, clarify objectives and resources, and select team members. These teams may be *ad hoc* and are formed for a specific JIT project. The steering teams are permanent. A member of one JIT team may subsequently become the leader of another. Leaders are selected, not on rank, but on ability to lead the project. JIT project team leaders are usually those who know most about the problem to be tackled and who will probably be most likely to be involved in implementing the results.

The teams thus formed use a number of techniques, most of which will be very familiar to those experienced in Quality Circle activities and other types of small group. The first teams, however, will not normally be at employee level; ideally they should represent the highest level of the organization. The problems they will tackle will often be strategic from a business point of view, and will have a direct bearing on major company policies, for example supplier relations. The first project teams will also be intended to start the process of cultural change in the organization: the concept of continuous project by project improvement; the continual challenging of norms. Breaking down the 'department first' spirit into a 'company first' mentality cannot start from the bottom. Experience has also shown that unless these changes are started at the top, there is little chance that the process will work.

Universal problem-solving sequence

Reference was made in earlier chapters to the fact that managers all too frequently attempt to make improvements by treating the symptoms rather than by establishing the true cause. For example, to overcome the problem of late deliveries, a case may be made out to purchase a sophisticated computer software package to improve scheduling. The arguments look impressive, but are in all probability based upon erroneous assumptions. The advocates of the proposals may have assumed that late deliveries are caused by inaccurate forecasting and poor-quality scheduling. This assumption has probably never been tested or challenged – why? 'Because it is time-consuming and complicated to collect the data' and, anyway, 'everyone knows that this is the cause of the problem'. How do they know?

Since the appearance in the 1980s of project by project improvement, based on concepts described by Dr J. M. Juran, literally hundreds – probably thousands – of cases have been reported where subsequent studies have shown that such assumptions, even those held by respected experts, have not been borne out by the facts. Unchallenged acceptance of the assumptions will invariably result in a costly discovery that the true problem lies elsewhere than in the forecasting or scheduling process. The real problem is more likely to be related to unpredictability in the supply and manufacturing process. Resolve these problems, and the need for the software will probably diminish markedly.

The reason managers repeatedly fall into the trap of jumping to conclusions is mainly that they are not properly familiar with the problem-solving process, and are therefore not sensitized to challenge assumptions.

Dr Juran states that all problem-solving, all breakthrough, follows a universal sequence of events. Avoiding this sequence is likely to lead to erroneous premises and non-solutions. All successful projects follow the sequence:

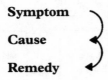

Symptom

Cause

Remedy

Thus there are two journeys: from symptom to cause and from cause to remedy.

In our example the symptom is 'late delivery'. It has already been shown that in many cases a remedy will be offered based upon assumptions. In this case the assumption was that late deliveries were caused by poor forecasting, and so on. That was a theory. The chances are that there are also a great many other theories held by other people. In the breakthrough sequence, these theories would be identified using the brainstorming process. This would usually be conducted by a project team formed for the purpose, and would form the start of the diagnostic journey as follows:

Symptom

● *Theories of causes*

● *Test of theories*

Cause (*establishment of*)

The brainstorming process is usually very revealing, and a great many ideas are brought to the surface. It is not unusual for there to be forty to fifty theories. Those who participate in such sessions are generally quite surprised at the number of possible causes highlighted in this way.

Brainstorming for causes of problems can be carried out simply by listing the ideas as they are suggested on a large sheet of paper, usually a flipchart. However, many of the suggested ideas will relate to each other, and this method of brainstorm recording makes it difficult to cluster the theories into cause types. While there are many ways in which this can be done, two approaches have proved popular and often extremely effective in this type of work.

PROCESS ANALYSIS

This technique will be considered again in Chapter 6.

Boxes are drawn on a flipchart, as shown in Figure 3.3, commencing on the right-hand side of the sheet, and working towards the left. The right-hand

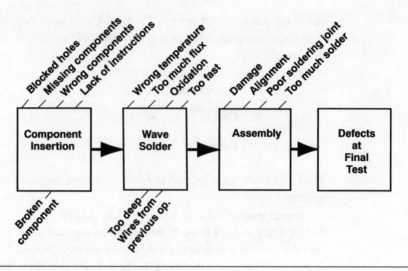

Figure 3.3 Brainstorming: the process analysis chart

box contains the name of the symptom or undesirable effect for which the causes must be found. In Figure 3.3 'Assembly' is shown as a simple operation. In reality this would probably consist of several operations in sequence, and these would each be indicated on the chart. When all operations or stages have been included, each box is brainstormed separately, usually commencing with the box on the left and working towards the right. This technique has several advantages:

1 It ensures that no process is overlooked. This could easily happen with a more indiscriminate form of brainstorming.
2 It will reveal at a glance whether some operations are more critical than others.
3 Occasionally patterns will emerge; for example, 'handling damage' may appear at several boxes, indicating that handling is something which needs specific attention.

Following completion of the process analysis chart, it is necessary to carry out some diagnosis or data collection. Many possible causes will have been revealed, but they are not necessarily of equal importance, or even realistic in some cases. They are only theories. As has been stated earlier, all assumptions must be tested. Many will turn out to be false – that is probably why the problem has not already been solved.

Following data collection and analysis, it may be revealed that one or a number of the theories turn out to be correct, and a true cause has been isolated. For example, suppose that it has been proven that a principal cause of late deliveries happens to be 'torn package' and that this occurs at four

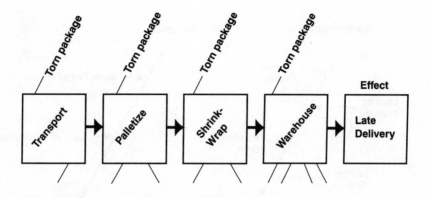

Figure 3.4   Process analysis of late deliveries

possible stages (as shown in Figure 3.4). Further data have been collected and it is discovered that the majority of the damage occurs in the warehouse.

At this point, it may be necessary to revert to brainstorming to determine the possible causes of 'torn package' in the warehouse. In this case a further variation of brainstorming might be used called the 'Ishikawa diagram' or 'fishbone diagram'.

ISHIKAWA OR 'FISHBONE' DIAGRAM

This technique is used when a very specific cause has been located, and it then becomes necessary to penetrate that cause and break it down into its minutest detail. Process analysis would not be used because we are only concerned with one specific element in the process.

Constructing a fishbone diagram is relatively simple. Again, the symptom or 'effect' is written in a box on the right-hand side of a large sheet of paper, with an arrow pointing to it as shown in Figure 3.5. It then becomes necessary to identify the most likely main cause groups. These can vary depending upon the situation, but there are frequently four, often described by a number of terms from each of the generic terms: manpower, machines, methods and

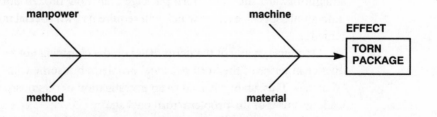

Figure 3.5   Cause classification of fishbone diagram

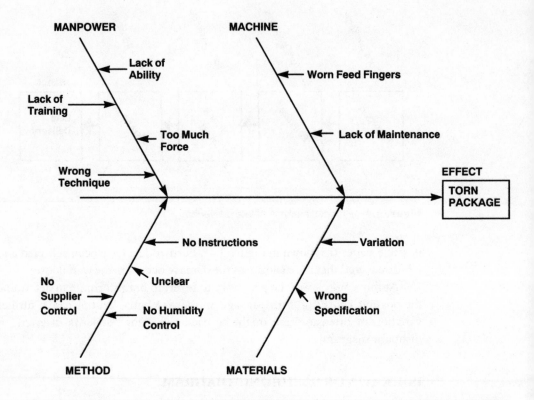

Figure 3.6 Cause classification diagram for torn packages

materials (conveniently referred to as the four Ms). These terms may not always be appropriate. For example, instead of 'machine', it might be better in some situations to use 'equipment', 'apparatus' or 'tooling', or instead of 'method' other terms more appropriate to the situation might be 'job instructions', 'procedures' or 'specification'.

When the diagram has been constructed in this way, the brainstorming begins. When completed, it may look something like Figure 3.6.

It can be seen from Figure 3.6 that what started out as a seemingly straightforward situation, 'torn package', has now broken out into dozens of individual aspects, each of which will require its own special investigation and remedy.

Of course, many of the items listed on the chart will not be of great consequence in terms of the 'torn package' problem, but some will. The question is 'Which?'. This again will lead to an investigation or diagnosis, to establish the leading causes of the problem 'torn package'.

Sometimes the true cause may itself lead to a further fishbone diagram. For example, suppose that it was discovered that 'grease on floors' turned out to be the leading cause of 'torn package'. A project team found that because of grease on the warehouse floor, fork-lift trucks were skidding into stacks. 'Grease on floors' might then become the object of a further fishbone diagram.

It can be seen that this process can be continued into more and more detail until eventually all the root causes have been identified. When this happens, rather than some superficial remedy such as motivate the workers, specific remedies are usually found for the very real problems which exist.

This example demonstrates that we have come a long way from the original belief that late deliveries can be solved simply by acquiring a computer. This will not solve the problem of grease on the warehouse floor, neither will it provide the means by which the problem is identified in the first place!

Of course, no one is suggesting that greasy floors are the sole cause of torn packages, or that torn packages are the sole cause of late deliveries. At each stage of process analysis with the fishbone diagram the problem is broken down into its specific elements. If there had been literally one single cause of late deliveries, the chances are that it would have been discovered long ago. It is most likely that there are two principal reasons why the problem remains:

1 It is not one problem but the collective symptoms of what could be literally dozens of specific problems, greasy floors being only one of them.
2 The vagueness of the description of the problem – late deliveries – usually leads managers to believe that the problem is more likely to be caused by someone else. They are therefore unlikely to set aside resources from their own department; they are more likely to accuse others.

So much for the diagnostic journey from symptom to cause. Once the true cause or causes have been identified it becomes necessary to consider possible remedies.

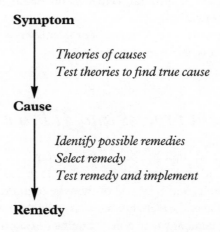

Symptom

Theories of causes
Test theories to find true cause

Cause

Identify possible remedies
Select remedy
Test remedy and implement

Remedy

Overcome resistance to change
Hold the gains

The remedial journey differs significantly from the diagnostic journey. It is frequently done by different people. For instance, suppose in the previous example that the cause of the greasy floors was found to be leaks in the sumps of fork-lift trucks: it is likely that the remedy would be in the hands of the maintenance department.

If, however, it turned out that the problem was caused by oily swarf being taken from the production department to the scrap tip, the remedy would be found by the production department. These transfers of responsibilities are discussed in more detail in Chapter 6.

Remedies can fall into two categories: reversible and irreversible. Examples of reversible and irreversible remedies can be found in the 'greasy floors' problem.

In the case where the grease is spilt by production workers carrying oily swarf through the warehouse, it may be that they are found to be overloading the transporters to the extent that the oil can drip over the side of the transporter. A remedy might be to instruct the workers not to overload the transporters. However, this would be a reversible remedy. Without proper surveillance, it is possible for the workers to return to their old habits. This would not be an unusual situation.

On the other hand, if the transporters were to be physically modified so as to make it impossible to overload them, or redesigned so as to prevent them from dripping however much they had been overloaded, this would be an irreversible remedy.

A choice between reversible and irreversible is not always available, but before applying any remedy it is always advisable to see whether there is a possibly foolproof way to prevent a future recurrence. The trouble with foolproofing is that each individual situation will have its own specific needs. The advantage of foolproofing is that, by definition, the problem will be solved on a permanent basis.

To ensure no recurrence of problems when reversible remedies have been applied, it is necessary to introduce a *process audit* to ensure that the gains are held.

The improvement process and JIT: a case study

This case example has been selected from a very wide range of possibilities as it encapsulates many of the points made in this chapter. It is based on a real-life example, and is typical of the type of improvement possible through the application of the techniques discussed in this book.

The company concerned manufactures products in the medium to heavy electrical engineering field. These may become part of large installations forming part of chemical plants, steel works, and so on. The product is basically a large steel container slightly longer than a double wardrobe and sprayed with a matt finish. Inside, it is literally packed with electrical components such as capacitors, transformers and contact breakers. The company's factory was built in the mid-1970s on a greenfield site, for a target turnover of £2 million.

Prior to commencing the improvement programme, the factory was working to capacity but achieving a turnover of only £1.6 million. It was totally congested with product at various stages of manufacture, or awaiting acceptance testing by the customer.

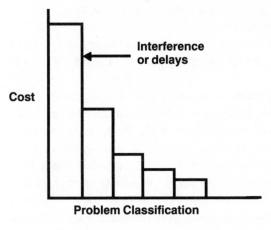

Project teams were formed with the object of identifying, analysing and solving problems relating to under-achievement of company objectives. Seven teams were formed initially and in this example the activities of only one of the teams will be followed. This team consisted of production workers engaged in the assembly of the products.

Initially, the team conducted a brainstorming session to identify major problems. Using the 'Pareto' technique for separating the important few problems from the less important many, the team selected 'hold-ups' or delays in production for its project, as shown in Figure 3.7.

Figure 3.7   Pareto diagram of brainstormed problems

Note: Pareto is the name of an Italian-American scholar who discovered in the nineteenth century that 80 per cent of the wealth was in the hands of 20 per cent of the population. It was later found that this curious 80:20 relationship occurred in many situations. For example, analysis may show that 80 per cent of the losses in a department are caused by 20 per cent of the problems.

In our example, the team then conducted a secondary brainstorming of hold-ups to determine the critical types of delay, as shown in Figure 3.8. A number of ideas were put forward including:

- lost tools
- misplaced tools
- broken or worn tools
- interference from other departments
- damage to product
- out of stock components
- wrong instructions
- lack of instructions.

Brainstorm List

Figure 3.8 Brainstorm list of 'delays'

It was the opinion of the team that 'out of stock components' was the biggest cause of delay. This opinion had been held for years. However, true to the process, the team collected data to determine the relative importance of each of these potential causes.

To do this, the team constructed a data sheet (as shown in Figure 3.9) and obtained the co-operation of other employees in the department to record the results over a one-month period. From these data a further Pareto diagram was constructed, as shown in Figure 3.10.

It can be seen from Figure 3.10 that out of stock components, far from being the primary cause of delays, were well down the list.

The number one cause, which incidentally had not previously made much of an impression on the team, proved to be the interruption caused on those occasions when the design was modified while the product was being assembled. Such events obviously occurred far more frequently, and caused a much greater time loss, than was realized. However, this problem was outside the scope of the team, and so it selected the second most important as the first project. This problem turned out to be 'lost and misplaced tools'. The team not only solved the problem, but managed also to introduce a self-managed

Data Sheet							
Delay Type	Mon	Tu	Wed	Th	Fri	Total	Time Lost
Material Shortage							
Worn Tools	20M			10M			
Misplaced Tools	1 Hr						
Engineering Changes	2 Hr		8 Hr		16 Hr		
Damage	20M		10M		20M		
Test	8 Hr						
Misc.	5M						

Figure 3.9 Data sheet constructed by the team

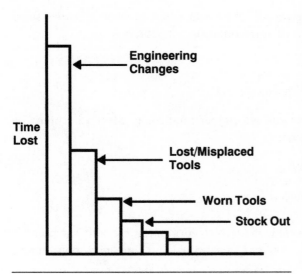

Figure 3.10 Pareto diagram showing results of data collection

planned maintenance routine. Eventually, project by project, the team got down to the 'out of stock components' problem. It found that 'stock outs' rarely if ever occurred with the major items in the product, only with the smaller items such as cable clips, self-tapping screws, and so on. The reason, it was discovered, was that the design department produced parts lists of only the main items. These lists were supplied to the buying department as a purchasing aid. The buying department therefore had very precise information as to the demand for these items. The smaller items were purchased on demand from the production department; it was their responsibility to warn the buyers when stocks were low. Sometimes this did not happen and occasional 'stock out' situations would occur.

The project team overcame this problem by counting all these small items as they were assembled into the product. The team then passed the resulting data to the buying department so that these items could be treated in the same way as the larger components.

Approximately one year after the improvement process was started, I visited the factory. Unlike the previous occasion, when there had been total congestion, the factory looked empty. At first impression it appeared that the company was short of work.

The production manager, who had steered and facilitated the programme, remarked 'No, we are not short of work. In fact we now turn over more than £3.5 million of product.' Through the projects described here, and those carried out by the other teams, they had effectively reduced the assembly time for one product from three to four weeks to an average of four days.

The major problem, which had proved to be outside the scope of the team, was found to occur at the design/customer interface and was largely due to a lack of clear information from the customer regarding certain product characteristics. A team comprising customers and designers was set up to review the situation, and a remedy was found.

This type of collaboration, together with the impressions gained by the customers on site visits, resulted in a significant increase in market share, hence the ability to make use of their much improved efficiency.

While this example would not necessarily apply in all other industries, it does nevertheless support the claims made in Chapter 1 regarding the potential offered by this approach. Note, also, that £2 million of market share had been diverted to this company from their competitors.

Summary

1 JIT cannot be achieved without proper motivation. Motivation must be considered in three categories:

- motivation for control
- motivation for improvement
- motivation for involvement.

2 Problems can be segregated into two categories, 'chronic' and 'sporadic'. It is mainly the 'chronic' problems which provide the greatest opportunities for JIT improvements.

3 There is a universal sequence of events by which all improvements are made and this applies equally to both chronic and sporadic problems.

4 The universal sequence involves two journeys – a journey from symptom to cause, and a journey from cause to remedy.

5 The remedial journey is not complete until the means for holding the gains of the improvement have been established.

6 Techniques available to help identify theories of causes of problems include process analysis and the Ishikawa or 'fishbone' diagram.

7 The case example indicated that dramatic improvements to productivity, quality and inventory reduction can be achieved through the project by project approach.

8 The improvement process described in this chapter is absolutely fundamental to the achievement of JIT. It applies at all stages in the product life cycle, for example:

- design
- manufacture
- package
- distribution
- after-sales support
- supplier quality
- administration.

9 Progress towards JIT might be made via MRPII, general housekeeping reviews and cost control, but endemic problems cannot be solved without the application of the improvement process. Without it, the chronic problems and buffer stocks, work-in-progress and so on, will remain.

Recommended further reading

Juran, Dr J. M. (1964) *Managerial Breakthrough*, McGraw-Hill – particularly Chapters 1, 'Breakthrough and control – a contrast', 2, 'Breakthrough – a panoramic view', and 3, 'The Pareto principle'.

4 THE DESIGN ASPECTS

This chapter and the next, which covers JIT in manufacture, are totally inter-linked and, while there is no logical point at which to divide the material covered, that division has been made, to provide two approximately equal and more easily digestible proportions, and to allow summaries to be made at appropriate intervals.

This chapter contains considerable checklist-type material which has been included to ensure a detailed understanding of the role of design in JIT – probably the least well appreciated aspect of the topic. The growing importance of product liability and its implications for design provide another reason for the detail included in this chapter. Finally, Dr Meredith Belbin's excellent booklet, *Quality Calamities and their Management Implications*, published for the British Institute of Management, further justifies this approach.

It must also be remembered that it does not matter how much care and attention is paid in manufacture; if the design is wrong any fault will exist in every product made – until the design is modified.

The role of design

During the past three decades there has been a fashionable view, largely encouraged by designers, that designers should design and production should produce and never the twain shall meet. It has been claimed that designers should not be constrained in their thinking or inhibited by having to consider the means of production. This, it was argued, was the responsibility of the production engineer. While there is undoubted virtue in allowing designers the luxury of total freedom of thought at the early stages of conceptual design, this approach is of dubious merit when allowed to extend throughout the entire design process. In fact, modern thinking suggests that the design process is only complete when it has been extended to include everything from original thought right through production, assembly, packaging, storage and even final distribution to the ultimate customer.

Under this concept, the designer is not merely designing a product, but also the means to produce and to supply customer satisfaction. Design could therefore be said to consist of three distinct phases:

- conceptual design
- functional design
- process design

> A design is valueless until the means have
> been proven to exist through which the
> design can be translated into a product or
> service to the satisfaction of the ultimate user.

The reader may recall that it was claimed in Chapter 2 that many instances of
JIT-related problems were a result of scrap, rework, supplier difficulties and
so on.

Design: a hatchery for JIT problems

Research has shown that a remarkably high proportion of JIT problems are
found to be related to design, in some cases as high as 80 per cent of all failures. Some may find this claim difficult to accept. This was the case when I
recently conducted a consultancy assignment for a company which manufactures sophisticated medical products used in hospitals all over the world.

The company had been losing market share to its competitors and did not
know why. Investigation of customer complaints and other internal failure
data indicated a major problem in design organization and that this was
responsible for over 80 per cent of quality-related losses. As with the example
quoted in Chapter 3, the factory shops were full of products, many of which
had been returned for modification. Some were waiting for parts from
suppliers, and things generally did not look good.

The company management had expected the consultancy to reveal shortcomings in the manufacturing processes and with suppliers. However, the
investigation revealed that not only were these good, impressive even, but also
that the paperwork and inspection procedures were adequate. There was an
immediate and hostile reaction to those findings which indicated that design
was at fault. Upper management had previously regarded design as a sanctu-
ary of excellence. The managers had pride in their products, even though
there were failures, and criticism of design was hard to take. They were then
asked 'How much time do you think that the forty designers are currently
spending on the development of new products, and how much on the
modification of existing products because they have been found to have some
inherent weakness?' They did not know the answer. In fact, at that time not
one of the designers was actually working on a new design. Every one of them
was involved in designing modifications; not as part of a policy for continuous
improvement, but in every case because it was being forced on them by the
company's dissatisfied customers. In one case, an incubator was being
redesigned. This was due to the fact that repeatedly opening and closing the

lid caused cracks to appear along the edges of the hinges. These had not been properly tested during the original design, and were only discovered nearly two years after the design had been completed, and the product in use in several places in the world. One design fault currently being rectified had actually led to a death.

Defective design may be manifested in many ways, and frequently appears as apparent manufacturing problems. Some of these are listed here, and all of them may lead to JIT-related problems:

1 Incorrect materials specified.
2 Vague or ambiguous specifications for materials, treatments, methods of test, and so on.
3 Inadequate allowance for fatigue and causes of strength loss during the specified life of the product.
4 Insufficient analysis of, and allowance for, environmental factors, including stress, shock, creep, dirt, fumes, gumming media, humidity, heat and cold, biological attack, and so on.
5 Poor design for manufacture, including weaknesses in the design of cast, forged, rolled or fabricated components, and the incorrect selection of processes; and insufficient consideration of design for ease of manufacture and reduction of cost.
6 Insufficient or incorrect specifications for corrosion protection.
7 Premature failure resulting from insufficient or badly designed reliability-testing procedures.
8 Lack of failure mode and effect analysis, resulting in failure in a dangerous mode. For example, a break in the linkage to the accelerator in a car should cause the vehicle to stop rather than accelerate to full speed.
9 Insufficient derating.
10 Inadequate user instructions.
11 Inadequate installation instructions.
12 Inadequate maintenance or service facilities.
13 Insufficient consideration of packaging and transport requirements, resulting in damage to, or degradation and contamination of, the product.

Part of the task of the design department is the creation of a whole range of specifications which together make up the recipe for the product. Some of this work simply entails calling up existing specifications and, for the remainder, the creation of new ones. This aspect of the design function can be, and frequently is, a highly complex task. A great many expensive mistakes are continually being made as a result of deficiencies in specifications, and a quality assessment team would do well to give thorough consideration to this aspect of a company's organization.

DESIGN – PREPARATION OF SPECIFICATIONS

Companies which have learned the importance of good quality systems give considerable attention to the detailed preparation of specifications. Those engaged in the manufacture of products for the Ministry of Defence will be only too well aware of the importance that customer places on this aspect of the manufacturing cycle. Fastidious attention to detail in the preparation and control of specifications will be repaid many times over, whereas neglect could almost certainly lead to product liability claims, product recall, and holding stocks of obsolete or slow-moving items. Basically, successful product design entails the preparation of a family of specifications, which break down into four main groups:

1 customer or performance specifications;
2 design specifications;
3 manufacturing specifications;
4 sales specifications.

Customer or performance specifications

In the case of domestic consumer products these specifications would be based upon market research information, or specified by a particular customer. In practice, these specifications can vary from vague statements, such as 'Provide a central heating system for my house', to detailed specifications which may lay down extremely precise criteria for each aspect of the customer's requirements. In the former case the two parties to the agreement may have very different ideas whether the specification requirement has been achieved, and therefore expose themselves to the possibility of subsequent legal wrangles which could turn out to be very expensive. It is by no means unusual for an unscrupulous customer to use the loose wording of this type of specification to claim breach of contract and to return goods when in reality he had simply over-ordered, with obvious implications for the achievement of JIT. Clearly it is worth giving considerable attention to this stage in the design process, and the collation and analysis of the following information should be regarded as essential before formally starting design activity:

1 the purpose of the product or design requirement (for example, removing dirt from carpets, communicating quickly over long distances, the destruction of missiles, and so on);
2 the degree of customer satisfaction already being achieved by existing products, and the known limitations in their design – including both structural and functional limitations;
3 selling price band;
4 whether a luxury or a necessity;
5 importance of aesthetic considerations;

6 safety requirements, limitations and hazards;
7 environmental considerations;
8 type of potential user;
9 the degree of variability acceptable to the customer in terms of performance, appearance, reliability, design life, shelf life, rate of deterioration,
   and so on;
10 service and maintenance considerations.

Design specifications

These specifications define the characteristics, capabilities and limitations of
the product. The content of a design specification should largely be based
upon test reports on prototype and preproduction models. Care taken in the
preparation of this specification and comparison with the customer's specification are probably the most important features in a programme aimed at the
avoidance of, or reduction in, product-liability risks. For this reason, much of
the remainder of this chapter will be concerned with the means by which
design specification information may be obtained and analysed.

The important features of a design specification are the following:

1 description of the product and ingredients, and so on;
2 design life: this may be specified in terms of time, number of operations or
   cycles of operation which should be expected under the specified conditions;
3 rate of degradation to be expected under the specified conditions;
4 output or performance parameters;
5 reliability to be expected during specified design life and under specified
   conditions;
6 effects on performance to be expected from environmental cycling, vibration, corrosion, noise, sunlight, dust, biological attack, fumes, and the like.

Manufacturing specifications

These specifications include a description of everything necessary for the
manufacture of the product. Such specifications are generally the most complex and frequently include:

1 component, sub-assembly and assembly drawings or ingredient specifications including tolerances;
2 drawings and details of tools, jigs, fixtures and measuring equipment;
3 calibration requirements for all measurement and test equipment needed;
4 material specifications;
5 instructions for processing and methods of testing at each stage of production;

6 instructions for testing incoming materials and components;
7 specifications for bought-in materials and components, including instructions to suppliers for materials testing and methods of production;
8 instructions for assembly and packaging;
9 instructions for storage and transport;
10 installation instructions and customer-training requirements;
11 details of all company, trade, national or international standards relevant to the product.

Failure to be precise or complete in any of these requirements will frequently result in quality losses affecting JIT.

Sales specifications
These specifications should include information necessary for the customer to decide whether the product is likely to satisfy his or her requirements. Such a specification does not need to be as detailed as either the design or the production specification but should include:

1 an illustration of the product's appearance;
2 a statement of the performance characteristics and claims;
3 where applicable, the dimensions or other features necessary to determine suitability;
4 promises of after-sales service, economy, maintainability, safety and reliability.

While the sales specification is considerably less detailed than the other three forms of specification, it must be remembered that it is this specification which will probably form the basis of the legal relationship between the buyer and seller of the product. It is, therefore, extremely important to ensure that all claims for performance, safety and reliability can be substantiated. There must be no ambiguity in the wording, and the limitations which may affect the safety of the product must be clearly stated. It is frequently the specification, or lack of a properly defined specification, which is responsible for many of the problems, the loss of orders or legal action, which can cost industry so much, so that it is well worth while to give a great deal of attention to this aspect of the manufacturing cycle. The following points are essential for the avoidance of JIT-related situations, but more detailed explanation of the requirements of specifications may be found in the British Standards Institution's 1967 guide to the preparation of specifications, which gives a comprehensive list of items which may be required in a specification.

1 The title must be unambiguous, and preferably of generic form to enable classification and cross-reference.

2 The number and dating system used should be designed to ensure identification with previous or subsequent issues.

3 Authorization and purpose of the specification, for example design, manufacture.

4 List of contents, including a description of all related specifications and standards.

5 Use British Standard symbols, terms, definitions, conventions, abbreviations and measuring systems wherever possible; otherwise define terms used and provide a glossary.

6 Define the period of useful life over which the product will perform to a tolerable level.

7 Define the 'total life' during which some performance may be obtained before safety is affected.

8 Items 6 and 7 must also state the conditions under which these periods can be expected, in terms of storage, maintenance and servicing.

9 Limiting levels for environmental factors affecting performance must be stated when appropriate, including the following: temperature, pressure, humidity, altitude, shock, vibration, terrain, atmosphere, noise, dust, infestation, radiation, fluid, chemicals, electrical interference. It must be remembered that combinations of these factors can often produce failures well below the levels of the individual parameters, for example stress corrosion in brass. These parameters must also include the acceptable duration at these levels.

10 The methods of test for the assessment of life and the limiting design features must be described.

11 Test and overhaul procedures necessary to ensure safety during the defined life of the product must also be clearly stated. The intervals between test, service or overhaul must also be defined.

12 Quality control, inspection and test procedures required during manufacture must be clearly stated, and reference made to appropriate British Standards and codes of practice.

13 Packaging and similar requirements must be clearly stated, having regard to the likelihood of damage during transportation and storage. This must include all instructions necessary for the correct installation and use of the product.

14 Wherever possible, quality parameters should be specified in the form of variables rather than attributes. Attributes usually create difficulties in definition, for example difficulties can arise when an instruction simply requires a surface to be smooth. It is not easy to stipulate the point when it ceases to be smooth and several people may have different opinions. However, if the instruction calls for 10 micrometres, it is possible to measure this, and discrepancies are less likely to arise.

The four types of specification are formulated at various points in the design process and the stages in the development of these can best be illustrated by reference to Figure 4.1.

Design review as a factor in JIT

The initial stages of design review will vary, depending upon whether the concept is determined by the customer or the manufacturer. Subsequent stages will usually depend upon the complexity of the product and the degree of innovation. The procedure of design review applies to:

1 feasibility studies for new products and new product designs at various stages in the design process;
2 existing products at intervals subsequent to their initial circulation.

The objective should be to bring together specialists from all relevant functions and, when appropriate, users, with a view to optimizing the design in terms of satisfaction of customer requirements, reliability, ease of manufacture, ease of assembly, ease of maintenance, service, appearance and safety. Basically there should be at least three design review stages in the design process:

1 The feasibility stage is the first, when all existing knowledge of customer requirements is compared with the feasible methods of satisfying those requirements.
2 Then follow intermediate reviews, of which there may be several, in which the results of feasibility studies, prototype tests information, performance claims, design life and reliability data are evaluated.
3 The final review will determine whether the completed product conforms sufficiently closely with the customer's requirements. This review is also concerned with the manufacturing methods, materials, processes and assembly methods, to ensure the optimum cost and quality of manufacture.

The specialists in a design review team should include at least one of each of the following, at the stages indicated:

Designers	All stages
Quality engineers	All stages
Production planners	Intermediate and final review
Specification and standards engineers	Intermediate and final review
Purchasing officers	Final review
Safety officers	Intermediate and final review

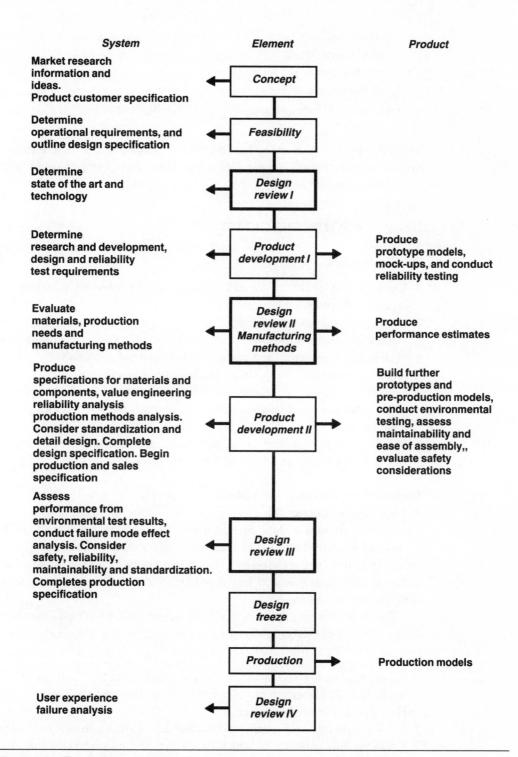

Figure 4.1 The design process

Technical sales representatives or market research	First and final review
Cost accountants	All stages
After-sales service personnel	First and final review

The following checklist shows suggested items which might appear at each of the three stages of design review. Obviously this could be extended or reduced according to circumstances.

DESIGN REVIEW CHECKLIST

Design review I

1 Interpretation of the customer's requirements in terms of performance, expected life and reliability.
2 Cost and selling price limitations.
3 Details and consideration of the state of the art, or technological limitations, of all possible concepts for meeting the customer's requirements.
4 Expected life of the product before technological obsolescence.
5 Consideration of all constraints, including environmental, safety legislation and considerations, assembly, operating, storage, transportation, size and interchangeability.
6 Development programme, including research and testing of new concepts.
7 Relation with mating products and aesthetic considerations.

Intermediate design review (design review II)

For a complex product this stage might necessitate the dissemination of a considerable amount of data. Should this be the case, the product should be considered item by item, or by individual assemblies, by specialist groups brought together for the purpose. This will save wasting the time of those only concerned with other aspects of the product and will allow development to continue where possible.

The product characteristics should be determined during these intermediate reviews. Essential considerations at this stage should include the following:

1 Failure mode and effect analysis, with particular reference to dangers which might arise in respect to product liability and risks under section 6 of the Health and Safety at Work Act.
2 Consideration of data relating to product degradation and contamination, including fumes, biological attacks, moisture, and health hazards, not forgetting pollution.

3 Analysis of prototype test data, including life tests, accelerated life tests and environmental tests.
4 Determination of performance parameters of items, assemblies and the complete product.
5 Value engineering considerations of components in particular, and cost reduction possibilities based upon the following questions:

    (a) Does its use contribute value to the product?
    (b) Is its cost proportionate to its usefulness?
    (c) Does it need all its parts?
    (d) Is there anything better for the intended use?
    (e) Can a usable part be produced at lower cost?
    (f) Can a standard item be used?
    (g) Is the tooling adequate, considering the quantity used?
    (h) Can another dependable supplier provide it for lower cost?
    (i) Is anyone buying it for less?
    (j) Does it increase variety unnecessarily?
    (k) Could another item from the standard range fulfil the function sufficiently well?
    (l) Has standardization been adequately considered in the range of component parts and dimensions?
    (m) Is it interchangeable with other designs?
    (n) Could alterations in design obviate the need for special tooling?
    (o) Does the design facilitate ease of assembly and ease of maintenance?
    (p) Has tolerance analysis been carried out and are tolerances compatible with both design requirements and manufacturing compatibility?
    (q) Has it been designed in such a way as to prevent the possibility of its being assembled the wrong way round, or in the wrong product?

6 *Review of manufacturing methods.* The object of design review of manufacturing methods should be to:

    (a) reduce the number of parts (simplification);
    (b) reduce the number of operations and length of travel in manufacturing;
    (c) utilize the best available materials;
    (d) use of least costly processes;
    (e) analyse tolerance and ensure use of statistical tolerancing where appropriate.

A checklist of factors to determine minimum cost designs should be run through at the appropriate design review, as follows.

Castings

- Eliminate dry sand (banked sand) cores
- Minimize depth to obtain flatter castings
- Use minimum weight considerations with sufficient thickness to cast without chilling
- Choose single forms
- Use designs which eliminate the possibility of hot tears
- Symmetrical forms produce uniform shrinkage
- Liberal radii – no sharp corners, thus avoiding possible hot spots and segregation
- If surfaces are to be accurate with relation to each other, they should be in the same part of the pattern if possible
- Locate parting lines so that they will not affect looks and utility, and need not be ground smooth
- Specify multiple patterns instead of single ones
- Metal patterns are preferable to wood
- Permanent moulds instead of metal patterns
- Avoid the need for loose pieces of multiple part patterns
- Provide draft angles such that precision machined faces may be cast downwards

Mouldings

- Eliminate inserts from parts
- Design moulds with smallest number of parts
- Use simple shapes
- Locate flash lines so that flash does not need to be filled and polished
- Minimum weight
- Avoid the use of designs which necessarily increase press cycle times
- Design moulds which use smaller presses

Punchings

- Use punched parts instead of moulded, case, machined or fabricated parts where possible
- 'Nestable' punchings economize on materials
- Holes requiring accurate relation to each other should be made by the same die
- Design to use coil stock
- Punchings should be designed to have minimum sheared length and maximum die strength with fewest die moves

Formed parts

- Use drawn parts instead of spun, welded or forged parts
- Design shallow draws if possible

● Provide liberal radii on corners
● Parts should be formed of strip or wire instead of punched from sheet

Fabricated parts

● Where possible, when economic, and when safety and reliability are not endangered, use self-tapping screws instead of standard screws
● Drive pins instead of standard screws
● Use rivets instead of screws
● Use hollow rivets instead of solid rivets
● Spot or projection weld instead of riveting
● Weld instead of brazing or soldering
● Use die castings or moulded parts instead of fabricated construction requiring several parts, where quantities allow

Machine parts

● Use rotary machining processes instead of the slower and more expensive shaping methods
● Use automatic or semi-automatic instead of hand-operated machines
● Minimize the number of shoulders
● Omit finishes where possible
● Use rough finish when satisfactory
● Dimension drawings from the same point as used by factory in measuring and inspecting
● Use centreless grinding instead of between-centre grinding
● Avoid tapers and formed contours
● Allow a radius or undercut at shoulders
● Give widest tolerances possible

Screw machine parts

● Eliminate second operations
● Design for header instead of screw machine
● Use rolled threads instead of cut threads

Welded parts

● Use fabricated construction instead of castings or forging, where safety and reliability allow
● Minimum size of welds
● Welds made in flat position rather than vertical or overhead
● Eliminate chamfering edges before welding
● Use 'burn outs' (torch-cut contours) instead of machined contours

- Lay out parts to cut to best advantage from standard rectangular plates and avoid scrap
- Design for circular or straight-line welding to use automatic machines

Treatments and finishes

- Use air-drying instead of baking
- Eliminate treatments or finishes entirely where possible and when corrosion is unlikely to reduce the appearance or life of the product
- Check finishes specified are suitable for the application and the environment

Materials

- Avoid expensive or exotic materials
- Use materials which are easily obtainable
- Use materials which are easily machined, formed and heat-treated
- Use materials which are stable
- Avoid materials which may suffer from stress, corrosion, fatigue or creep
- Avoid materials which may suffer biological degradation in the user environment
- Avoid the use of dissimilar materials in juxtaposition
- Consider effects of temperature, vibration, humidity, shock, corrosive environment, shelf life and likely storage conditions

Assemblies

- Make assemblies simple
- Make assemblies progressive
- Make only one assembly to eliminate the need for trial assemblies
- Make component parts right in the first place so that fitting and adjusting will not be required in assembly
- Design parts so that they cannot be incorrectly assembled or located the wrong way round
- Make parts accessible
- Use quick-release mechanisms and snap fasteners

Remember – complex or badly designed and inaccessible assemblies will increase service and maintenance costs, increase work-in-progress and may lose subsequent orders.

General

- Reduce number of parts by standardization
- Reduce number of operations
- Design for ease of maintenance
- Design for ease of assembly

7 Check that all drawings, specifications, test reports, and so on are clearly identifiable, and that the issue numbers of documents and their circulation are strictly controlled.

Final design review (design review III)

This review will include a complete reapproval of all the items listed in the previous stage, together with a detailed consideration of all manufacturing requirements. Comprehensive data obtained from tests on pre-production models should be analysed. In the case of manufactured products it is essential that these tests are carried out on products manufactured by tooling and production personnel rather than those previously produced in the model shop by craftsmen. In the rush to put a new product line on the market, this stage is frequently overlooked. The risks inherent in this practice are considerable. Craftsmen may easily alter a dimension to ensure a good fit, and this may not always be written into the production drawing. An internationally known car manufacturer recently suffered the consequences of such an occurrence. The result was a catastrophic seizure of the components in the gearbox, which resulted in three fatal accidents, and an extremely expensive product recall.

Items to be considered in addition to the above must include the following:

1 A review of all long-delivery items, such as special materials and special tooling.
2 Consideration of purchasing needs, including vendor appraisal of new suppliers.
3 Critical review of all tolerances and other specification limits.
4 Consideration of all inspection and test requirements. The appropriate visual standards must be set and agreed and the appropriate means of assessment determined.
5 Analysis of training requirements for all production quality control and inspection personnel.
6 Review of the quality plan for the manufacture of the product.
7 Review of the packaging and labelling arrangements.

At this last stage – point 7 – the following questions should be asked:

1 Are the potential dangers which may be inherent in the use of the product *clearly marked* indelibly *on the product,* and on its carton or container, and on the instruction leaflet?

The importance of this aspect is well illustrated by a 1971 case, *Vacwell Engineering Ltd* v. *BDH Chemicals Ltd.* The defendants manufactured a chemical which they marketed for industrial use in glass ampoules bearing a warning label 'Harmful Vapour'. Following discussion with the defendants, the plaintiffs used the chemical in their business of manufacturing transistor materials. To prepare the chemical, the labels were washed off the ampoules in sinks containing water and a detergent. In the course of this procedure there was a violent explosion, resulting in the death of the operative and extensive damage to the plaintiffs' premises. It appears that one of the ampoules had been dropped into the sink where it had shattered, releasing the chemical into the water. The ensuing reaction had broken the glass of the other ampoules, which had then also mixed with water and caused the major explosion. At the time of manufacture the effect of water on the chemical was not known to the defendants, but the dangers had been detailed in scientific lectures dating from the nineteenth century.

It was held that the defendant manufacturers were liable in respect of the damage suffered, because they had failed to carry out adequate and proper research into the scientific literature and to give full warning of the changes accompanying the use of the product. Research consistent with the exercise of 'reasonable care' would have reduced the likelihood of the chemical being mixed with water.

2 Are the claims made on the advertising literature more positive than may be justified?

An example of this is shown in an American case involving a two-gallon container of carbon tetrachloride carpet cleaner. Sold under the trade name 'Safety Clean', it had on its packaging the word 'Safety' so clearly marked on all four sides that the word 'Caution', the admonition against inhaling fumes, and the instruction to use only in well-ventilated places, seemed of comparatively minor import and was missed by the consumer, resulting in her death. The manufacturer was aware of the danger, but misapplied his intention in not carefully expressing his wishes and warning to the consumer.

3 Are the packaging instructions sufficient to ensure that the product will not be exposed to the elements or degrade in any way during storage or transit, and will the product be protected against all possible forms of contamination?

4 Are the labels sufficiently distinctive, such that the product is unlikely to be confused with another product? This is particularly important with chemicals and pharmaceutical products.

5 If containers of substantial construction are used by the company's customer to pack the customer's own products, does it state clearly on the container that it must not be used again?

It is possible that an ingredient in the packaging material may react with the product, and it is not certain that the customer could not sue the supplier of the box on the basis that it was purchased with the supplier's goods. It is also possible that the containers may collapse when stacked if used subsequently.

Reliability in design

JIT implications of design do not finish when the product leaves the factory. 'Reliability' can be regarded as the life aspect of quality. The field performance and characteristics of the product will influence not only the reputation of the company, but also decisions related to the supply and stocking of spares. Apart from some military products, where formal reliability prediction and testing is a contractual requirement, the importance of this aspect of JIT-related concepts is generally grossly underrated. It is for this reason that the topic is given broad treatment here.

Decisions such as whether to produce enough spares for a given product to last the life of the expected demand, or whether to produce, distribute or stock on a continuous basis, will depend upon expectations relating to reliability. If our expectations differ markedly from reality, we can have some nasty surprises. It makes sense therefore to consider the ways in which reliability can be determined and monitored effectively.

The implications behind the definition of quality require a product which not only performs satisfactorily when purchased but also continues to give satisfactory service throughout its design life. This life aspect of quality is generally described in terms of reliability, and is determined by the probability that the product will perform satisfactorily for a specified period of time under specified operating conditions. For the effective application of JIT, it is essential that all plant, means of transport and equipment generally should perform constantly and predictably. It is essential that the probability of failure is taken into account.

Unfortunately this probability does not usually remain constant throughout the life of the product. Most texts on the subject describe three main phases which can be distinguished in the majority of cases:

1 The 'wear-in' or 'infant mortality' period, during which the failure rate of the product decreases rapidly. The causes of failure are frequently to be found in faulty workmanship, inefficient inspection or possibly bad installation.
2 'Normal working life', during which the failure rate is roughly constant and, for a well-designed product, usually low. The causes of failure during this phase are random in nature and therefore unpredictable.
3 'Wear-out period', the onset of which can be fairly precisely predicted with such products as tungsten light bulbs. With others, the onset of wear-out failures can be spread over a very long period for individual items of a particular product type, and be influenced considerably by servicing, maintenance and general care of the product during the previous phase. The failure rate will increase with time, and this increase may be abrupt or gradual, determining the appropriate maintenance or replacement strategy.

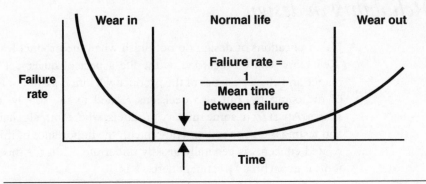

Figure 4.2   Phases of product life

The curve in Figure 4.2, frequently described as the 'bathtub' curve, describes these phases in the life of a typical product, when plotted against time.

Failure mode and effect analysis should normally be carried out at each stage in the reliability programme, and the consideration of such situations resulting from product failures will require serious attention.

A knowledge of reliability concepts, and the underlying theories of planned maintenance, preventive maintenance and breakdown maintenance, is essential for good maintenance management and the reduction of work-in-progress.

THE STATE OF THE ART

While it requires a knowledge of mathematics to be able to quantify reliability, even the most non-numerate person is quite happy to compare the products he or she owns in terms of their reliability. Much of the pioneering work on the development of reliability concepts has been conducted in the electronics and aerospace industries, and a great deal of the published matter on this topic is of a highly mathematical nature and therefore daunting to those unfamiliar with the mathematical processes behind it. In many ways this is unfortunate, because there now appears to be a strong reluctance on the part of industry generally to apply the principles, many of which do not require a great depth of knowledge of statistical method.

Fortunately, recent developments in this field have now greatly simplified many of the techniques, and reliability engineering can now be regarded as a management science which has its own discipline, its own techniques and its own standard terms and criteria, which may be specified in contractual form. This section is devoted to an outline of the management approach, an explanation of reliability terminology and a brief explanation of the most easily applied techniques.

Reliability, ultimately, is a question of confidence. One must have confidence that the car will start in the morning, that a fire extinguisher will operate after being attached to the wall for many years, that an aircraft with two hundred or so passengers will land 'hands off' in thick fog, that a missile will explode when in range of the target, that the thousands – if not millions – of systems in operation when flying men to the moon will continue to operate with such reliability that all are returned safely to earth. None of these events is being achieved consistently and predictably by accident. They require planning in the most intricate detail, the testing of every minute component part, and the most meticulous attention to every relevant aspect of management and organization.

Of course, a well-designed reliability programme can be very costly. Many of the tests required can be expensive both in terms of time, equipment required, and also in products when the tests are destructive, which they frequently are. However, against this cost must be weighed the alternative cost, which might mean scrapping large numbers of products, a product recall which may cost millions of pounds, a disaster which could cost hundreds of thousands of lives, or excessive work-in-progress while a major item of plant is undergoing an unscheduled repair or overhaul. Of course, these ideas apply equally to our own products, as they do to plant and equipment. Also, it will be necessary to be able to evaluate our suppliers' ability to achieve reliability, whether for products or services. The following discussion applies in both situations.

A reliability programme, therefore, must be based upon a trade-off between the cost of testing and the cost of trouble. While to solve a problem at the design stage may cost 10p plus the aid of a pencil and rubber, at the manufacturing stage it could cost hundreds of pounds in scrap material and components, alterations to jigs and fixtures, and so on, or tens of thousands if not millions of pounds when such a product has been distributed on a wide scale.

Responsibility for the framework for the reliability procedures will usually be a senior management function, but responsibility for the co-ordination of a specific product development programme will usually be delegated to a senior engineer. He or she will be responsible for the reliability aspects of the development programme from inception through to final design acceptance, and will be required to produce a plan which includes the following items:

1 Prior to design review I:

   (a) analysis of customer performance requirements and consideration of all environmental factors relevant to the product;
   (b) relevant legislation, including safety considerations;
   (c) customer test specifications and relevant British and other standards.

2 After design review I:

(a) produce an outline plan for the reliability test programme, listing the major features;

(b) gather reliability data regarding existing mechanisms and components;

(c) start reliability testing on prototypes and mock-ups;

(d) start analysis of systems reliability;

(e) produce estimates for men, materials and equipment required;

(f) estimate the total cost of the programme, including cost justification for any capital equipment requirements. This information is vital if a realistic go/no-go decision is to be made whether to proceed beyond design review II.

3 After design review II:

(a) In a complex project, design review II is unlikely to be a single event, although a final appraisal will usually be made after the major reviews have been completed. After this event, the testing being carried out before the review will be continued, particularly if protracted-life testing is necessary.

(b) At this stage the finalized product will be beginning to take shape. The testing activity will then be focusing more on product testing, failure mode and effect analysis, tests to ascertain safety and maintainability and the like, environmental testing, and testing pre-production models produced on production equipment. This is an important point: frequently, major problems have resulted from taking chances at this stage. The problems often arise because the prototypes which have appeared satisfactory were made by craftsmen who, when small difficulties such as ill-fitting components are encountered, make adjustments and occasionally forget to make these known to the draughtsman. Consequently, the product may go into production with a serious unknown fault, which is unlikely to be put right by semi-skilled operatives at shop-floor level, and in any case may cause expensive alterations to jigs, fixtures or process parameters. Worse still, the problem may go unnoticed until long after the product has gone into service.

BASIC RELIABILITY CONCEPTS

When equipment is tested to verify or determine the desirable reliability characteristics, testing can realistically be carried out only by means of statistical sampling techniques. This is because many of the tests are of necessity destructive, and it is therefore normally impossible or impracticable to test the entire population. Samples may be obtained from the following:

1 random samples taken from a given population of items to be tested;
2 a sample of time taken from the life of a product;
3 the time taken to obtain a predetermined number of failures;
4 the number of trials to obtain a preselected number of failures;
5 a combination of 1, 2 and 3.

The population might consist of:

1 the entire life of a simple product;
2 development models and mock-ups;
3 assemblies, sub-assemblies or components;
4 a pre-production run;
5 production runs.

As with other forms of sampling, care must be taken to ensure that the items selected for test are as representative as possible of the population. Quantified reliability data may be obtained in two ways:

1 by reliability prediction, using synthetic data based upon known character-istics of existing equipment;
2 by reliability assessment, determined by conducting reliability tests.

Reliability prediction
This is usually carried out early in the design process and entails the arrange-ment, in block diagram form, of the component parts of a system. The data used are usually obtained either from previous testing or from data sheets relating to the component parts. The data always relate to the normal working life portion of the 'bathtub' curve, and therefore assume only random failures.

Mean time between failures (MTBF)

1 This is only constant during the normal working life period of the product. It therefore implies the mean time between random failures. During this period only unpredictable failures will occur.
2 Being the 'mean' or average time between failures, it follows that half the population will have failed by this time. This is frequently not realized and is often misinterpreted to mean the time before a failure can be expected.
3 Since the quoted MTBF only considers random failures, it does not neces-sarily follow that the product will survive for that time before reaching the wear-out failure period. A human being, for example, only suffers a random failure on average once every 500 years or so!

Mean time to failure (MTTF)
This is similar to MTBF but is used only to describe the failure of 'one-shot' devices such as lightbulbs.

To calculate the MTBF for a system, based upon a knowledge of reliability of the component parts, it is necessary to understand one or two simple statistical ideas. Failures, when they occur, are generally distributed in a manner which will be described by a specific mathematical model. For reliability prediction we are concerned with only one such model, known as the Poisson distribution. Fortunately the Poisson distribution is one of the most basic of the distributions, and an understanding of its basic concepts is by no means a daunting problem for anyone with even the most modest mathematical background.

Reliability assessment

A full treatment of this aspect of reliability is well beyond the scope of a book of this type. For this reason, the text will be restricted to an outline of the most important features and useful techniques.

WEIBULL ANALYSIS

Unlike reliability prediction, we are unable to make assumptions regarding the failure distribution from which the data have been obtained; those readers familiar with curve fitting will realize that without the aid of a computer this could be a long-winded process. Fortunately, since a fairly recent discovery made by a Swedish engineer named Waloddi Weibull, this need no longer be the case. To solve problems involving a study of fatigue failures, he produced what he described as 'a mathematical model with wide applicability'. The formula for this model appears rather daunting at first sight, and is probably responsible for causing many less mathematically minded engineers to shy away. Basically:

$$F(t) = 1 - e^{-(\frac{t-\gamma}{\eta})^{\beta}}$$
$$\& R(t) = 1 - F(t)$$

$$\text{where } F(t) = \text{Cumulative percentage failed at time (t)}$$
$$R(t) = \text{Proportion surviving at time (t)}$$
$$\eta = \text{is a scaling parameter}$$
$$\beta = \text{the shape parameter}$$
$$t = \text{time}$$
$$\gamma = \text{locating parameter (which in most situations is equal to 0)}$$

It can be seen that when $\beta = 1$ we have a special case of the Weibull distribution which is equivalent to the Poisson distribution,
i.e.

$$R(t) = e^{-(t/\eta)}$$

If various values are substituted in the formula, it can be demonstrated that the Weibull distribution can also be used to approximate the normal, hypernormal and many other probability distributions.

All this may be very well for the mathematician. Fortunately, a graphical approach has been developed, which saves the reliability engineer from having to juggle with formulae. The necessary graph paper may be obtained from Chartwell, plus an example of reliability tests using the paper to give some idea of the power of the technique.

When $\gamma = 0$

$$\ln \ln \left(\frac{1}{1-F(t)}\right) = \beta \ln{:}t - \beta \ln \eta$$

which is of the form $\gamma = mx + c$ and hence a straight line graph of slope β and intercept $(-\beta \ln \eta)$, for example when

$$\ln \ln \left(\frac{1}{1-F(t)}\right) = (\gamma \text{ axis})$$

plotted against $\ln(t)$ (x axis).

Chartwell Weibull graph paper is constructed to enable such data to be plotted directly with no need for any sophisticated calculations, as can be seen from Figure 4.3.

The effect of this graph paper is to ensure that failure data will always plot a straight line, regardless of the underlying distribution (except in the specific case where γ does not equal 0) but this is easily dealt with. Consider the following data:

Time period	Cumulative percentage failures
1	3
2	30
3	76
4	88
5	99.9

Figure 4.3 shows these data plotted on Chartwell Weibull paper.

The points are seen to fall on a straight line. At right angles to this line we construct another straight line which is drawn to pass through the 'estimation point' in the top left-hand corner of the page. This line will pass through the β scale and the $P\mu$ scale at some point, depending upon the slope of the plotted line (β means the estimated value of β). Thus, we have a method of estimating this parameter of the Weibull distribution.

It has already been shown that when $\beta = 1$, the data have been obtained from a Poisson distribution indicating random failures, and a constant failure rate. For β values less than 1, the data indicate a reducing failure rate, suggesting that we are dealing with the wear-in period of the product's life. For

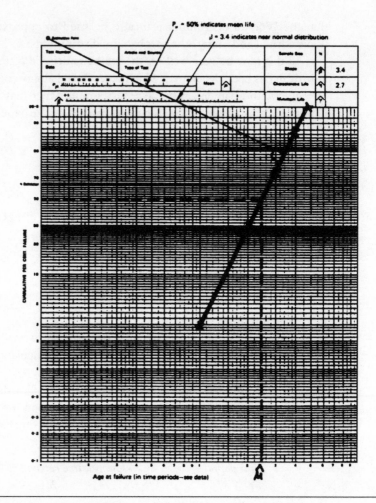

Figure 4.3   Weibull analysis

β values in excess of 1, the data indicate an increasing failure rate, suggesting that we may be dealing with a wear-out situation.

When $\beta = 3.44$, the distribution approximates to the normal distribution, which is a classical wear-out situation. This is characterized by a long period during which no failures occur, followed by a rapid increase during which the entire population will normally expire.

Data relating to plant breakdowns and so on can all be plotted on Weibull paper, and the resulting knowledge which enables prediction of wear-out failure modes is obviously beneficial to the JIT objective.

RELIABILITY TESTING

The main problem with reliability testing is to obtain the maximum information from the minimum of tests. Basically, there are two reasons for conducting tests:

1 Reliability demonstration: tests are performed on samples from a population, and inferences are drawn from these results about the reliability of the population – usually to determine the specification limits.
2 Acceptance testing: to determine whether the specification requirements are being met by the product.

In both cases there are two alternative situations which will determine the type of test:

1 a 'one-shot' device, such as a missile, a fire extinguisher or a match;
2 a device where failure may be a function of time.

RELIABILITY DEMONSTRATION

For reliability demonstration, and dealing with a one-shot device, it is usually a matter of taking a sample from the population, say twenty products, and testing them. If two fail, the reliability confidence limits may be estimated by using tables of the binomial or, in favourable cases, the Poisson distribution.

In the case of time-related tests, several tests will show how confidence limits can be applied during the constant hazard phase of the product life. Where this assumption cannot be justified, it will be necessary to make use of Weibull plotting paper, and the application of confidence limits by means of the Weibull method is simple, provided tables are available.

ACCEPTANCE TESTING

For one-shot devices the method is exactly analogous to attributes acceptance sampling, as described in BS6000. This technique is well covered in most texts on statistical quality control.

Since it is most desirable to obtain an accept/reject decision with the destruction of the minimum number of items, it would be as well to consider the use of sequential test methods. A good example of a practical application is given in US government specification MIL STD 781B, *Reliability Tests: Exponential Distribution*.

LIFE TESTING

The life testing of a product can be an extremely time-consuming business, and therefore expensive, but essential. Before life testing can begin, a number of questions must be answered:

1 How can an artificial environment which includes all the hazards of the real environment be created?
2 How can the tests be accelerated without undermining the value of the results?
3 How can we be reasonably sure we have included all the failure modes which are likely to occur in the normal life of the products? And have we fully analysed their effect?

Environmental testing

The environment should be considered under three headings:

1 The natural environment, in which the product will suffer degradation from normal climatic conditions, rain, winds, biological and entomological attack, temperature and diurnal temperature fluctuations, humidity, dust, dirt and fumes.
2 The product environment, created by the equipment or by interacting equipment, such as voltage variation, vibration, shock loads, corrosive media, gumming media, electrical or kinetic heating, dissimilar metals in juxtaposition in the presence of an electrolyte causing electrolytic action, static electricity, radiation, fire, and so on.
3 Exceptional environmental conditions, like earthquakes, particularly violent storms, radiation, fire, explosion, collision, extremes of temperature, humidity, salt spray and biological degradation.

Accelerated tests

For long-life products it may often be desirable to telescope the product life by increasing the severity of the tests. However, great care should be taken to ensure that the results remain valid under these changed conditions. It is quite possible that failure will occur in a different mode from that which would have been experienced under normal operating conditions. For example, the rate of stress reversal in a metal structure undergoing fatigue tests is limited by the local heating caused in the material. This could easily affect the structure and thereby falsify the results.

When accelerated testing is impossible, owing to the nature of the product or component, or when the test time is in excess of the time which can practically be allowed for a test programme before the start of production, there are three useful strategies which can be adopted:

1 Start testing pre-production prototype models well before production begins, and log as many hours as possible with these prototypes. Continue testing until destruction, even after the production and circulation of the product in the marketplace, making sure that the prototype always has as many hours lead time over production items as possible. This means that

the period of wear-out failure will be known well in advance of a similar condition in the production model.

2 The step test. Again, begin testing a number of pre-production models as soon as possible before the start of production. After a reasonable number of hours have been logged, remove one prototype from the test and, on this item, increase the severity of the test. Continue to increase the severity in steps until the product fails. Carry out failure mode and effect analysis on this product, to determine the likelihood of a similar failure occurring in a production model. After further time has elapsed, remove another item from test, and repeat the procedure.

3 If 1 and 2 above are not possible or are impracticable for some reason, it may be necessary to specify a very short time life on certain safety-critical components in the first production models. After a number of these have been replaced prematurely, and no failures or the likelihood of any failures have occurred, the time life may be extended slightly, and the procedure repeated; this may be continued until, eventually, the components are used for their full design life. This practice can of course be adopted even when 1 and 2 are being carried out, and is a standard procedure in aircraft maintenance.

FAILURE MODE AND EFFECT ANALYSIS (FMEA)

This can be started at the earliest stages of the design process and should continue through all the stages of design, all reliability testing, and out into the field when the product is in service. From a product liability point of view, this is probably the most important aspect of the entire reliability programme. FMEA has recently become a basic requirement of many reliability specifications. A wide variety of different approaches to the procedure exists, varying from very informal to highly formal, as in the case of sophisticated missile programmes.

The basic objective is to list every conceivable type of failure, under the widest possible variety of environmental conditions, and then to consider their effect. It is necessary then to assess the probability of such events occurring, with the object of reducing these probabilities to the absolute minimum. It can be seen that this procedure can be used as a means of monitoring product safety through a development programme, and over several product changes. A further classification or grading can be applied to the seriousness of the failure in terms of danger to human life.

One example of the application of failure mode and effect analysis was the pre-production testing of the Ford Fiesta. During these tests a number of the pre-production models were destructively tested by simulating various types of impact. It was found that the battery leads would be cut in a head-on collision, and thus could easily be the cause of a fire; the leads were then redirected, thus alleviating the risk.

The terrible tragedy of the Townsend Thorenson ferry might well have been avoided through the application of FMEA. FMEA can also be applied to the distribution process relating to JIT. For example, 'What would be the effect on the supply of raw materials in the event of the Baltic Sea being frozen or strikes at Heathrow, and so on?' 'Which shipping line has the best approach to dealing with the former risk?' Seatrans Shipping Line of Norway has given considerable thought to these JIT-related problems.

Clearly, the design process is of fundamental importance to the achievement of JIT and this aspect is considered in greater detail in Chapter 5.

Summary

1 Design is a frequent prime source of JIT-related opportunities and these can have their origin in conceptual design, functional design and process design. Design includes everything through to and including the means of after-sales product support.
2 Design can be responsible for as many as 80 per cent of all failures.
3 Vague or inadequate specifications may be a source of such failures. These specifications include:

   ● customer or performance specifications
   ● design specifications
   ● manufacturing specifications
   ● sales specifications.

4 The design review process is a most effective way of reducing the likelihood of design-related problems.
5 Design review should be carried out by teams comprising personnel from both inside and outside the design function, and principally those who will be involved in meeting the design requirements.
6 Reliability is the life aspect of quality and must be 'designed in' to the product.
7 The importance of reliability prediction and testing is often grossly underrated by industry. This is surprising since it is usually the reliability of a company's products which gives them their long-term reputation.
8 Reliability failures can occur at three distinct phases in the product life cycle:

   ● wear in
   ● normal working life
   ● wear out.

Wear-in failures can be reduced through better manufacturing techniques, and product testing.

Wear-out failures can be deferred through well-designed maintenance routines and the product's accessibility for regular service through good product design.

Reliability in the normal working life period is a feature of the quality of design.

9 Reliability assessment and prediction can take place at each stage in the design process.

10 Reliability factors are frequently truncated due to pressure to bring a new product to market. The cost of such strategies will frequently outweigh the benefits when subsequent defensive modifications are taken into account; particularly when the inevitable failures result in loss of reputation and hence market share.

11 Reliability testing requires skills in the application of statistical techniques such as Weibull analysis.

12 Reliability prediction and improvement require use of fault tree analysis and failure mode and effect analysis.

Recommended further reading

Belbin, Dr R. Meredith (1970) *Quality Calamities and their Management Implications*, British Institute of Management.

Juran, Dr J. M. (1974) *Quality Control Handbook*, 3rd edn, McGraw-Hill – Chapter 8, 'New product quality'.

O'Connor, Patrick D. T. (1981) *Practical Reliability Engineering*, Heyden (2nd edition, 1985, John Wiley).

5 THE MANUFACTURING ASPECTS

In earlier chapters it was noted that Just in Time is dependent upon the ability to produce products manufactured to specification on time every time. It was explained that while zero defects may be something to aim for, the current state of the art in Japan is to achieve quality levels in terms of parts per million (ppm). To achieve such levels it is necessary to go beyond the traditional ways of thinking and to take a fresh look at the way things are done. That is the purpose of this chapter. In the West defect levels of parts per hundred are more the norm. Hence the application of BS6000, MIL STD 105D and the like. Parts per million levels cannot be achieved through traditional methods; it requires the intensive application of the quality sciences and disciplines.

Initially, this chapter further expands ideas introduced in Chapter 4. We then move into the area of Process Capability. Process in this sense does not simply mean the manufacturing process, but includes everything an organization does in the execution of the tasks involved in a commercial enterprise. The concepts are just as applicable to a service organization as to manufacture, although the text considers the latter.

The importance of design to production

Manufacturing has been the focus of quality-related attention ever since the industrial revolution. More has been written about manufacture than any other industrial subject, and yet problems abound. One reason is that many of the problems experienced in manufacture have their origins elsewhere and frequently result from a lack of collaboration between manufacturing and related departments. Chapter 6 covers this in more detail, but some discussion is relevant here.

The most critical interface which will influence the performance of production is that with design. This is not to say that other interfaces are not important; high performance can only be achieved when all these interfaces are properly managed.

As has been stated earlier, the design function is central to the achievement of all the company's goals, and must take account of manufacturing feasibility. It is not good enough to suggest that design is responsible only for design, and production for production.

DESIGN-RELATED DISASTERS

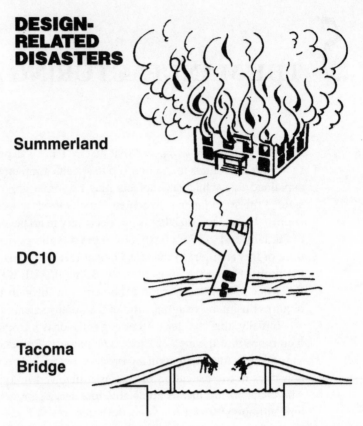

Summerland

DC10

Tacoma Bridge

A good production engineer will find a way to make anything – at a price! A designer who does not take account of manufacturing feasibility must be made to realize that he or she has an open chequebook to the company's coffers. Unlike a manufacturing fault, which may only affect a single product or batch, the design fault, whether it be customer related or process related, will be present in every single item which is made.

A design flaw found at the drawing stage can be corrected with a pencil and rubber. A flaw not detected until manufacture will involve modifications to tooling, jigs, fixtures and process set-ups, not to mention the additional hazards of having drawings and parts in existence which have been manufactured to different standards.

If the flaw remains undetected until after circulation in the marketplace, the cost can then be inflated to astronomical proportions which may in some cases threaten the company's very survival, particularly if it proves to have violated the rapidly developing consumer protection laws.

This could of course apply to manufacturing faults, but to a much lesser extent. Proof of this can easily be found. Just pick up any book which describes disasters caused by man, and study the circumstances. In most cases the original design will be central to the situation. For example:

- the Summerland disaster in the Isle of Man caused by the wrong selection of roofing materials at the design stage
- the cargo door of the DC10 – again a design fault
- the Tacoma bridge disaster, and so on.

Only rarely are the causes related to human error, negligence or the wilful behaviour of production personnel or users. Even when they are, many could have been avoided by foolproofing the design.

All this discussion is intended to emphasize the fact that the design department carries a heavy responsibility, not only to ensure that the product is functional but also that it can be made with ease and at low cost. Generally, cost increases with the complexity of the design. The more complex the design or the more precise the design requirement, the greater will be the cost of manufacture. This is evident from Figure 5.1, which shows that the designer must take account of manufacturing feasibility if he or she is to produce successful designs which are profitable to the company.

While this chapter covers manufacture, this is in itself regarded as being part of the whole design process. Many industrial processes fail for not recognizing this.

In effect, the design process is incomplete until process design has been integrated with functional design and conceptual design as depicted in Figure 5.2.

Process design itself does not rest simply with the design of the individual elements of a product. In this context the process includes everything which happens, from design for manufacture through to the point of sale to the ultimate user. Consider, for example, a product familiar to everyone – the tea bag.

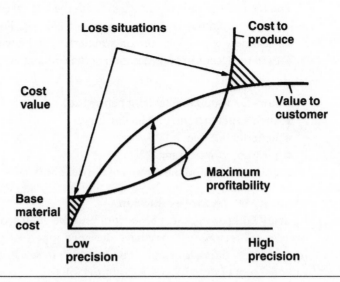

Figure 5.1 Degrees of precision in design specification

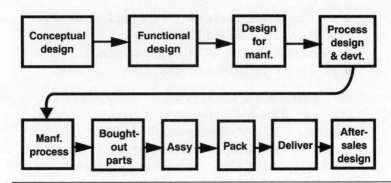

Figure 5.2   The integrated design process

Follow this seemingly simple product through each stage of the process.

Stage 1: Conceptual design

Prior to the invention of the tea bag, was customer satisfaction being obtained from loose tea? Evidently not. Obviously, at least a proportion of the market would have preferred to avoid the need for either the teapot, the strainer, or both.

Of all the possible alternative ways of overcoming the problem, it is clear that the concept of the tea bag prevailed.

Stage 2: Functional design

To operate successfully and to be competitive with loose tea, it is necessary to meet certain requirements. Not being an expert in tea bags, I can only guess at these, but here are some likely considerations:

1 The tea must be able to diffuse through the bag material easily, and prefer- ably at approximately the same rate as loose tea. This implies the need to test a variety of possible container materials, and forms of perforation.
2 This in turn leads to consideration of the container material. It must be:

   ● non-toxic
   ● non-biodegradable (at least before use)
   ● such as not to contaminate flavour
   ● light but durable
   ● pleasant in appearance
   ● able to withstand the rigours of the distribution system.

Stage 3: Design for production

In many companies, this phase would not be regarded as part of the design process. Therefore, we may have designed a perfect product which will be unnecessarily difficult or quite impossible to make. In JIT thinking this is an essential part of design. At this point the following questions are certain to be asked:

1 Do we have the means of production?
2 Do the means of production have the capability to produce the product in volume, consistently, batch after batch, under normal process conditions? How do we know? Do we have the data?
3 For bought-in parts, do our suppliers have the capability to produce consistently in volume? How do we know? Again, where are the data?
4 If the answer to question 2 or 3 is either 'don't know' or 'no', what can we do about it? What will it cost to find out? Is it worth the trouble? Can we modify the design so that existing capabilities will be certain to be adequate?

How many times are these questions ever asked? The temptation to take a risk at this point is always strong. At this stage in the design process companies often fear that a competitor may beat them to the market with an equivalent product or, perhaps, they are being pressurized to enter the market with a hasty improvement to an existing product which has been found to contain some unfavourable characteristics. Either way, the pressure on designers and product development personnel is usually so great that the questions are never asked – with sometimes disastrous results.

The effect may be that either manufacturing or the supplier is subsequently faced with the prospect of high rejection rates, 100 per cent inspection, massive rework and a wide range of associated JIT-related problems.

Stage 4: Process design
This process must be broken down into many separate elements. In the case of our tea bag, these elements would be:

1 *Manufacture*

- manufacture of the bag
- manufacture of the box or pack
- processing the tea and flavouring, and so on

Are these adequate to ensure the consistent production of a saleable product? How do we know?
2 *Assembly*

- insert the tea into the bag
- insert bags into the box or pack
- test
- palleting, shrink-wrap, and so on

Are these adequate to ensure the consistent production of saleable product? How do we know?
3 *Storage*

- transport into warehouse

- store – conditions of storage – environment, and the like
- remove from warehouse into transporter

Are the conditions such that the product will remain in saleable condition, and does everyone know what is expected of them? How is this controlled?

4 *Distribution*

- by train, lorry, aircraft, ship or other means
- the means of transport and conditions during transport
- heat, cold, humidity, handling

Does the product have suitable protection to withstand all the rigours of these elements? Does the product give adequate warnings? Are we sure?

5 *Storage prior to sale*   Again, the conditions of storage are vital to ensure that the customer receives a saleable product.

Sometimes, elements 4 and 5 may be outside the direct control of the producing organization but, if this is the case, does the design department have adequate information about the risks at this stage to be able to 'design in' adequate protection to ensure the quality of the product?

In the case of our tea bag, it is likely that any Western sales outlets – such as Waitrose, Marks and Spencer or Safeway – would ensure that the products were palleted and stored away from other products with strong odours or flavours which might interfere with quality. However, with export markets it is quite possible that in, say, some Third World environment the product might not be palleted, and could well be stored next to bleach or some other toxic or heavily odoured product. Does the design of packaging take these possibilities into account? Are we sure?

This may all seem to be going a long way from the connection with JIT, but it is not. Failure at any of the above stages will result, and does result every day, in JIT-related situations. The contaminated product will result in slow-moving lines, sales turnover lower than forecast, and sometimes total market failure.

Recently, nine cans from a carton of 12 on a merchant's display shelf were seen to be dented. The cans were still there the following week, with the brand name showing for all to see. It is likely that the cans were in good condition when they left the factory. The point is that the manufacturer's reputation is now in the hands of his distributors and customers. What can be done to ensure that the product is kept in good condition? This is all part of the process, and is all part of JIT – if not in our warehouse, then certainly on the display shelves.

Stage 5: After-sales design

The manufacturer's responsibility does not end at the point of sale. We may have designed a perfect product; we may have produced the components perfectly; they may have been assembled to perfection, packed with loving care, and supplied to the user in kid gloves – but if he does not know how to install or set it up, or how to obtain the best possible use from the product, because we have not told him, we are unlikely to obtain customer satisfaction, return business or increased sales.

How many of us have ever bought a product containing inadequate instructions? There is a body of opinion that the instruction books which accompany computers are written by people with IQs of over 200 – who assume that the user has a similar IQ. Again, this is also relevant to JIT for the same reasons as are described under stage 4 above.

CONTROL OF DRAWINGS, SPECIFICATIONS AND DOCU-MENTS

While this function should be controlled from the drawing office, the production department should take care to ensure that drawings used for production are the most recent issue or, in the case of replacement parts, the appropriate issue. Care should also be taken to protect drawings and instructions from dirt, oil and grease. Many a production defect has been caused by a dimension being misread as the result of dirt obliterating a number.

Quality in production

PRODUCTION PLANNING

The aim of production planning is to ensure that the resources required for production are in the right place at the right time. Inefficiency at this stage can often lead to 'make do and mend', with the consequence that alternative materials may have to be used owing to shortages of those specified by the design. This situation is ripe for JIT problems.

Production planning in the West increasingly emphasizes the application of MRPII, frequently linked to computer-aided design, computer-aided manufacture, computer-aided engineering and so forth. Technology in these areas has become extremely sophisticated and is still advancing at an astonishing rate. While sophisticated shop-loading and scheduling techniques are undoubtedly beneficial to the smooth running of any organization, there is one fundamental flaw in these systems which must inevitably limit their scope with respect to JIT. They are almost all based upon forecast sales demand. For MRPII to be effective, it is necessary to obtain and record fluctuations in process-related factors such as scrap, rework, machine breakdowns and so on. The more information that is obtained on these aspects and the more specific the data, the more effective will be the scheduling. However, there is nothing in these systems which can eliminate the causes of the problems. Neither will sales forecasting eliminate sales fluctuations. Both these facts will place limits on the optimum performance of MRPII and other forecast-based concepts.

The only possible way to go beyond these limitations is to:

1 implement the project by project improvement process described in Chapter 3; and
2 reduce the dependence on forecast sales demand by developing the system to respond more rapidly to changes in demand.

In the ultimate case, as depicted in the Toyota example in Chapter 1 – the Kanban two-card system where each department puts demands on its suppliers upstream – the process of producing only against demand for the product is almost complete. Such a system virtually obviates the need for forecasting and scheduling, at least on a day-to-day basis. However, it must be realized that such an achievement must be a long-term objective. It has taken Toyota some two decades to reach this level of sophistication and then only through the total application of the concepts concerned.

ASSEMBLY

A great many quality problems can be detected at the assembly stage. From a cost point of view this is perhaps a little late in the day, but better than after shipment.

From a quality viewpoint assembly has several aspects, and the following points may serve as a useful guide for quality audit purposes:

1 Does the design facilitate ease of assembly? If not, is the relevant information being fed back to design to be used in subsequent design reviews?
2 Does the design allow incorrect assembly? For example, a component may be interchangeable with another from a different product, giving rise to incorrect performance. Valve nozzles with differing orifices would be a good example of this problem. Alternatively, the component may be so designed as to be capable of the wrong orientation.
3 Data relating to faults in previous processes may be obtained in assembly operations. Some of these operations may serve as a form of 100 per cent inspection.
4 If a product is difficult to assemble, it will probably also be difficult to service and maintain. In the case of consumer products this could lead to customer misuse when 'do it yourself' repairs are attempted, and could lead to product liability claims.
5 Paced or unpaced assembly operations may markedly influence the number of defects produced, and incorrect assembly is frequently related to working conditions on the line, particularly in the case of conveyor assembly

work. Changing levels of human performance can be found at different times in the work shift, and at differing conveyor speed rates.

6 Paced conveyors also present problems for inspectors. Research has shown that there is an optimal speed for paced inspection – too fast and the inspector fails to notice the defect, owing to insufficient viewing time; too slow and the defect is missed because the inspector has become bored. There are also differences between old and young inspectors. Older people generally require more time to view, although they may be just as efficient in other respects. Older people also require more light. The nature of the human eye is such that, as a person grows older, he or she needs progressively more light to view the same apparent contrasts. This may present no problem, provided due allowance is made when designing the inspection task.

QUALITY ACCOUNTABILITY

The most common cause of quality problems in production is directly related to the apparent conflict between the need for high levels of production and the need for quality. This conflict is a direct result of over-specialization and diversification. In many cases this has resulted in situations where one person is responsible for production and another for quality. In most cases production norms are continually being raised while the means for improving or maintaining quality at the new levels of production are ignored. Quality control, therefore, becomes an appendage to production rather than an integral part.

The situation is exacerbated when products become more sophisticated with higher levels of demand. Because quality has become divorced from production, there is unequal pressure applied for the establishment of more efficient production methods in terms of quantity, and the respective quality control considerations tend to be overlooked.

In these situations quality control can only maintain the balance by constant vigilance and toughness – hence the conflict. This problem may be overcome by looking back to the days of the craftsman. By definition a craftsman is responsible for the quality of the work he or she produces, and there is no reason why this should not still be so if care is taken to organize the tasks correctly.

Consider the organization chart in Figure 5.3. For this type of organization it may be seen that all aspects of product quality have been assigned to the quality assurance department. By definition it follows that no one else shares any responsibility for quality. The quality control department becomes a police force, and generally fights a losing battle against marketing pressures to meet delivery targets regardless of quality.

Consider now an alternative approach. If Figure 5.3 is rearranged so that operators are responsible for checking their own work, and inspection and test are included as an integral part of the production process, as shown in Figure

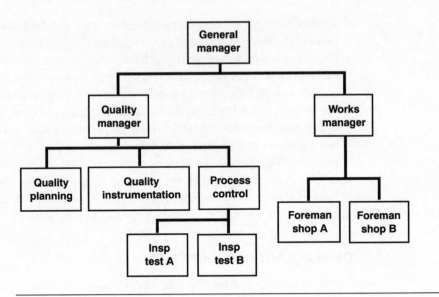

Figure 5.3   Bad organization of the quality function

5.4, all the disadvantages are negated, and operatives are made to feel responsible for the quality of the work they produce. However, we must ensure that the closed-loop feedback, mentioned earlier, is effectively closed, and we have to be very careful that this principle is applied. In the example given the quality plan is produced by quality assurance, but the measurements are taken by production. If they do not comply with the planned procedures, the only way

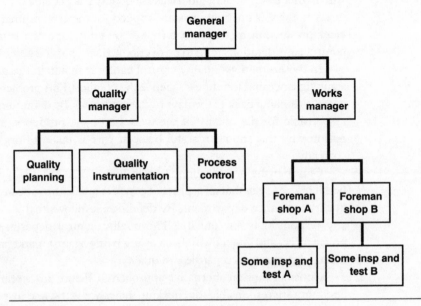

Figure 5.4   Good organization of the quality function

in which quality can re-establish its requirements is by being given more day-to-day management authority than was intended. This will not work in practice, and conflict will again arise. It is necessary, therefore, to build safeguards into the scheme. It is essential that those concerned with quality audit, either of their company or a supplier, should be thoroughly acquainted with these safeguards, and be aware of the problems which will arise if they do not exist. The necessary safeguards to ensure the closed-loop feedback, using operator control and inspection by production personnel, are as follows:

1 the procedures used and the amount of inspection and test must be determined by quality control, even though others may perform the tasks;
2 all inspection equipment must be recalibrated and controlled by quality control, and the control programme strictly adhered to by production;
3 quality control must participate in the control of tools, jigs and fixtures, and verify their continued suitability;
4 quality control is responsible for identification of the relevant training to be given to production personnel, and for ensuring achievement of a satisfactory level of competence;
5 quality control must conduct a continuous audit of items 1, 2 and 3, and of outgoing product quality;
6 quality control and quality assurance must have means of participation in changes to the plan when it is found that deficiencies exist.

INCENTIVES AND PAYMENTS BY RESULTS

In general the application of incentive schemes is detrimental to the achievement of JIT and these do not occur in Japan. By definition, if a person is paid for the quantity of work he or she produces, they will pay little regard to quality. Some firms who operate these schemes claim that their operators are not paid for defective work. In general this is highly unpractical, particularly in cases where work cannot be identified with a particular individual. However, there are examples of cases where operators have been paid quality bonuses. Many such schemes recognize that an operator is likely to produce a small amount of scrap work, and offer to pay him or her a bonus provided that they keep within this figure and that they check their own work. Generally speaking, it is better to find ways to motivate other than through direct incentive, if a spirit of company-mindedness is to be achieved.

QUALITY CIRCLES

By far the best approach to motivation is to use Quality Circles. These are small groups of workpeople, usually under the leadership of their foreman, who meet regularly for about an hour every week with the object of solving quality problems. The concept was first introduced in Japan in 1962 and there are now well over one million such groups operating in Japanese factories.

Subsequently, the Quality Circle approach spread to Brazil, the United States, Scandinavia and Europe. British success with Quality Circles has been patchy with a high incidence of failure. These failures have not been due to shortcomings in the concept, but in most cases to a lack of understanding of both the concepts and the organization necessary to ensure success.

Advantages which may accrue from effective application include:

1 dramatic reductions in quality failure costs (manufacturing defects in many Japanese products are of the order of one hundred times fewer than in their Western counterparts);
2 improvements to quality and productivity;
3 increased effectiveness of supervisors;
4 higher morale, reduced labour turnover and increased job satisfaction;
5 substantial improvements to the competitiveness of the company.

This concept is further discussed in Chapter 6.

HUMAN RELIABILITY

Even allowing for the ultimate development of quality systems with emphasis on prevention, there will always be a need for a considerable amount of inspection, both during and after manufacture and subsequently, throughout the life of the product. It is extremely important that the inspection function should not become the 'poor relation', overlooked in any quality system. The resulting quality-related costs, possibly from product liability claims or an expensive recall programme, would be greatly reduced. It is essential that inspection should always be as efficient as possible; unfortunately this is rarely the case. In fact, even when 100 per cent or higher levels of inspection are being used, it is always highly probable that defects or errors will be over-looked. Error figures of 25 per cent or higher for even the most experienced inspectors are not uncommon.

It has been claimed that:

1 10 per cent of production costs are inspection activity;
2 90 per cent of inspection is visual;
3 80 per cent of inspection has no specialist aids of any kind;
4 *people miss about 15 per cent of defects.*

These statistics show that significant improvements in product quality, and reductions in cost, may be possible if the causes of low inspection performance are properly understood and remedies applied.

Although the major aspects of this topic have been researched and clearly written up in magazines such as *Applied Ergonomics*, there are few textbooks on the subject other than those written in a very scientific manner. Most text-books on quality assurance give only scant treatment to the subject.

Process capability

One prerequisite for the achievement of JIT is the provision of a capable process. It was mentioned earlier that parts per million defects represented the state of the art. Actually, some Japanese companies are now talking in terms of parts per billion (ppb).

This section shows how this is being achieved, and indicates what the JIT-practising company will need to do both in its own organization and in those of its suppliers. Hence the remainder of this chapter will be devoted to the topic of process design and development.

Fundamental to process design and development is a knowledge of the capability of the process, or 'Process Capability' as it is known. This is neces-sary for three principal reasons:

1 to enable the preparation of product design specifications which can be achieved by existing processes;
2 as an aid for process control, to ensure that the process continues to satisfy these requirements continuously under operating conditions;
3 as a base for continuous process improvement.

Of these three considerations, Western managers familiar with the concept of Process Capability are most likely to use the techniques for item 2, and to a limited extent item 1. Whilst some may be aware of the importance of Process Capability for item 3, there are very few companies in the West who use the concept for this purpose.

In contrast, this would be a principal application of the techniques in Japan, not only within their own companies but also as a means of judging suppliers, and helping them with the process of continuous improvement.

PRINCIPLES OF PROCESS CAPABILITY ANALYSIS

Process Capability Study is basically a statistical technique, and is an essential prerequisite for Statistical Process Control or improvement.

Many managers who do not have a mathematical background – or indeed many who do! – are nervous about statistically based concepts. This is unfor-tunate because while statistical techniques can sometimes become quite com-plex, the Pareto principle usually applies. In other words, about 80 per cent of the applications require only the simple or basic techniques and concepts.

While it is possible to conduct Process Capability Studies in great depth, and using extremely sophisticated statistical tools, the bulk of the applications require no such ability, and can be handled by anyone with a degree of common sense.

The treatment of Process Capability in this chapter is addressed, with no apology, mainly to the non-mathematical manager. The mathematically inclined manager who already possesses a knowledge of statistics might find this approach to be a useful way of overcoming the suspicions of colleagues and others less inclined in this direction. The best way to achieve anything of this nature is to *keep it simple*, and that is what we are about to do.

Process Capability Studies usually concern the collection and analysis of data obtained from a process. This includes any kind of process. For instance:

- dimensional accuracy of machined parts
- ability of a furnace to hold temperature
- accuracy of a typist
- reading errors in printing
- variations in credit period
- stock levels on specific items
- number of defects per 100 units of production
- reading accuracy using precision instruments
- missing components
- delivery times.

At first glance it might appear that there must be different ways to treat each of these other situations, but fortunately this is not so. Basically, there are only two kinds of data:

1 attribute or countable data; and
2 variable data.

'Attribute data' means data which are attributable to something. For example, typing accuracy. The typist either makes an error or does not. If the typist does, the data are discrete, that is, one, two, three or whatever number of errors will be made in a given time. All attribute data can be treated in the same way.

With attribute data events always occur in the form:

- good/bad
- right/wrong
- error/no error
- black/not black
- on/off
- is/is not – and so on.

For the purposes of this analysis all attribute data will be considered as a single entity. For a more scientific approach, it would be necessary to distinguish between attribute data which have a finite limit to the total possible number of occurrences, for example the number of green pills contained in boxes of 100 bottles (binomial data), and data where a theoretically infinite number of occurrences is possible, for example oil stains (Poisson data).

Attribute data also include an important sub-group known as 'subjective data'. These data are subjective to the senses – feel, touch, smell, taste, for instance – but again can be classified in the same way as above.

In the case of the tea bag, for example, the resulting cup of tea either tastes like Earl Grey or does not. Of course there are degrees, and different people may have different opinions, but this is a problem of finding suitable standards. It is not a problem for the techniques involving attribute data.

Variable data are different. These are obtained from any process which varies on a continuous basis, and are mostly analogue, although there are digital data forms as well: there must be continuity, for example temperature, volume, speed, current, resistance, diameter, length, weight, and so on.

Regardless of the sources of attribute or variable data, the same basic techniques or concepts for Process Capability Study can be applied.

Most Western texts on Process Capability concentrate more attention on the collection and analysis of variable data. This is unfortunate, because while it is acknowledged that variable data are more powerful (by a factor of ten) than attribute data, attribute situations are considerably more numerous. Also, if by 'process' we include office services and other non-manufacturing situations, the bulk of the data available will be in attribute form.

ATTRIBUTE DATA

The basic technique for recording attribute data is the frequency diagram. Data from the process are recorded on the diagram to see if a pattern exists: this is usually the case. After about fifty samples of a hundred items per sample have been taken, the result will be similar to that shown in Figure 5.5, showing typing errors for two typists, A and B.

It is obvious from the two charts that typist A is producing better work than typist B and is doing so consistently. If the reason for typist B's poor performance can be found, the way may be open to bring B's work up to the level of typist A.

It is also apparent from the charts that there is a distinct pattern in each of the two workers. In the case of typist A the variation either side of the average is quite small. These variations are caused by chance, and it does not mean that A is working less well on the occasions when his or her errors are 3 and 4. The same applies to B as well. The variation is much greater, but this will always happen when the average moves away from zero, provided that the laws of chance are at work and that there is no other factor which could influence the result. Any other worker who had an average of 7 errors per sample would show a similar variation because these variations follow fairly precise laws.

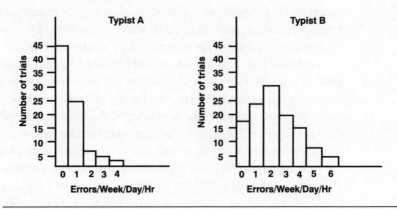

Figure 5.5 Frequency diagrams of typist errors

It requires only a rudimentary knowledge of statistics to be able to determine from mathematical tables the likelihood of any number of chance errors, once the basic variation is known. This applies to any situation involving attribute data whether it be torn packs in the warehouse, absenteeism, machine breakdowns, or whatever.

Now let us assume that we have located the reason for B's less satisfactory performance and B is now working at the level of typist A. Provided that we are happy with this achievement, we would wish to ensure that B did not revert back to the previous level. What we have in fact done is to conduct a Process Capability Study, albeit in its simplest form, and used the results to make an improvement. We also know that unless we can find some way to improve the performance of A, this is the standard we must expect for the time being. Any improvement on A's performance will require a project to gain a better understanding of the relationship between process variables and product result.

To ensure that B did not revert to the previous level it would not be necessary to keep on taking samples of fifty or more items.

At this point we can take advantage of another basic statistical concept. If we look at the chart for A, it will be noted that 4 errors occurred only on one of fifty occasions. Also, there were no occasions when there were more than 4. In other words, 4 errors could be regarded as a relatively rare event. We know that if a sample were taken from time to time, 4 errors would occasionally occur. If, however, we obtained a sample with more than 4, or if two consecutive samples both contained 4, it could reasonably be assumed that the process had changed.

We know instinctively that a rare event will, by definition, occur occasionally. But we also know that when the same rare event occurs consecutively, it is unlikely still to be a rare event. We come to suspect that something has changed. We would do this, even if we had received no statistical training at any time in our lives, because we learn by experience that the same rare event almost never happens on consecutive occasions.

In the case of the typist, particularly B, what is quite probable is that B has reverted to the old ways, and 4 errors is no longer a rare event. A glance at B's chart indicates that in fact 4 errors is quite common at that level of performance. On the other hand, assuming that this occurrence of 4 errors is in accordance with statistical theory, this represents a 1/50 chance. The probability of a 1 in 50 chance occurring on consecutive occasions is $1/50 \times 1/50 = 1/2500$. This is sufficiently unlikely to be a chance occurrence and therefore the process should be investigated to find the cause of the change. What we have now done is to use the Process Capability data as a basis for process control.

VARIABLE DATA

The treatment of variable data does not differ a great deal in conceptual terms from the treatment of attribute data.

Data can be obtained from a process in the same way, and charted using the frequency diagram. However, differences do occur in several ways. In theory, there is no zero origin on the variable chart. While this is unlikely in practical terms, the mathematics which form the basis of most everyday variable data analysis assume that the data could range from plus to minus infinity. The key part on the variable chart therefore is the average or mean of the data.

Most data used in the Process Capability Studies will be characterized by a mean or target value. This could be a dimension, a temperature setting and so on. It is known that variation around that target figure is likely to occur, and the Process Capability Study will usually be conducted with two objectives:

1 to compare the process average with the target average;
2 to discover the dispersion around the average – in the case of existing product specifications, this variation would be compared with specification limits.

When completed, the Process Capability chart would probably look similar to Figure 5.6. It can be clearly seen, without statistical aids, that the mean of the process is off centre from the target mean, and that a number of the samples show that the process is incapable of keeping within the design requirements.

This lack of capability is unlikely to be due to negligence. It is more likely to be inherent in the process. Only a change to the process or a widening of the tolerance will produce a satisfactory result. It may be surprising to some readers, but this type of simple Process Capability Study is used only in a small proportion of companies.

Of course, those who are familiar with the concepts of Process Capability

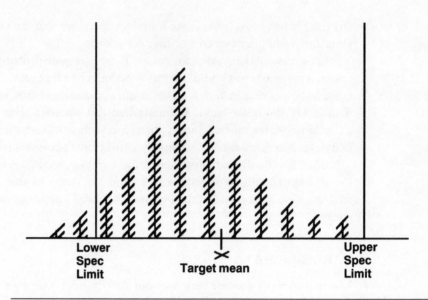

Figure 5.6 Process Capability chart of temperature readings for digital thermometer

will agree that the treatment of the subject given here is extremely basic and that it is possible to take this process to very sophisticated levels, but that is not the point. The point is that even at this level a great deal of process knowledge can be easily gained. Once the facts are known the way is open to provide designers with essential process knowledge to bring harmony to the relationship between design requirements and process capabilities. In Japanese companies all workers, supervisors and managers would be well acquainted with these techniques, even to very sophisticated levels.

PARTS PER MILLION

In the foregoing examples of attribute and variable Process Capability Studies, it will be noted that the charts contain one essential common characteristic. In both cases they exhibit rare events in the tails of the distributions. In the variables chart (Figure 5.7) there are two tails, one at the high temperature end and the other at the low. This is typical of the majority but not of all situations involving this type of data.

In the case of attribute data, A in Figure 5.5 had only one tail, whereas B had two, as with the variables chart. However, since one of the two tails was at the 'good' end, we do not normally worry if results better than this happen to occur. Of course this might indicate the presence of some factor which has brought about an unexpected improvement. In this case, it could be worth while attempting to locate the cause so that the gain might be held in the future. In the well-organized JIT company, this would be certain to happen.

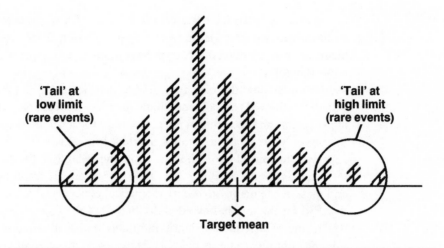

'Tail' at
low limit
(rare events)

'Tail' at
high limit
(rare events)

×
Target mean

Figure 5.7   Frequency diagram indicating the 'tails' of the distribution

Further calculation concerning attribute sampling for A in Figure 5.5 indicated that the average number of errors per sample of 100 sheets of the typist's work was one. This could be stated as 10 000 errors/1 million sheets, which sounds a large number. But it may be that this level of error is representative of the current state of the art in respect of typing and therefore quite a reasonable achievement by typist A. But in JIT thinking, quoting performances in this way enables comparisons to be made and will focus attention on the need for improvement. In JIT thinking, the total of fifty errors found during the Process Capability Study would be analysed to find the causes. Some of these might be classified as 'management controllable' and others as 'operator controllable'. In the case of the typist, typical causes of 'management controllable' errors might be 'illegible handwriting', 'poor maintenance of the typewriter', 'poor lighting', 'crowded environment', and so on. Examples of 'operator controllable' errors might be 'transposed letters', 'wrong letters', 'poor spelling', 'carelessness or not paying attention', and the like.

In the JIT organization, assuming that typing errors were found to be an important opportunity for improvement, data on them would be collected to establish the causes and seek remedies. Because the Process Capability Study had been carried out, it would soon become evident whether or not a real improvement had been achieved.

A fairly graphic example more directly related to manufacture is that of the Quasar television factory in the United States. Around 1980 the factory was sold to a Japanese company. Prior to the sale, the average defect rate was 150/100 sets. This figure was not uncommon in the industry. Shortly after the sale to the Japanese, and employing the same labour, the defect rate was reduced to 4 defects per 100 sets. More recently, it has been claimed that the rate has been reduced to 0.5 defects per 100 sets, or 5 000 parts per million. It is said that these 0.5 have been further broken down and classified into 0.35 management controllable and 0.15 operator controllable, and that project teams are now working on these defects to discover the precise causes and to apply remedies.

Consider now the case for variable data in terms of parts per million. Figure 5.7 showed two tails containing the more undesirable results, one at the high extreme and the other at the low. Unlike the attribute situation where it is usually only necessary to control one tail, in the case of variable charts it is necessary to control two. The basic thinking relating to the data is essentially the same as for the attribute data. However, there are important differences, and these relate mainly to the mathematical concepts which underlie variable data. So far the text has avoided discussion of the theories and mathematics which underlie frequency distribution and statistical charting methods, and this will continue so far as possible. However, in the case of variable data it is impossible to avoid at least a peripheral treatment of these concepts, if the text is to be understood by the non-statistically inclined.

Figure 5.7 indicated that the frequencies were at a peak around the mean or average of the data, and then reduced fairly rapidly and uniformly at points progressively away from that central point with the result that the data appeared to produce a bell shape on the chart. While this is by no means typical of all variable situations, it is extremely common. So common in fact that when the resultant chart does not look bell shaped, the trained analyst will probably try to find if there is a reason for this before doing anything else. Frequently, such an investigation will lead to the discovery of a cause of excessive variability. If a remedy can be found and applied, the overall process variability will have been reduced. This is the essence of JIT thinking, and can lead ultimately to the elimination of the need for inspection.

In one of my earliest experiences with this type of work our Process Capability Study was carried out on a 3-inch Butterworth semi-automatic lathe. The machine was turning steel components to 2.5-inch diameter, with excessive variation in the diameter.

The resulting chart showed a distribution which was nothing like the expected bell shape. Subsequent investigation revealed that the bed of the machine was cracked. When this had been repaired, a further study was carried out. Although the results were better, they still did not conform to those expected. Further investigation revealed that different setters were regrinding the tools in a variety of different ways, and this led to undesirable results. By the end of the exercise several other faults were revealed, each of which when resolved led to reductions in variation, and ultimately to the production of an almost textbook bell-shaped distribution. It is almost certain that if the concept of the bell-shaped distribution had not been known, the improvements would not have taken place. By the end of the project, the machine was so precise that inspection of parts during production was only necessary as a precaution against a sudden and unexpected deviation, for example chipping the tip of the tool from a local hard spot in the material. Scheduling was made easier, and the improvement had a ripple effect all the way down the line to the final process.

The bell-shaped distribution, or curve as it is usually known, is more usually referred to as the 'Gaussian' or 'normal distribution' and follows precise mathematical laws involving two parameters:

1 The location of the central point. This would be the mean or average of the data.
2 A measure of the dispersion or spread either side of the mean value. Obviously this spread will vary depending upon the precision of the process or variability of the data.

The measure of dispersion is known as the 'standard deviation' and can be calculated from data which are known or estimated to be 'normally distributed'. Standard deviation is usually denoted by the lower case sigma symbol, σ.

Once the standard deviation has been estimated or calculated, it becomes possible to use this value as a means of estimating the probability of data occurring at any point from the mean value. For example, in Figure 5.8 the standard deviation has been calculated as 2 degrees either side of the mean of 80°C on the chart.

By calculation or by the use of statistical tables, it can be found that 68 per cent of the readings will fall between $\pm1\sigma$ or conversely, 32 per cent will fall outside that value: 4.5 per cent will fall outside $\pm2\sigma$. This approximates to a chance of 1 in 50 above and to 1 in 50 below, and only approximately 1 in 1000 will fall outside either plus or minus 3σ. It can be seen therefore that σ is an extremely useful value to obtain when using variable data.

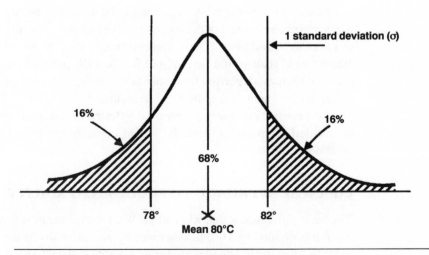

Figure 5.8   Proportion of readings within 1 standard deviation

For Process Capability purposes, σ is used almost universally as a measure of comparative capability. Capability in this sense means the capability to achieve the requirements of a specification. Here there is a marked difference between typical Western and Japanese thinking. In both cases, Process Capability is determined by first estimating standard deviation (σ) of a process through data collection and analysis. At this point Japan and the West take a different path at a fork in the road.

WESTERN APPROACH TO PROCESS CAPABILITY

In the West, and certainly in the UK, the traditional approach is to divide the drawing tolerances by 6σ. The reason is that ±3σ is estimated to contain all but approximately 1/1000 of the total population of data. Therefore, if $T/6σ$ is equal to or greater than 1, it is assumed that the process is capable of meeting specification requirements.

The full argument is as follows:

$$\frac{T}{6σ} = \text{Relative precision}$$

where T = tolerance and σ = standard deviation.

If $T ≈ 6σ$ the process is said to have *medium* relative precision.
If $T < 6σ$ the process is said to have *low* relative precision.
If $T > 6σ$ the process is said to have *high* relative precision.

Obviously high relative precision is desirable but it is frequently argued in the cost that such an effect results in the under-utilization of high precision or expensive resources. This thinking is not shared by the Japanese, or by those who understand the full implications of JIT.

Medium precision, while appearing to be adequate, has the disadvantage that very precise control of the mean or the dispersion is required to avoid 'out of tolerance' conditions. These controls would need to be very much more sophisticated than would be required for the high precision process because even the slightest departure from standard conditions would result in over- or under-achievement of specified requirements.

Low relative precision is obviously undesirable and such processes should be avoided wherever possible. JIT could certainly not be achieved in these conditions.

JAPANESE APPROACH TO PROCESS CAPABILITY

The basic difference is that while in the West the tolerance is divided by 6σ, in Japan it is divided by 10σ! In other words, the variability of the process must be far less than would be regarded as acceptable in the West.

Alternatively, using 6σ as the basis, the Japanese look for a figure of 1.33 or greater from the equation $T/6\sigma$. For companies such as Toyota, the figure 1.33 is a basic process requirement for subcontractors, and the Process Capability Study is a major aspect of supplier evaluation and audit – unlike the West where most attention is given to documentation, traceability and so on.

The value of Process Capability is also used as a yardstick by which inter-firm comparisons are made. The Japanese company would not therefore be satisfied with simply achieving the designated 1.33 value. It knows that its competitors will always be trying for an even better figure, and some companies aim for as high as 15σ or $T/6\sigma = 2.5$.

The reason for the 10σ target is because 10σ roughly corresponds with one fault in one million, the ultimate in ppm.

The Japanese know that if a process can be improved to such an extent that it can achieve the level consistently product after product, there is no need for any form of inspection, or checking by the user. By the time the process has been improved to such an extent it will have become almost totally predictable. This is the essence of JIT. Parts leaving a machine can be assembled immediately with other components without the need for any form of checking and they *will always be right*!

Dr Taguchi, a famous Japanese quality specialist, has shown that all variability is undesirable. In contrast, it is traditional in the West to attempt to alter the maximum variability on the basis that precision is expensive. More recently, the more sophisticated Western companies have been forming the conclusion that Dr Taguchi is right. For example, Figure 5.9 contrasts the two approaches diagrammatically.

It is only through this means that Toyota has been able to create the incredible JIT assembly line described in Chapter 1.

PROCESS CAPABILITY TO PROCESS CONTROL

Having determined the capability of the process, and where necessary started the improvement process based on the ideas covered in the text, it becomes necessary to control the process to ensure continued capability.

Process control can be effectively achieved through an extension of the basic concepts applied to determine Process Capability, and the approach varies only slightly for attribute data compared with variable data.

Control of attribute data

Let us return to the typists and assume that A's work is regarded as satisfactory, even though we would like further improvement if we can locate the causes. The fifty samples which were taken to determine Process Capability indicated that a sample containing four errors would occur on average once in fifty samples. This means that samples can be taken from time to time, and

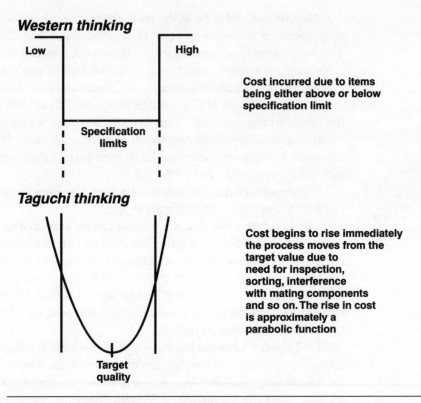

Figure 5.9   Western and Taguchi thinking contrasted

compared with the results of the Process Capability Study. If these appear to follow a similar pattern, it can be assumed that all is well.

This can be done by means of the 'time to time trend analysis chart' which is illustrated in Figure 5.10. This type of chart is extremely popular in Japan and can be found in almost all work situations. There are slight variations in the form of these charts for attribute data, depending on whether the data is Poisson or binomial (as shown in John Oakland's book referred to on p.128)

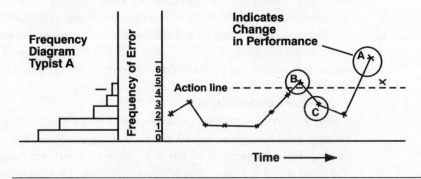

Figure 5.10   Time to time trend analysis chart

and whether the errors, defects or events are in terms of 'defects' or defects per 100 or whatever. However, the basic concept is the same.

It can be seen from Figure 5.10 that three aspects have been ringed around as A, B and C.

In the case of A, one result has fallen outside the warning limit. This was the 1/50 level. Since the 1/50 value will occur on average 1/50 times anyway, it is reasonable to assume that this is the case here. If, however, it had occurred on the next consecutive sample, the possibility of this being by chance is so small that this will not be thought to be the case. It is more likely that a change has taken place and this should be investigated.

Notice that plot B is outside a line labelled 'action line'. It has been estimated that a sample containing five or more errors will only occur by chance on 1/330 occasions. This is thought to be unlikely to be such a chance event and again an investigation would be made. Notice that on this occasion there was no need to wait for a second occurrence.

The third type, C, shows seven plots all within the limits, but note that they also appear to show an upward trend. Usually in this form of charting it is conventional to assume that if a trend of seven readings all point in the same direction, it can reasonably be accepted that an adverse trend has taken place even though no sample has actually gone outside the limit. There is a high chance that some of the items which were not sampled had in fact gone outside but they were missed.

Control of variable data

The general approach to control charting using variable data is similar to that for attribute data, but the mechanics are different, and we are again dealing with a two-tailed distribution rather than one as in the case of attribute data.

The treatment given to the topic under this heading is simple, practical and could be used in any situation involving variable data. However, it must be stated that the techniques available for the control of variable data can become very sophisticated and well beyond the scope of this text. The advantages of greater sophistication lie in increased sensitivity to changes when they occur. The advantage of the approach described here is that it is simple enough for anyone to understand and use.

The belief is that it makes sense to start with simple techniques to get everyone involved, and then to extend them once confidence has been achieved. In Japan, control charts are understood and used by everyone from machine operators upwards, and the techniques are used at their most sophisticated levels. JIT as achieved in Japan would probably be impossible without them.

The best way to understand and use control charts for variables is to imagine the bell-shaped frequency diagram on end, as shown in Figure 5.11. The chart can then be plotted in the same way as with attribute data. The

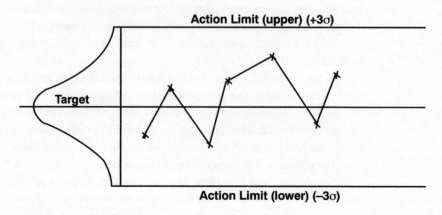

Figure 5.11   Control chart for variables ($\bar{x}$ on average chart)

same arguments relating to the identified features A, B and C hold good with variable charting as with attributes.

Taking variable just one stage further, the chart in Figure 5.11 is an extremely crude but effective means of control. However, it is not very sensitive to changes and the method can be made more effective by plotting not single results but the averages of a number of consecutive results, say four. In other words, a sample of readings will be taken, the results totalled and averaged. The average value is then plotted on the chart. Of course, the range from smallest to largest sample can vary, but the average will remain the same. A further chart is therefore constructed on which the ranges are plotted, similar to that in Figure 5.12.

It can be seen from Figures 5.11 and 5.12 that both the movements of the average value and movements of the dispersion or range can be controlled, and that these results give good visual impact of changes when they occur.

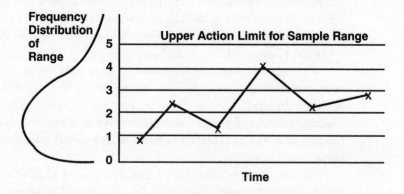

Figure 5.12   Control chart for sample range

These charts are variously referred to as Shewhart control charts after their inventor Dr Walter Shewhart, or X/R control charts, 'X' meaning average and 'R' being range.

Although invented in 1936, these charts have until quite recently been hard to find in Western companies. However, as a result of Western studies of Japan, and awareness of the importance of this approach to the achievement of JIT in production, and high quality from suppliers, many prominent Western companies have acknowledged this importance. Some, notably the Ford Motor Company, have put considerable resources into implementing the control chart concept in their own organization and encouraging their suppliers to do likewise.

JAPANESE APPROACH VERSUS WESTERN APPROACH

While the West is now beginning to respond to the fact that Japan is making good use of the concept of control charts, there remains a fundamental difference in the two approaches to the concept.

In the West, the charts are normally used for control or early warning purposes. Most of the Western textbooks indicate that this is their main use. In Japan this is not the case at all. There, the charts are used for the sole purpose of *eliminating variability*.

In the West, an 'out of control' indication from the chart will only stimulate the response, 'Stop and reset the process', and hence return to the previous status until the next occurrence. In Japan the 'out of control' indication would stimulate a project team not only to find the cause but to apply a remedy to avoid a recurrence.

The effect of this improvement would be to reduce the total variability. This would lead in turn to a further Process Capability Study and recalculation of the action limits, which would then be closer to the control target value. This process of continuous improvement has enabled the Japanese to achieve phenomenal gains in the reduction of process variability to the extent that in many cases they are able to produce parts almost exactly to size, and hence achieve parts per million.

Western supplier relationships

In recent years many Western automobile manufacturers have visited Japan to find out how the Japanese relate to their suppliers. Most of them have been surprised to discover a totally different form of relationship from the customer–supplier relationships which are typical in the West.

In the West these relationships are based upon standards similar to ISO 9000 and the like. Using these standards Western manufacturers frequently formed adversarial relationships with their suppliers, based on strong contractual requirements and the use of multiple sourcing as a means of executing maximum muscle-power.

Standards such as those mentioned place considerable emphasis on procedures, documentation, the role of quality assurance and quality control as police-style activities parallel to production, and usually require the supplier to apply the same approach to its own suppliers and so on. This standardized approach makes little reference to Process Capability, process control techniques, improvement team activities or Quality Circles, and is based entirely on the audit and review process. It makes no provision for collaborative teamwork between customer and supplier.

Other Western approaches include:

1 *Buying to established standards* Those standards are ISO, CEN or British Standards, including certification schemes such as the European CE mark. The aim of this method is that the customer can rely upon the product having been approved and tested by an independent body.

2 *Approved firms systems* This means buying from firms already approved by other authorities, for example on the defence contractors list, ICI- or Marconi-approved or the like. This method has the twin benefit that it is both unnecessary to produce one's own specifications, and also avoids the need to conduct appraisals; but it makes no provision for collaborative arrangements.

3 *Goods in* An informal approach, with or without sampling schemes, this operates through the use of existing suppliers. Confidence may be gained with time, but the risks will always be largely unknown. This approach is usually confined to firms who do not appreciate the principles of quality assurance, and should be regarded as a danger signal by assessment teams for JIT.

4 *Acceptance by final inspection on site* This may be a practical approach in some instances, particularly in the case of 'one-off' items such as machine tools bought 'off the shelf'.

5 *Centralized batch acceptance* All goods must be 100 per cent or sample-accepted on receipt at warehouse. This approach will recede as JIT becomes more popular.

6 *Monitor by customer on site (in process)* This is often necessary when the purchase of specialized products is required from a company which lacks the required quality control functions.

7 *Test by use* This can often be a cheap and cheerful but satisfactory method if a locating jig can be used as a go/no-go gauge. For example, to check the dimensions of a television chassis the first operation can be designed such that if the product is under- or over-sized it will not fit the locating pegs; the defective product may then be placed aside. The combined operation

forms a very effective method of 100 per cent inspection at low cost, but could be disastrous in a truly JIT factory if things go wrong. It is likely to disappear when JIT really gets going.

8 *Vendor rating* There are numerous schemes available for monitoring the performance of existing suppliers. Basically they may be compared on their record for quality, price and delivery. Points may be awarded for each item against a weighting determined by relative importance, for instance quality 40 points, price 30 points and delivery 30 points.

Points for quality may be calculated as: percentage of batches accepted = 90 per cent; therefore 'quality points' = $0.9 \times 40 = 36$, and so on.

More sophisticated schemes may include packaging, maintainability, after-sales services, and the like. Vendor rating is an essential element in JIT.

Japanese supplier relationships

In contrast, the Japanese approach is totally different.

Instead of the adversarial relationship, Japanese manufacturers take the view that since their own success is likely to make more future work for the supplier as well, both parties have a common interest in meeting the goals of the enterprise. The Japanese manufacturer will therefore seek a long-term collaborative relationship based on teamwork and mutually agreed improvement projects involving personnel from both organizations.

It is not possible to staff this type of collaborative arrangement adequately when multiple sourcing is being used. There is also a strong implication of a lack of trust in this approach. The Japanese therefore aim towards single sourcing with long-term agreements based on mutual visits and sharing secrets and technical knowledge.

The supplier would be expected to operate the improvement process in the same way as the customer, and many such projects would involve personnel from both.

Supplier evaluation is based not so much on standards such as ISO 9000, but on the results of Process Capability Studies, and the way in which control charts are used. Education, training and employee involvement activities such as Quality Circles would be key indications of the supplier's general approach to customer satisfaction, and the extent to which the supplier's upper management is supportive and enthusiastic about those activities would make far more impression than sterile adherence to procedures, important though they may be.

A further important difference between Western and Japanese companies is the tendency in the West to impose new concepts on suppliers before they are properly understood by the procuring company. This is definitely happening in relation to JIT. In many instances it is apparent that companies think that JIT simply means that the supplier is required to arrive at the goods inwards store at a specific time on a particular day. I know of one instance where the requirement imposed on the supplier states that if he fails to arrive between 10.15 and 10.45 on a certain day the lorry will not be allowed into the site, and must return double loaded the following day. This requirement appears in a contract entitled 'Just in Time'. This prompted the supplier to attend a conference at which he said that many of his other customers impose similar demands and he is certain that JIT means nothing more than that to them.

A Japanese organization would invariably research any new concept extremely thoroughly prior to implementation. It would then be normal first to introduce the concept internally. Only after it had acquired considerable expertise would suppliers be approached. In the case of JIT the supplier would then have the option of agreeing to collaborate or lose the business. If collaboration is accepted, the customer would offer consultancy and training to enable the supplier to meet the requirements. This would be in their mutual interest.

Location of suppliers for JIT

A more practical problem currently facing Western companies is the question of the supplier's location.

Prior to the advent of JIT and the general acceptance of the need for stockholding, warehousing and so on, motorways and marshalling yards were nothing more or less than a form of live storage. Now, with more and more companies beginning to realize the potential offered by JIT, it has become apparent that proximity of supplier to procuring company is most important.

In the Baltimore truck plant (see Chapter 1) the company had begun to purchase large areas of industrial land in the vicinity of the factory and was actively encouraging suppliers to move their premises to these locations. There is much evidence that other major companies are beginning to think the same way.

Summary

1 Just in Time requires defect levels measured in parts per million levels. Defects in parts per million cannot be achieved simply through the application of the traditional methods, such as sampling and batch inspection. It requires the intensive application of the quality sciences and disciplines.

2 Design and manufacture cannot be separated since manufacture is only one aspect of the design function. In JIT thinking, product design also embraces process design and the process means everything from conceptual design through to user support.

3 Planning and scheduling concepts based upon forecasting are limited in their applicability to the achievement of JIT. The main effort must be to improve the rate of response of the system to sudden changes in demand. This obviates the need for long-range sales forecasts, and stockholding part-finished or finished goods.

4 Quality-related and therefore JIT problems frequently arise from the need for line managers to meet competing objectives simultaneously. Accountability for quality must become more clearly identified with the line manager.

5 Incentives and payment by results schemes generally produce inferior results when compared with those achieved by a well-motivated labour force using regular payment methods.

6 Quality Circle programmes are proving to be a very effective way of achieving both the co-operation of the workforce in improvement activities while at the same time creating a better working environment.

7 Inspection by human inspectors cannot result in the achievement of the necessary quality levels. The only means by which these can be achieved is either by non-human methods of inspection or preferably through eliminating the causes through improvement projects.

8 Process Capability Studies are central to the elimination of process-related defects, to process design improvement, supplier evaluation and to product design. The West has yet to appreciate the extent to which these aspects form part of JIT in Japanese companies.

9 Process Capability Studies are an essential prerequisite to process control, and process control provides the essential information for the selection of process improvement projects both for management project teams, and for teams involving the workforce such as Quality Circles.

10 In the West, Process Capability and Statistical Process Control techniques are generally used to maintain the current capability of the process and to limit variation. In Japan these techniques are used to *eliminate* variation.

11 In the West a process is thought to be satisfactory if the product is held within specification limits. In Japan the influence of Dr Taguchi's teaching has led to the belief that all variability leads to quality-related failures and costs.

12 In the West manufacturers attempt to control the quality of suppliers through:

- multiple sourcing, short-term contracts
- adversarial contractual requirements
- application of third-party schemes such as ISO 9000.

13 In Japan manufacturers achieve high consistent quality from suppliers through:

- single sourcing, long-term contracts
- collaborative contractual relationships
- use of Process Capability as a means of ensuring supply quality.

14 In Japan suppliers are encouraged to locate close to the premises of the customer. This is beginning to happen in the West as a result of attempts by the Ford Motor Company, General Motors and others to compete with their Japanese rivals.

Recommended further reading

Goldratt, Eliyahu M. and Cox, Jeff (1986) *The Goal – Beating the Competition*, Gower.

Hutchins, David (1985) *Quality Circles Handbook*, Pitman.

Oakland, John S. (1985) *Statistical Process Control*, Heinemann – Chapters 3, 'Using quality data in problem solving', 4, 'Measuring process variation by variables', and 9, 'The control of processes using attributes data – defectives'.

Rosander, A. C. (1985) *Applications of Quality Control in the Service Industries*, Marcel Dekker Inc.

Schonberger, Richard J. (1986) *World Class Manufacturing*, Free Press – Chapters 1, 'Faster, higher, stronger', and 2, 'Line operators and operating data'.

6 INVOLVING THE WORKFORCE

The *Gestalt* effect of 'the whole being greater than the sum of the component parts' represents the primary philosophy which underpins every successful drive for JIT. Ultimately JIT is the almost inevitable outcome of a labour force dedicated to the ever-increasing success of the company.

In the Toyota example described in Chapter 1 it is obvious from the first impression that near total harmony has been achieved between workers and management, managers and other managers, workers and other workers. Contrary to popular opinion, this harmony is not the result of some unique genealogical feature inherited by the Japanese from their forebears. Recent evidence suggests that the same qualities are latent in all people of all races. This is borne out by the fact that those Japanese companies established in many parts of the world are found to exhibit the same harmonious relationships even though they employ the indigenous population. In many cases, the non-Japanese plants have been found to outperform the parent company in Japan. This was claimed to be the case with Nissan in Washington, Co. Durham in the UK, and with other Japanese-owned companies in the south of Wales.

The philosophy behind the achievement is based upon a number of fundamental beliefs regarding people:

1　People are social and have a need to belong. This applies to working relationships as well as to social and domestic relationships.
2　People have a natural desire to feel part of a team or group.
3　It is natural for people to desire recognition for their contribution to the success of their group.
4　Groups also have an identity, and groups have a need for recognition.
5　Groups want to be, feel and appear successful.
6　People develop a strong sense of pride in the team to which they belong, particularly when it is sympathetic to their needs, provides recognition and is successful in the achievement of its goals.
7　People have an innate loyalty to their group and to their company, even when their needs are not satisfied, and even when they are unsuccessful.
8　Loyalty is strengthened by care and maintenance of the needs of the members, and through good communication.
9　Fully participative members of high-performing teams will give everything to ensure the continued success of the group.

10 Competition between teams can be either constructive or destructive depending upon the established codes of behaviour. Constructive competition is essential to JIT and can be developed to the extent that each team can be made to feel part of a larger team represented by the company itself.

11 Social divisions within an organization are destructive, divisive and negate the forces required to build the *Gestalt* culture.

12 Whilst hierarchy may be necessary for decision-making purposes, discipline is normally more effective when it is achieved through peer pressure.

13 Trust and responsibility are essential features in the development of homogeneous working relationships. No one wants to feel treated as nothing more than a number on a clock card, a cog in a wheel or an extension of the desk or bench.

All these points are relevant to the achievement of JIT and the goal of galvanizing the resources of everyone in the organization to work towards making their company the best in its business. To develop a spirit of corporate pride and corporate identity and loyalty has now become essential to success in today's and tomorrow's world.

The question is how to achieve these things. Basically, the answer is to involve everyone in some form of teamwork. In essence there are three or sometimes four types of teams to be found in the more successful organizations.

Types of project team for process improvement

SINGLE-FUNCTION TEAMS

These comprise groups formed amongst personnel who do identical or similar work. Examples are teams of salespeople, service engineers, wages clerks, fork-lift truck drivers, and so on. (See Chapter 10 on Total Productive Maintenance.)

CROSS-FUNCTIONAL TEAMS

These teams are formed for a specific purpose. Examples would be to find the causes of some major problem and to propose remedies.

AN ENTIRE DIVISION

These would not hold regular meetings, but in a successful company which managed to create the spirit of involvement, employees can be made to feel part of a team.

THE COMPANY AS A WHOLE

Recent management books such as *In Search of Excellence* and *Theory and Management* all remark on the fact that a sense of corporate identity is a common feature of all the world's most successful companies. In essence, it is the summation of all the other types of team, integrated in such a way as to represent the company as a whole.

Teams in the first two categories form the basis of the remainder of this chapter. How to achieve divisional and company teams will be discussed in Chapter 9.

The 'no blame' concept

The 'no blame' concept is also fundamental to successful JIT programmes. This concept is based on the belief that no one comes to work with the intention of deliberately doing a poor-quality job. If, therefore, poor quality is the outcome, it is possibly caused by an organizational deficiency rather than through negligence or the deliberate action of an individual or group.

To identify, analyse and solve such problems it is necessary to establish an organized and systematic approach. As has been stated earlier, all improvement is made project by project and in no other way. Teamwork has been found not only to be an effective approach to dealing with these problems, it also fits perfectly with the beliefs listed earlier in this chapter.

TRIPLE ROLE CONCEPT

A second concept which has been developed extensively in recent years is the 'triple role' concept. Through this concept every employee, at all levels and in all functions, can be regarded as operating in three modes, more or less simultaneously. Any one individual might at any time be acting in the role of either customer, processor or supplier.

The terms customer and supplier are usually associated with persons or organizations outside one's own. In the case of the triple role, the supplier can be any person or function which supplies either a product or a service, and the customer is any person or function which may receive either a product or a service. In many cases they may even be the same person.

A person in an organization will often receive a product which could be either a drawing, specification, material, component, sub-assembly or the like, or alternatively a service in the form of information. In this situation the receiver will be the customer. At this point, he or she will then become a processor, either by carrying out an operation on the goods received, or by some manipulation of the information. Following this, the result will be passed downstream to a 'customer'. This customer will then become the processor by performing a subsequent operation, and so forth.

As with external customers and suppliers, the product or service offered and received may or may not be totally satisfactory. In such cases it is usually claimed that a 'quality' problem exists because the supplier did not achieve customer satisfaction. In most cases, this is not entirely the fault of the supplier. It is often because the supplier was unaware either of the needs of the customer or the facilities available to the customer to make best use of the product or service supplied.

To take a familiar example, consider the case of the supplier–processor–customer relationship which exists between marketing, design and production.

The design engineer is (or should be) supplied with information by market research, and from technical sources. His or her principal customer will probably be the production department. If the information received from market research is incomplete, misleading or indigestible, the design engineer may well design a perfect product which almost totally misses the requirements of the customer.

Taking the designer's relationship with production, if the design engineer has inadequate information or knowledge regarding process capabilities, both current and future, he or she may well design a product which proves to be difficult or, in extreme cases, impossible to make. Design faults of this type usually have a cascade effect which works in the opposite manner to a wave in a pond. The ripples in a wave become smaller the further they move from their cause. In the case of design faults the reverse is usually true, resulting in costs which increase by an order of magnitude for each successive stage in the process right through to detection by the ultimate user.

Figure 6.1 shows that the design engineer is at one stage the customer of the market research department, then a processor when producing the designs and, finally, a supplier to production when the design has been completed. In each case it is likely that the supplier believed he or she was meeting the needs of his or her customer. The fact that he or she may not have done may not be known to him or her because there is no feedback from the customer.

To illustrate, let us return to the example. A drawing is sent to production

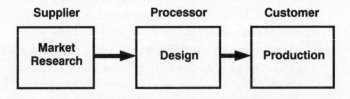

Figure 6.1   Internal customer/supplier relationships

by the design engineer. Various dimensions will have tolerances of accuracy required. Some of these may be easy for the production people to achieve, others may not. In some cases the tolerance might be beyond the capability of the process or the operator, but this may be unknown to the designer. Production assumes that the tolerances are required because the working of the completed product depends upon that level of accuracy. Rather than challenge the hopes of the designer, production is faced with two alternatives:

1 Find more precise manufacturing methods. These could well be costly, or require the services of an outside supplier with the inevitable effect on lead times and costs.
2 Use 100 per cent inspection to sort good from bad. The effect of this alternative on the requirements of JIT is obvious.

If the designer had been aware of these difficulties, he or she could:

1 review the tolerance to determine whether it really did need to be that precise;
2 transfer the tolerance to making parts which could perhaps be manufactured more easily;
3 change the configuration of the design to avoid the difficulty.

These problems can be greatly reduced by the introduction of the 'closed feedback loop' into the process.

The closed feedback loop of control

The performance of a management system is similar in form to an electro-mechanical system, which requires monitoring to ensure compliance with the overall plan, and any discrepancies between plan and performance analysed and corrected. A system built in this fashion is known as a 'closed-loop feedback system' and in terms of an electro-mechanical control system can be described in the diagram shown in Figure 6.2.

From a management point of view this may be reinterpreted as plan, perform, analyse and replan, thus completing the loop, as shown in Figure 6.3. A management control system simply cannot work properly if the loop is not closed. Generally, this fact is not sufficiently well appreciated in industry and is the cause of much inefficiency in many spheres. Quality problems, which will inevitably result in JIT problems, will invariably be the result of an open-loop system.

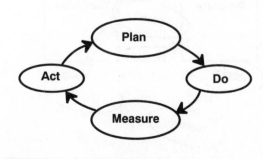

Figure 6.2 Closed-loop feedback system

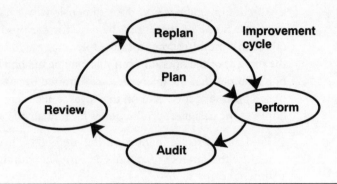

Figure 6.3 The completed loop

In the case of the internal supplier–processor–customer relationship, the closed feedback loop concept becomes an integral part of continuous annual improvement, as shown in Figure 6.4. Output from the processor becomes input to the customer. In terms of the feedback loop, the output from the processor, which is received by the customer, is the result of the 'plan', irrespective of whether it was correct or not. Under the 'no blame' concept it is unlikely that the processor would deliberately supply goods or services which were unsatisfactory. However, unless he or she receives feedback from the customer he or she has no way of knowing whether customer satisfaction has been achieved or not. Therefore the processor, or supplier, needs the information.

The 'plan' therefore consists of two elements:

1 the supplier must be made aware of the needs of the customer;
2 these needs must be compared with the ability to supply, and if necessary, they must be compromised and agreement reached.

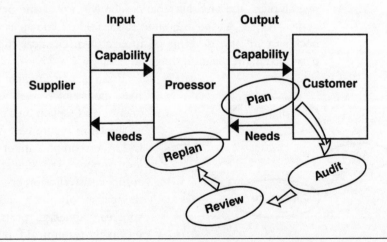

Figure 6.4 Closed feedback loop applied to customer/supplier relationships

The resulting 'plan' thus developed will form the basis both of the expectations of the customer and the standards set for the supplier.

Only after agreement has been reached should supplies be offered to the customer. This is followed by energizing the 'measurement' element of the feedback loop. The means of measurement will vary according to the circumstances, but in most cases will be carried out by the customer, either formally or informally, and usually in the form of the question 'Am I receiving what I expected to receive, in the right time and at the right place – and in the agreed form?'. Feedback of resulting information must be given to the supplier so that the loop may be closed. In the event that supplies do not meet expectations, the third element in the feedback loop is energized and corrective action takes place.

Corrective action can take several forms. In many cases it may simply consist of an informal discussion between customer and supplier. In other cases the differences may be both significant and important, and resolving the problem beyond the capacity or resources of the customer and supplier. This may lead to the use of specialist help in the form of systems analysts, production engineers, and the like, but the modern approach is for the increasing use of project teams. Such teams normally comprise members of the respective departments involved plus others with useful specialist knowledge.

Experience suggests that those who will be directly affected by the resulting proposals should always participate in the project.

This type of project improvement is at the very heart of JIT thinking. If such an approach has never been used before, the number of possible projects will initially go far beyond the digestive capacity of the resources available for making the improvements.

Even in small organizations, internal customer–processor–supplier networks will be quite complex. Also, the flows are not always in one direction. For example, in some situations the design department will supply the finance department with data relating to new products to enable the finance department to prepare forecasts for managerial decision making. In this case the finance department could be regarded as the customer of design. On other occasions the design department will require financial information relating to actual costs of previous designs, to improve the accuracy of future cost estimates. In this situation the finance department will be acting as a supplier to design. This 'to-ing and fro-ing' is of course happening all the time throughout the entire web of interdepartmental relationships. Which of these are critical to the achievement of JIT? There is no single answer. Prior to any improvement activity, it is necessary to conduct an analysis of the whole organization using the Pareto principle to identify the biggest opportunities using the least amount of effort or resource.

Effective achievement of this objective requires a structured and systematic approach. In later chapters, a detailed discussion of the basic planning requirements and general structure should help to illustrate the types of structure which are typical in successful organizations.

Getting started

IDENTIFICATION OF INTERNAL CUSTOMER/SUPPLIER IMPROVEMENT OPPORTUNITY

Two systematic approaches have been found to be particularly effective means of identifying opportunities for customer/supplier improvements, and involve all the teams from up- and downstream operations. Both approaches involve brainstorming of one form or another.

Team-to-team interaction

This approach requires two teams, one from each of two interrelating departments; for example, research and development may form one team and, say, finance the other.

Each of the two teams, located in separate rooms, is then required to brainstorm all the ways in which it sees itself as supplier to the other department, and then to reverse the process and brainstorm the ways in which it believes it is a customer. For both situations the two teams, still independently of each other, will analyse the lists they have created to identify which elements of customer/supplier needs they believe are being satisfied, and which are not. In the case of non-satisfied needs, the team can take the process further to clarify why it does not think the requirement is being met.

Typically, it is usual to find that where the team sees itself as supplier, it has a higher opinion of satisfaction than when in the role of customer.

When this process has been completed, the two teams are brought together, and each will present its results to the other. The results can be highly educational. What frequently happens is:

1 the lists have little in common – many items which appear on one list are missing from the other, and vice versa;
2 items which are in the form of information supplied as opposed to products are often criticized as being in a form which is unintelligible to the recipient (this frequently applies in the case of financial information), or in the wrong format, or the information arrives too late or too infrequently to be of great value;
3 it becomes evident that there is a lack of a common language between the departments.

The element of surprise at the differences is usually high amongst the participants in such sessions, and a strong desire to work some of the key issues rapidly becomes evident. In one case in recent experience a participant from a finance department remarked 'I have worked for this company for twenty-six years and this is the first time I have sat in the same room as people from production and I had no idea as to the problems they had.' This was by no means a unique experience.

Ideally, this type of team-to-team process should continue, department to department, until all the possible interactions have been worked through. In every case, both customer and supplier issues should be identified individually, and the results shared.

Following each of these sessions, the teams should then identify which of the issues must have priority as projects for improvement.

To guide the teams towards the most important objectives, it is necessary to set out the parameters and expectations of the organizing body. If the aim is to identify opportunities relating specifically to JIT, this should be made clear to the teams at the outset.

The list below shows how many interactions are possible in a simple organization. In reality, even those interactions can be broken down further; for example, production can be broken down into production engineering, planning, operations, assembly and so on.

R&D + Finance	Finance + Production
R&D + Production	Finance + Marketing
R&D + Marketing	Personnel + Commercial
R&D + Personnel	Commercial + Finance
R&D + Commercial	Production + Commercial
Production + Marketing	Commercial + Marketing
Marketing + Personnel	Personnel + Production
Personnel + Finance	

When each of these interactions is also considered, the opportunities for improvement are immense. This should not lead to dismay. Most readers of this book will currently be employed. Therefore the company for which they work is still surviving. That being the case, any improvement based upon the opportunities which may be brought to the surface via this process means that future, continued survival is more likely. However, if the opportunities are not taken, survival becomes severely threatened by competitors who are using such means for improvement, notably the Japanese.

Customer/supplier improvement through process analysis
Sometimes it may be more effective to identify customer/supplier opportunities through process analysis or process dissection. This approach can be extremely effective when a clear objective has been established at the outset, as would be the case with JIT.

Typically, a company team formed for the purpose of progressing

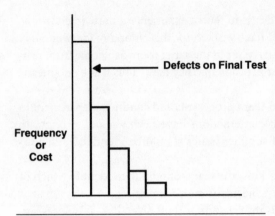

Frequency
or
Cost

Defects on Final Test

Figure 6.5 Pareto analysis of JIT issues

towards JIT would commence the process with a brainstorming session to identify JIT-related opportunities, and list them as shown in Figure 3.8. This list would be analysed to identify the most obviously important key issues.

Pareto analysis of the key issues will then indicate the most important from the JIT point of view. Suppose for example that a Pareto analysis of the brainstormed items indicates that 'stockholding' is the most costly or important item. Then 'stockholding' would become a project theme, and 'reasons for stockholding' would be brainstormed. The resulting ideas would then also be evaluated using the Pareto principle, and might appear as shown in Figure 6.5

A typical example might be 'defects on final test'. For most modern products, the term 'defects' would cover a broad range of specific items, for example:

- blocked holes in printed circuit boards
- bridged tracks
- open circuit
- wrong component
- missing component
- dry joint.

Many of these could easily occur at a number of different operations, and for many different causes. In a great many cases they may be the result of poor customer/supplier relationships. Process analysis can be an extremely effective technique to highlight these situations when they occur. For complex projects the boxes might extend over several sheets.

In the illustration in Figure 6.6 a few causes have been identified. In practice, a considerable number will be clustered around each box. Usually, this form of analysis will reveal patterns which might not have been obvious even to those well acquainted with the process, and their identification will frequently lead to a solution of the problem.

To give an example, I recently conducted a consultancy assignment at a printing works involved in extremely high-quality and demanding work. Prior to the assignment the client had conducted some personal research and was shocked to discover that over a six-month period he had lost over £1.8 million in business due to quality-related customer complaints: this, he claimed, was a conservative estimate. Subsequent analysis of the complaints indicated that few of them actually resulted in any form of rework so there was no direct cost

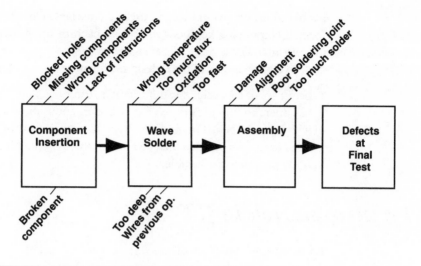

Figure 6.6 Brainstorming: the process analysis chart

involved. However, in most cases the client, while accepting the product with some deficiency, would place the next order with a competitor as a form of punishment.

Process analysis was used to identify or locate the department or function where the faults originated. Analysis revealed that the two functions most heavily involved were sales and computer typesetting. While faults occurred in other areas, they were minimal compared with those established to have their origins with these two functions.

Further analysis indicated a close association between causes identified in the two functions. Of greatest importance were:

1 computer typesetters frequently misinterpreted the handwritten instructions on works order forms given by sales;
2 the sales personnel varied in the terminology used in these instructions depending upon the age of the salesperson.

Printing technology has changed dramatically during recent years, and with it the terms used to describe various requirements and processes. The older salespeople felt more secure when they used terms which would now be regarded as out of date. Generally, the computer typesetters could interpret the meaning of these instructions and make allowances. Occasionally they got it wrong.

These and other discrepancies might not have been revealed had not process analysis been used.

The information revealed by the analysis indicated the need to redesign the works order instruction document. However, it was agreed that the best people to do this would be the users themselves. Consequently, a team was formed comprising key personnel from each of the functions shown on the process analysis diagram (Figure 6.6).

Two key features of the redesigned form were:

1 better space allocation for important instructions;
2 key operations being printed on the document using agreed standard terms, with boxes to tick. This had the effect of compelling up-to-date terminology to be used, and avoided the need for handwriting, much of which had previously proved to be illegible.

Project teams: role in JIT

Basically, there are three distinct types of project team:

1 cross-functional;
2 within function – but inter-disciplinary;
3 within function – single discipline.

Types 1 and 2 have certain things in common and are usually formed for similar purposes. Type 3 is quite different from both 1 and 2, and for the most part has a quite different purpose.

CROSS-FUNCTIONAL TEAMS

In terms of JIT improvements, the degree of power of each of these types of group is likely to reflect the order in which they are listed above. Evidence suggests that in most organizations the problems which have proved to be the most persistent, time-consuming and costly are usually cross-functional. This is because the major problems span functions, or at least appear to, and each function is convinced that blame lies elsewhere. Consequently, everyone blames everyone else and the problem remains in the middle.

If it were obvious that the problem was solely the concern of a specific department, the management of that department would probably have found the time to tackle the problem, particularly if it was known to be important and recurring.

By way of example, consider a situation which is probably well known to most.

A manufacturing company has consistently found that a particular product line is under-achieving on its production targets and that levels of work-in-progress are high. The topic has been raised for discussion at one of the monthly management meetings.

The production manager is defending himself: 'I have three machines which keep breaking down on that line, and if the maintenance department got their act together, I could meet the schedule requirements.' The maintenance manager also has a theory: 'I think the breakdowns occur mostly on the night shift and if you got your people to look after the equipment better, they wouldn't break down so often. In any case, I'm short of labour on the night shift, and if personnel would let me have another fitter and two more electricians, then I could fix the machines.' Personnel then replies: 'That's unfair, we are already up to budget on the wages bill, so I can't let him have anyone else. If the finance department would allow more money, I could let him have his labour' – and so it goes on. Everyone has a theory, but no one is going to tackle the problem because each is convinced it is someone else's responsibility. Analysis will show that a great many serious problems fall into that category.

The best way to avoid the impasse would be to form a project team involving all the managers with a vested interest in various theories. These theories will often challenge each other, but the project by project, systematic approach – symptoms–cause–remedy – will allow these theories to be tested, causes found, and solutions offered.

Cross-functional teams of this sort will frequently solve in a matter of days or weeks problems which have defied solution for years, and which have sometimes threatened the very survival of the company. When asked afterwards why this approach has proved to be so effective, the reply is often 'This is the first time we have ever sat together in the same room and none of us appreciated the other's situation'. In the United States, a project team of this type recently solved a problem which saved nearly $8 million, by means of a few meetings – for just such a reason.

While there may be slight differences in approach, the tendency in modern companies engaged in international competition is towards the establishment and development of this type of small-group activity.

WITHIN-FUNCTION PROJECT TEAMS

The second form of group is the 'within-function interdisciplinary group'. In essence, these groups are identical to the cross-functional and have similar objectives. The only difference is that the core members of the team will all be from within the same functions.

On the whole, the projects will tend to be somewhat smaller than for the cross-functional teams, and will often include members of lower status, although this will not always be the case. Also, the groups will usually be organized and controlled from within the function, whereas the cross-functional teams will normally be organized on a company-wide basis. Projects chosen by within-function groups will normally be those where it is evident that the cause also lies within the function. For example, 'blocked holes in printed circuit boards' would probably be tackled by a production function team, whereas a problem such as 'failed product launch' would more likely be tackled by a cross-functional team involving market research, research and development, production, finance, commercial and after-sales. These teams can be even more effective when involved in Total Productive Maintenance activities.

SINGLE-DISCIPLINE GROUPS

The third type of team, the 'within-function single-discipline groups', are quite different from the others in many respects although they also tackle work-related problems. These differences are quite important, and it is my belief that it is essential that they are well understood by anyone who contemplates the development of this aspect of JIT.

One way to clarify the differences and purposes of these groups would be to show how they evolved in the first place, so let us take a look at the Japanese history which led to the development of small-group activities and then, in the following section, at the evolution of JIT itself.

JAPANESE SMALL-GROUP DEVELOPMENT

The historical development of these groups dates back to the end of World War II and the period from 1945 to 1951, which represents the American occupation period. During this period the Americans had two key policy elements:

1 to change the culture of Japan to such an extent that it would not develop a postwar militaristic society;
2 to help in the postwar reconstruction so that Japan could stand on its own feet economically and would not require an indefinite series of handouts from the USA. Many people now feel that the Americans may have overdone that part of the policy.

For the first part, General MacArthur, the Supreme Commander of American forces in Japan, sacked all the influential managers in government, commerce and industry over the age of forty-five. Because the Japanese tend towards policies of lifetime employment, and managers progress upwards only by age and competence, this meant that all the senior managers were suddenly swept aside. Younger people therefore found themselves elevated to senior positions years earlier than they would have expected, and with no one to copy. To learn quickly, these young managers flooded over to the United States to attend business schools, under the slogan 'copy the West'. At the same time, for the purposes of the second element in the policy, the Americans sent some of their most eminent management consultants to Japan as part of an educational package in their postwar redevelopment.

All this assistance was masterminded by the American military, to which quality control is of the utmost importance. The military buying agencies know better than anyone that wars can be won and lost just as much by the quality and reliability of the equipment in the field, as by the bravery and organization of the fighting forces. Consequently, the help they gave to the Japanese at this time had a strong quality-related bias.

Pioneers of JIT-related concepts

DR W. E. DEMING

In 1950 the Americans sent to Japan an expert in Statistical Quality Control, Dr Edwards Deming, to give a series of lectures on the topic to the country's leading industrialists and opinion influencers. In effect he was able to convince the Japanese nation that their future and standard of living depended upon being able to compete effectively in world markets on the quality and reliability of their products. At that time the Japanese had an unenviable reputation for being junk merchants to the world and their products were regarded as being cheap, grossly inferior imitations of Western products.

Deming convinced the Japanese that the statistical techniques of quality control were an essential means to the elimination of this reputation and to being able to produce high-quality products at low cost.

Following Deming's visits the Japanese launched a massive nationwide programme in all levels of organization, mainly on the techniques of Statistical Quality Control.

DR J. M. JURAN

In 1954 the Japanese invited Dr J. M. Juran to visit Japan, also for the purpose of lecturing on quality.

Dr Juran's message was somewhat different. In effect he was saying 'Of course, the statistical approach is important. In fact it is essential to good results, but it is only one aspect of a much broader and more complex subject.' In essence, while the statistical approach is in some form applicable at all levels of organization, the techniques really relate to the control of specific production processes, and this is where the main thrust of effort had been made.

Dr Juran convinced the Japanese that quality was ultimately the responsibility of upper management – not just as a means of giving legitimacy to the activities of others at lower levels, but in ways which imply total and continuous involvement. The main thrust of Dr Juran's message was that:

1 Upper management controls the direction of the company's resources. Therefore, only upper management can decide how much should be spent

on quality improvement, how it should be spent, and how this investment should be monitored.

2 Only upper management can identify the major strengths and weaknesses of the company compared with competitors, and only upper management can make the final decisions about which markets to attack, where to change direction and so on – in other words, to design, monitor and develop the strategic plan for the organization.

3 Since all these decisions are quality related, only upper management can ultimately control quality.

Juran then suggested and showed how all quality improvement is made on a project by project basis and how this might be achieved.

In his lectures he suggested that upper management identify opportunities for improvement. This could be done using the brainstorming technique.

The resulting list would in all probability exceed the digestive capacity of the resources available for tackling the problems identified; therefore they should be prioritized. The Pareto technique should be used to separate the vital few from the less important many.

Some of the major problems or opportunities for improvement might be tackled as projects by the upper managers themselves. In other cases, teams of senior managers would be formed.

The Japanese accepted the advice and a number of large companies began pilot schemes, initially involving only upper and senior levels of management. Meanwhile, the development of Statistical Quality Control continued at all levels.

As the teams got started, a new development took place. The teams of senior managers which had been formed to tackle the problems identified by upper management had their own ideas about future projects and began to submit proposals for these upwards. Upper management now found themselves vetting these proposals and setting priorities.

In some cases the projects identified by the senior managers did not require upper management approval, and the managers were sufficiently senior to make the decisions themselves. They could also set up project teams at lower levels to themselves. The process therefore began to progress downwards through the hierarchy.

This was intended and encouraged from the outset and, by 1960, in some large Japanese companies the project team approach had progressed all the way down to front line supervision (see Figure 6.7).

PROFESSOR K. ISHIKAWA

At this point a leading Japanese professor, Kaoru Ishikawa, made a major contribution.

He had noted that the less important many problems on the Pareto

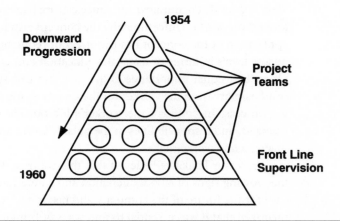

Figure 6.7 Progress of project by project approach in Japanese companies

diagram were not being picked up and tackled by the managers because there were always 'more important' problems to tackle. In addition, he noted that the majority of these problems were more in the category of 'operator controllable' than 'management controllable'. In many cases the managers may not even have known of the existence of some problems let alone their detailed make-up. Professor Ishikawa realized that the only way in which these problems could be effectively identified, analysed and solved was through some form of involvement of the workers themselves. Since Statistical Quality Control was being extended to supervisory level at least, it seemed to make sense to find ways of involving the operating forces in the project by project improvement process as well.

Another problem which significantly influenced Professor Ishikawa's thinking was the fact that labour alienation had become a real problem in Japan, as had the diminishing role of the foreman or supervisor, in line with similar events elsewhere in the world. He saw this deterioration as being due to the widespread introduction into Japan of the so-called Taylor System of Management. This will not be discussed in detail here but it is discussed in many other texts including the author's *Quality Circles Handbook*.

The Taylor System is based on the idea that management is a scientific process beyond the scope of the workforce and supervision. The planning and management of work should therefore be separated from the 'doing' aspects. In its most developed form, 'management manages and people do'. The concept was developed in the United States at the turn of the century as a direct consequence of the lack of skilled craftsmen resulting both from the rapid expansion of industry and the influx of largely unskilled labour. It therefore became essential to 'de-skill' work and elevate all problem-solving upwards. In terms of productivity, the concept was spectacularly successful and, following

World War II, encouraged by American management consultants it spread around the world. Unfortunately, the concept also has its downside. Rigorous application of the concept has the effect of reducing work to the most meaningless levels in terms of using the education and creativity of the workforce. Of at least equal importance is the fact that this approach also removes all responsibility from the worker for the quality of the product, or influence over the process. In contrast, the worker's life outside the factory gates has not changed, and responsibilities in the outside world are much the same for both manager and worker alike.

Professor Ishikawa believed that this contrast was largely responsible for the growing signs of labour alienation and a deterioration in the worker's concern for the future of the company and his or her own work performance. He theorized that it was essential to find ways of bringing back the craftsmanship concept, but at the same time preserve the economic advantages of the Taylor System. The result was that he postulated the possibility of bringing craftsmanship back to groups of people under the leadership of their own supervisor, through the project by project process.

The idea was that teams of workers from the same department, sharing common work interests and with common work experience, could, if they so desired, be trained in problem-solving, and should be given time on a regular basis to identify opportunities for improvement, make recommendations and, where possible, themselves implement the improvements. In this way Professor Ishikawa effectively found the answer to a range of problems which have bugged Western management for decades. Through this approach it becomes possible to:

1 re-establish the role of supervisor or foreman as leader of the group back to the same relationship which existed under the craftsmanship regime;
2 provide opportunities for leadership development of supervisors and potential supervisors;
3 enable supervisors to develop a better relationship with the working group and to earn greater respect from higher levels of management;
4 make better use of the creativity and education of direct personnel and make work intrinsically more interesting, rewarding and enjoyable, irrespective of the repetitive nature of some tasks (see, for example, the Toyota situation described in Chapter 1);
5 develop a spirit of company-mindedness and concern for the achievement of company goals;
6 provide a vehicle for the continuous development of staff.

The model in Figure 6.8 shows how Professor Ishikawa's suggestion takes the project by project approach down to the workforce.

Ishikawa suggested that because of the Taylor System, it was neither possible nor desirable to form groups of direct employees in precisely the

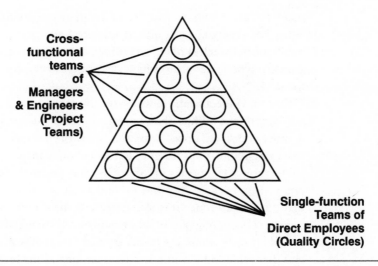

Cross-functional teams of Managers & Engineers (Project Teams)

Single-function Teams of Direct Employees (Quality Circles)

Figure 6.8   Integration of Quality Circles into Company-wide Quality Improvement

same way as with managers who expect to be directed towards improvement activities, and who also expect to receive additional 'in career' training as part of the management development process. The differences suggested by Professor Ishikawa were basically as follows:

1   Groups of workers should be set up but only on a *voluntary* basis. Those who volunteer were thought more likely to make a contribution than those who had been compelled. It also implies that they have volunteered to accept the rules, provided that these have been made clear from the outset. People should also be free to leave a group if they so wish.

2   The teams should be given freedom to *select projects of their own choosing* even though suggestions may also come from others. The object is to show trust. If the workers think a problem is important, this must be accepted, as it would be under the craftsmanship concept. A craftsman is by definition responsible for the quality of his or her own work. It was also felt that, by virtue of the Pareto concept, it would not be good use of management time to identify projects for the groups. In addition, many of the problems known to the workers may be unknown to the managers. As an American speaker said recently, 'The guy that knows that 25 square feet of floor space best, is the guy that works there.'

3   In addition to point 2, it was not thought a good idea to allocate time to projects by judging each project on its merits. Many difficulties could arise if large differences in time allocation emerged. It would also be difficult for upper management to control the process if this were to be the case. In contrast, with management project teamwork the time allocated for projects can vary widely depending upon the nature of the project and its urgency.

It was therefore thought to be better for a fixed allocation of time to be made to each group irrespective of the merits or complexity of the project. What has emerged is an almost universal acceptance that approximately one hour per week is practical both from the point of view of project work and the avoidance of too much disruption of the function of the department.

4 Unlike the project teams in which the life of the team is *ad hoc*, these groups are continuous. When they have completed one project, they will select another and so on, on a continuous basis. Each project is followed by a formal presentation of its findings to the section manager.

The project teams may in some cases stay together after the completion of one project because they have found another which is equally relevant to that particular group. It is also likely that the group will disperse, with the members becoming part of new teams formed to tackle different projects.

5 As with project teams, the teams are all trained in the problem-solving skills, and these should be continuously developed as the team members develop skill and confidence in their abilities.

6 While projects form the basis of the activities of these small groups of workers, management must not lose sight of the fact that the re-establishment of the advantages of craftsmanship, pride in the job, improvement in morale, corporate pride and identity and so on are at least equal in importance to cost reduction. Also, the Pareto principle indicates that only a few of the projects selected at this level will have a major impact on the company on an individual basis. It is the *collective* result which is important.

Experience suggests that a well-run programme involving teams of this type will produce a return on investment of 4:1 upwards. This is obviously desirable but management project teams will usually produce a substantially larger yield in most organizations.

Because of these fundamental differences between the two types of group, Professor Ishikawa suggested that these teams be called 'Quality Control Circles'.

In mid-1962 the Nippon Wireless and Telegraph Company reported that it had set up nine of these groups along the lines of Professor Ishikawa's suggestion and that they were enormously successful. By the end of the year, over thirty-five other companies had followed suit. By 1978 the numbers of groups had risen to a staggering one million, involving an estimated ten million Japanese workers.

At about this time the West, which was beginning to respond to the growing competitive challenge from Japan, discovered the existence of these groups. The group approach was of course fundamentally different from typical Western manufacturing practice, and it was not easy to understand the context in which the groups operated. The project teams of managers are given much lower visibility as is the whole framework of an organization supporting company-wide quality and within it the JIT objective. Consequently, Westerners have obtained a biased impression of the importance of Quality Circles.

This book should go some way towards putting all these elements into context. None of them stands on its own. They are all integrated and inter-active elements in a cohesive whole which has helped to make Japan one of the most productive countries in the world.

Summary

1 JIT depends upon involvement and participation and requires a concen-trated and continuous drive at all levels towards making the company even more successful than before.
2 This involvement must be organized and co-ordinated, and usually results in the establishment of project teams.
3 Project teams include:

   ● teams of managers
   ● teams of specialists
   ● teams of direct employees.

   These teams are trained in the techniques described in Chapters 3 and 5, principally the symptom–cause–remedy sequence.
4 The 'no blame' concept and the triple role of supplier/processor/customer form the basis of project identification.
5 The closed loop of management control enables quality planning and action to be followed by review, audit and replay, both systematically and through the project team process.
6 Process analysis enables JIT problem causes to be highlighted and analysed at macro-level.
7 The Ishikawa or 'fishbone' diagram enables problem analysis at micro-level.
8 Concepts which led to the achievement of JIT in Japan were influenced by Dr Edwards Deming, Dr J. M. Juran and Professor Kaoru Ishikawa.
9 Professor Ishikawa's observations and teachings led to Quality Circles and the breakdown of the so-called Taylor System of Management.

Recommended further reading

Belbin, Dr R. Meredith (1981) *Management Teams – Why they Succeed or Fail*, Heinemann.

Hutchins, David (1985) *Quality Circles Handbook*, Pitman.

Sasaki, Professor Naoto and Hutchins, David (1984) *Japanese Approach to Product Quality*, Pergamon.

7 MOTIVATION

Motivation means people

It has frequently been said that *people* are industry's most important asset. If people do not really care, or if they just do their jobs according to instructions, no amount of sophisticated processes will produce the intended results on a constant basis. People cannot be eliminated from the system. Even if products are made by robots, it takes people to maintain them, to write and verify software, plan the system and so forth.

The subject of motivation is therefore absolutely critical to the achievement of JIT and, in my opinion, this chapter is therefore the most important in this book. If for no other reason, the objectives discussed in other chapters could not be achieved without some consideration of the aspects covered in this.

When the subject of motivation is raised, it is usually applied to the behaviour of the operating forces. In this chapter, we are talking about motivation at all levels – upper management, line management, off-line management, technical specialists, trade unions, supervision, outside sales, suppliers, purchasing, maintenance, administration and the workforce. In fact not only everyone in the company but everyone throughout the supply chain as well.

Consider the implications for an important customer in a supply chain based upon JIT if a supplier suffered an industrial stoppage. This happened in the 1980s at a major supplier to Austin Rover. The risk of such an event was one of the principal matters requiring consideration by Japanese Nissan executives when they decided to select a British site for their European car production. They knew only too well that an unpredictable industrial relations climate is totally unsuited to the introduction of JIT. It was only after they had gained confidence in their ability to develop a sufficiently highly motivated workforce in the United Kingdom that they made the decision to go ahead.

Motivating *managers* is a far bigger problem than many people realize. No one would deny that most managers are highly motivated and responsive to firefighting situations. Most spend a high proportion of their working lives engaged in such activities, and a high proportion probably think that this is what management is all about. Many managers believe that fighting sporadic 'fires' is the most important aspect of their job, and for this they are highly motivated.

Unlike improvement projects, firefighting is both dramatic and exciting. It also gives a sense of achievement. The manager, out in the department with his sleeves rolled up, leading the action, can feel like Rambo and believe he is giving the impression of energy and leadership. However, Chapter 3 indicated that such an approach to management is ineffective because it only addresses sporadic problems, and does nothing to attack the chronic problems which hold the secret to JIT success.

The chronic problems are numerous, they have always been there, they are not dramatic like the sporadic problems. Many of the chronic problems will not individually change the world, but the key factor is that unlike the sporadic problems, which come and go, they are there all the time. When they have been successfully identified, analysed and solved, in the manner discussed earlier, the benefits accrue year after year. JIT can only be achieved through the successful solution of these problems.

It takes time to identify these problems on an individual basis; time to collect data to identify and analyse the causes; time to find a remedy, test a remedy, apply the remedy, overcome resistance to change, and to hold the gains. Few managers have the time available since they are so busy firefighting, but *the time must be found*. It is precisely because these problems have been accepted in the past that managers find it difficult to become motivated to solve them in the present and the future.

It is only the highly motivated manager who will find time to attack these problems. This frequently means additional time in the early stages, in the form of an up-front investment. It is not unknown for such highly motivated managers to hold their first few meetings out of hours, and to adjourn to a local bar to get the process started. If the initial projects are well selected, the resultant remedies may well reduce the need for firefighting as an activity and make more time available in the normal working week for JIT improvement activities. In the early stages, such an investment must be made if JIT is to be achieved.

A second feature of management motivation is the motivation required actually to motivate the workforce. In many cases, this will involve motivating the unions as well. This can be both tedious and time-consuming. In many cases it will mean gaining a better understanding of the way people think, and finding out what is important to them in their everyday lives. The firefighting manager will have little time available for such involvement and, again, it comes back to the question of motivation.

On a trip to Japan a few years ago I was talking to a British manager who had worked in a Japanese company in Tokyo for the past seventeen years. He told me that British visitors frequently say to him 'Of course, you are lucky managing in Japan, you don't have to spend so much time dealing with your workpeople as we do.' His reply to such a statement was 'That's where you are wrong. We spend probably ten times as much time dealing with our workpeople as you do, that's why we don't have the problems which you have!' Again, the question of time becomes a critical factor.

The problem is that we are faced with a vicious cycle. We do not have time to concentrate on the care and development of our people or on identifying and solving chronic problems because we are so busy fighting sporadic 'fires'. Consequently, more sporadic 'fires' break out due to this lack of attention, giving us even less time to tackle these problems.

The process of breaking out of this spiral cannot be initiated by line management. As long as such managers are being judged on their firefighting ability, and not on their improvement achievements, the spiral becomes even more vicious. This spiral can only be broken by upper management. It is upper management's job to identify the areas which need to be tackled first, to estimate the time and costs involved and to provide those resources. They also have to take time out to convince their managers that this is not another quick fix, a flavour of the month, but the beginning of a process which will ultimately become a way of life within the company. This in itself requires deep commitment and motivation from upper management. It is not something which the upper managers can achieve by initiating the process with a fanfare of trumpets in the expectation that they can then walk away and leave the results to others. JIT requires *continuous* involvement and considerable visibility by upper management. It must be realized by upper management that JIT involves a massive cultural change within the organization. This in itself means a changed relationship between managers and other managers, managers and their subordinates: a change in the criteria for the selection of replacement managers and supervisors, a change in criteria for job evaluation, annual appraisals, team briefing, and general communications. Goals and targets must be reviewed with the emphasis given to improvement activities gaining status against the priorities given to control activities. Merit rating schemes must be similarly reviewed.

Internal customer/supplier relationships must be given continuous atten-

JUST IN TIME
NOT A
QUICK FIX

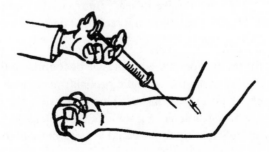

tion, and positive action taken on any weaknesses exposed. The 'no blame' concept must become a reality. This concept is based upon the belief that no one comes to work deliberately to do a poor-quality job. Therefore, if poor quality is the outcome there must be an organizational problem which must be resolved. The customer/supplier relationship concept described in Chapter 5 provides an effective approach to tackling these problems.

The relationship between management and workpeople must also be changed. JIT cannot be achieved effectively in an environment where management 'manages' and people 'do'. This approach – unfortunately all too typical in modern organizations – is anathema to those who are planning the factory of the future, using JIT and related concepts.

Workpeople can only become properly motivated when the company's objectives are consistent with their own. This requires managers to obtain a belief in and commitment to the idea that workpeople have loyalties, goals and needs similar to their own. It is essential that managers wholeheartedly accept that their subordinates have the following basic qualities:

1 An innate loyalty to the company and to their colleagues at work.
2 A desire to see the company as a community in which they share their lives with others, including the managers, all year round, and not just at the annual Christmas party if there is one.
3 A wish to be proud of the company's products, and to share in the process of making these products successful in the marketplace.
4 A need to feel trusted, respected and cared for as whole human beings and not just numbers on clock cards or extensions of their machines or desks. (In my opinion, the human resource development 'specialist' who first coined the term describing workpeople as 'units' is in the wrong profession.)
5 They want security and continuity of employment, and a long-term relationship with their friends and colleagues. They do not want to be in a position of uncertainty, financial unpredictability, and constantly moving from job to job.
6 They like to think that the company is concerned with their long-term development and not just the narrowly based skills which might be the requirement of their present task.
7 They would like to see a future in the company for their own family and friends. An opportunity for their own children to develop and grow.

If a company can realize these needs and expectations, it is highly unlikely that the motivation of the people will be found wanting.

Most managers would probably agree with these seven points, and would like them to be achieved. However, while the caring manager can go a long way towards achieving some of these ideals in his or her own department, it is unlikely that he or she could achieve more than local success. It would also be impossible for a single manager to make significant changes if the whole culture of the company is tending towards a different direction. Generally, although cultural change is dependent upon the support of individual managers, it is largely outside their personal control. Only upper management can provide the appropriate environment to enable such a cultural change to take place. To do so requires upper managers to understand the changes which are involved.

The respective roles of the various levels in the motivation for JIT may be summarized as described in the following sections.

Upper management

First, upper management will study JIT seriously, with particular emphasis on the approaches of leading Japanese companies, and compare these with Western initiatives to identify strengths and weaknesses. Factors dependent on Eastern cultural values and those based on sound management practice must be clearly distinguished.

Second, the programme must commence from the top down, with phase 1 being a clear boardroom initiative. The more that upper management is seen to have been involved in the detailed planning of the process, the more easily others will be convinced of its commitment. One British company which has recently developed a programme which includes JIT spent almost a year planning the programme at boardroom level before even involving top line managers. The rewards of that planning are now being reaped even before the programme has been fully introduced.

Third, it will identify the cultural changes which must take place for JIT to be fully successful. This will require comparisons between the ideal culture and the current culture. Since cultures cannot be changed overnight, it will be necessary to identify the elements of culture individually, and then set priorities for change. Key elements of culture include:

- Internal customer/supplier relationships
- 'No blame'
- Interpersonal relationships within functions and across functions
- Relationships between managers/supervisors and subordinates
- Personal development programmes, including training both in skills and in behavioural aspects of work
- Status identity in use of car-parks, canteens, working areas and the like: also payment systems, start and finish times, clocking on and off and other perks/penalties
- Internal communication methods such as briefing, notifying, newsletters, and so on

- Degree of disclosure regarding company performance
- Use of scoreboards as performance indicators, and the priority these give to quality/quantity
- Criteria for management performance reviews
- Structure and content of meetings
- External customer/supplier relationships.

This list is by no means exhaustive, and it is recommended that any board of directors who might be using this book as guidance should conduct a brainstorming session among themselves to identify specific aspects relating to motivation for JIT pertinent to their own organization. When completed, such a list will include a number of major items, each of which would result in a key company initiative and involve a great deal of upper management time.

It must be emphasized that these items are not prerequisites to the commencement of a JIT programme, but they are essential to the long-term ultimate achievement. Some of these elements do not have to be worked on immediately. Others do, but even so they do not need to be completed in advance of JIT. However, it is important that a start is made on some of these and, perhaps equally important, that a start is *seen* to have been made. Those items which are known to cause offence to others at lower levels will be high priority, progress of such items giving a clear impression to all that upper management is seriously taking the company's problems in hand and is doing something positive to improve performance – in other words, to make the company a better place to work.

Recently a British company in the north of England, producing medical products, began an initiative to improve its market share and the company's reputation, both internally and externally. My organization was commissioned to help as external consultants. Our initial assignment was to conduct an audit of the company to determine its strengths and weaknesses. The chairman of the company said 'I do not want to wait for the final report before we begin to take action on our weaknesses. If you find anything serious, I want to know straight away so that we can begin the process of putting things right.'

A number of aspects soon emerged. A Quality Circles programme had been started some two years before but it never really came to anything. Work to put this right began immediately.

While quality checks were being carried out at various points, no obvious priority was given to quality as such. The company did not have a clearly defined quality policy, neither were there any obviously defined quality systems and practices although these existed on an informal basis. A great deal of quality-related data were regularly collected, but never put to good use.

When these points were put to the chairman, immediate action was taken, and training given to the appropriate personnel. One action was the development of a clear policy statement on quality. This was subsequently printed in a quality typeface, and framed copies were hung in every manager's office and in the reception area.

Several months later, during a review of the progress made with the improvements, it was claimed internally that even though a number of very tangible savings had been made due to quality improvements and associated cost reductions, the most significant benefit came from the raised morale, not only of the workforce but of line management and supervisors as well, due to upper management being seen to be actively involved in a programme aimed to restore the company's reputation. Everyone wants to be part of a winning team!

Middle management

It is a fact that middle management will not become motivated for JIT or indeed for any other company-wide programme unless it is clear that upper management is not only committed but also fully involved. Also, that this commitment and involvement is almost certain to be sustained and continuous and to become a way of managerial life.

While this commitment and involvement is easy to demonstrate in the short term, it is difficult to ensure that it will continue into the long term. One of the biggest single handicaps to the demonstration of this long-term commitment is the transient nature of the upper managers themselves. One of the more regrettable features of American management to be incorporated in Western Europe since World War II is the concept of management development through frequent job changes. As a young man in the 1950s and 1960s, I was advised even by my own boss that it was in my best interests to change companies every two years or so. The theory was that to stay longer indicated a lack of motivation, or 'get up and go'. The ambitious young man was told that it was necessary to move around like a grasshopper to gain as wide a spectrum of experience as possible. The young manager who had experience in only one company would be unlikely to gain promotion to a higher position against competition from an outsider with 'greater experience'.

This concept does not apply only to young managers. In more elevated positions it is argued that a senior executive takes one year to learn the job, one year to perform and to make an impression, and should then move on, trading upon the successes achieved. This approach was encouraged in the 1980s by Sir Michael Edwardes, who suggested that others should follow the example he set in British Leyland, or Rover Cars as it is now known. While there was an undoubted need for some drastic surgery at British Leyland, requiring someone of the calibre of Sir Michael, there can also be little doubt that grasshopper management is a considerable disadvantage to the achievement of JIT or for that matter any related concepts, such as Company-wide Quality Improvement, which also require cultural change. The reason is that cultural change is a long-term process. With any change of such magnitude, there are always a number of managers who favour the change, others who do not, and many between these extremes who could be convinced, but only if they are confident that the change will be permanent. Few managers would be prepared to go overboard on any scheme if they had the slightest suspicion that they might be seen to be numbered amongst the believers when the next flavour of the month is introduced and everything returned to its previous state.

The most likely reason for this suspicion is uncertainty regarding the continuity of upper management. There are many examples where an enthusiastic chief executive has begun the process of cultural change, only to be moved to another part of the organization or to go to another job elsewhere. It is rare that a replacement will want to continue with an initiative which does not bear his or her stamp, with the result that the initial achievements will have been lost. Those involved in such failures will be less likely to support any future initiatives for fear of similar failures. In some companies so many such initiatives have been started and failed that managers have become immune to any further changes however attractive they may appear.

A further big disadvantage of short-stay management is the tendency for such managers to opt for decisions which show short-term rather than long-term gains. The hope is that a quick killing will provide the manager with a reputation for success which can be traded elsewhere. Quite often, these short-term gains have negative long-term consequences. It is also likely that long-term decisions are never made.

Of general importance is the fact that in a society of transient managers no one enters into long-term management development programmes, because they believe they will be spending money on training staff for their competitors. The hope is that the competitor will do the training, and we can cream off or headhunt those who show promise. The result is that no one does the training, and this becomes a loss to society generally.

The lesson is that for the long-term achievement of JIT, the transient management process must be stopped. It is not natural to our society and its disadvantages far outweigh the advantages.

Managers who realize that their own long-term future success and development lie with the long-term future and success of the company are far more likely to become motivated to support JIT. This applies at all levels, right to the top. This is a key principle in the success of Japanese companies, and is typical of a number of industries elsewhere. It is not a cultural concept. Transient management was invented in the United States, and exported to the rest of the world after World War II. Prior to that time it existed in only a minimal number of industries. There is therefore no reason why a return to something approaching lifetime employment cannot be reintroduced into Western society if the will to do so is there.

A point which may be of value to those concerned with this aspect of cultural change relates to one of the methods designed to maintain this concept, used by the Japanese.

In Japanese companies salaries for all levels of employee are to a greater or lesser extent related to years of service to the company. In addition, very large bonuses are given based upon the previous year's performance of the company. Promotion is also related to years of service. An outsider transferring employment from one large Japanese company to another would almost certainly suffer a drop in pay regardless of his or her status, and would also be awarded a very much smaller bonus than the longer-serving employees. The logic behind this approach is based on the fact that the company's performance is founded on the years of dedicated service of the existing employees. In Toyota, for example, it was recently claimed that over 900 000 employee suggestions were currently being implemented per year! It is believed by Japanese managers, probably rightly so, that since the new recruit would not have contributed to this improvement, an entry salary equal to or greater than that of existing employees would be greatly resented, and thus creativity would be threatened.

Further, because movement from company to company is regarded as unusual and disloyal, such personnel are regarded with great suspicion, particularly when they have taken a drop in salary to make the move.

In contrast, not only is such movement encouraged in Western society for the reasons given above, but it is usual for such moves to result in higher salaries than those being paid to longer-serving employees. The resentment caused by this approach is only too obvious. In addition, such transient personnel usually have little loyalty to the company and are probably more concerned with what they can take out rather than what they can put in. The long-term future of the company may be irrelevant to them since they are unlikely to be there for that long.

Any organization intending to introduce JIT or to develop the concept further would do well to consider the implications of these points very seriously indeed. Long-term company loyalty is a major element in the development of international competitiveness.

A second main aspect of middle management motivation relates to motivation for the involvement of the workforce. Most managers would agree that some form of involvement of subordinates is desirable; most political parties recommend various forms of participation in their manifestos; the EU has produced a directive on the topic; and yet involvement of such personnel is at a lamentably low level. Why? If everyone is for involvement, and the operating forces themselves want to be involved, how come we do not seem to be able to achieve anything significant in this area? Also, why is it that the Japanese on the other hand seem to have little difficulty in finding ways to involve their people? Again, the question of cultural difference arises. The traditional Western belief is that Japanese workers have an innate loyalty to their companies and to each other. The inference is that Japanese managers have this loyalty simply as a bonus to give them a standing advantage over their Western counterparts. The facts are squarely to the contrary.

THE JAPANESE EXPERIENCE

Japanese workers are loyal. So too are their managers and indeed everyone else, both in the company and right through the supply network. The reason is not due to cultural differences. The main reason is that Japanese managers *recognize the importance and value of loyalty*. They also recognize that loyalty is not something which you have as a right, *it has to be won*! The Japanese company and the Japanese manager give much time and thought to the question of loyalty. They also spend a significant proportion of the company's profits on winning, deepening and developing this loyalty. The process does not start merely at the point of induction into the company: it starts with children at school.

Yet again, Toyota provides an example. In Toyota City, the Toyota Motor Company has built a large exhibition, approximately the size of the Albert Hall in London. At the front of the building there is a large car- and coach-park. It is usually full of coaches which have brought schoolchildren from all ages from a wide area of that region of Japan. Through the main doors, the visitor enters a large hall or reception area. The area is usually packed with children, assembled in rows with guides carrying identification flags. The visitor then progresses from room to room around the building. Rather like the exhibit rooms in the Science Museum in London, each room contains a number of exhibits featuring some aspect of industrial development in the world, mostly related to the automobile. At one point the visitor enters a planetarium. In the centre stands a space capsule which had been used by the United States in the early stages of manned space flight. Children could enter the capsule and view the sky, imagining they were Neil Armstrong or some other space hero. It was obvious that Toyota's intention was to capture the hearts and minds of these young people at the earliest possible stage of their development. Not only was the company investing in its own future, it was also contributing to the future of Japan by presenting technology as an exciting, social and meaningful way of life for future generations of Japanese. How different from our own approach, where the media consistently tell us that industry is dead, that manufacture is in a state of permanent, if not terminal, decline – that the Science Museum is nothing more than a relic of days gone by.

The lesson is that we must work to achieve loyalty, we do not have it as of right.

Another example of this can be taken from the Honda Company. Every year the company closes the factory for two working days. Prior to these two days, workers are encouraged, either as individuals or groups, to develop crazy inventions and to make them into working models. These models are then demonstrated at the two-day event. Families are invited, and the object is to create a carnival, a fun atmosphere. Prizes are given for the craziest, most creative or most innovative inventions. Honda claims that approximately two of these ideas are incorporated into successive designs of Honda products. The main objective of the function, however, is to develop a sense of community, loyalty, identity and harmony between family and work.

Much space could be given in this chapter to describe other quite different examples taken from Japanese companies, but the point of all these examples is that the Japanese do not take employee loyalty for granted – *they work for it and they work to retain it*!

THE LEGACY OF THE TAYLOR SYSTEM

The real question for Western managers is 'Why are we in the West so much less highly motivated for, and aware of, the importance of motivation and involvement that we devote so little time and resource to achieve it?' Obviously the question does not have a simple answer. The reasons are many and complex. Some are hidden in the complexity of human psychology and physiology. However, one theory (which I support) is that, here again, the Western world is suffering from ideas imported from the United States, and that at one time there was a greater awareness of the importance of loyalty and involvement but it has been lost in the fairly recent past. The particular import in this context is the so-called Taylor System of Management. We have already seen how, under this concept, management problem-solving is regarded as being beyond the ability of supervisors and workforce and, consequently, how all problem-solving is devolved upwards to management.

We have also seen that these problems are too numerous for managers to tackle by themselves. In addition, many of the problems are so intrinsically related to specific tasks that it is likely that managers are not even aware of the specific nature of such problems, let alone the means to find suitable solutions. Only the workforce has the know-how and creativity to solve such problems. Consequently, they remain unresolved. Not only do the workers gain the impression that managers are ineffective due to this lack of awareness, they see them as being incapable of solving those problems which, together with their solutions, are only too obvious to the workers. Apart from the loss of respect resulting from this experience, the workers see the managers as being remote and uncaring. For their part, the managers interpret the fact that the workers are not always producing good work as a lack of interest and a negative approach to work. Based upon this erroneous assumption, managers sometimes seek remedies through the use of incentives, penalties and propaganda. Thus the division is made ever wider.

The real tragedy is that West European companies need never have got themselves into this situation in the first place. The reason why the Taylor System was incorporated into Western Europe following World War II was because organizations were mesmerized by the phenomenal effect on the productivity of the United States since it incorporated the System in the early 1900s. Following World War II the Taylor System was responsible for making the United States into the most productive nation on earth. In the years that followed, company after company in country after country adopted the Taylor System as a way of managerial life. Interestingly, even though the Taylor System was fundamentally different from the concepts of management which evolved in our cultures, the cultural argument against its introduction never arose. Consequently, the Taylor System swept the world, to create an entirely new culture all of its own.

What is perhaps surprising is that the cultural argument has surfaced, and is proving to be a major hindrance to the adoption of the concepts being discussed in this book. It is surprising because many of the ideas suggested here have in the past been part of our own cherished cultures.

For example, prior to the incorporation of the Taylor System, management relied upon the know-how and experience of the craftsmen, gave recognition for achievement and adopted a paternalistic approach to the workpeople. The company was regarded as a family, even though the workpeople may not have participated in ownership or shared in profit. The foreman or supervisor was seen as the leading craftsman, and was probably appointed as a result of superior skill and know-how and his relationship with subordinates. He would take apprentices into his care, and would regard it as his responsibility to develop their skills. Of course, industry was not always like that and there are many horrific stories of exploitation, mainly in the unskilled industries. But in the era of the craftsman, the foreman had high prestige and the ambition of many was to reach that status. How different today!

What must be realized is that the Taylor System was developed not out of cultural considerations, or indeed as the panacea many thought it to be, but as a natural response to a need which prevailed in the United States at the time.

At the end of the last century, industrial growth in the United States outstripped the supply of skilled craftsmen. At that time the USA was faced with an unskilled immigrant population who came mainly from Western Europe. They were mostly illiterate, and did not want to work in the factory environment. Their main intention was to earn as much as they could as quickly as they could to travel west as pioneers. Consequently, American industry was faced with a largely illiterate labour force, with high labour turnover.

What more natural therefore than to develop a system where the skill is taken out of the work? The Taylor System achieves this to such an effect that in many cases the work is almost devoid of meaning to those performing it. What must be done is to find ways of reintroducing craftsmanship, pride in the job, and a sense of hope into our workforce. In this way we can use the education and creativity of our workpeople.

Returning to the original point of this discussion: why we are unable to provide participation and involvement even though most would agree that it was necessary. The reason is probably because this is impossible without first dismantling the Taylor System. This is by no means easy. The system has been around for a long time. It has infiltrated every type of work in every type of industry. Jobs are designed and constructed based upon the system, and it is intrinsically interwoven into our society. Even the teaching profession is Taylor-based. Teachers have very little opportunity for self-realization or to display their own creativity. Syllabuses are rigidly set, in many cases even down to the last detail of a weekly schedule. This is not necessarily wrong, but it does indicate the scale of the problem if changes to the system are to be made.

THE PROBLEMS – AND WHAT CAN BE DONE

What is necessary is to find an approach which takes advantage of the many good aspects of Taylorism, all the good aspects of craftsmanship, of which there are also many, and then create a new system which has none of the bad aspects of either. Chapter 6 discussed the means by which this has been achieved in Japan.

Another difficulty which needs to be addressed is the fact that successive generations of managers and supervisors have been selected on the basis of their ability to operate in a Taylor environment. What is not certain is whether those managers would be able to operate effectively in a changed environment. The managers themselves would probably also have fears on this account, and many would be likely to resist any changes which threaten their personal ability to manage.

It is this aspect which provides the biggest threat to cultural change. It is almost certainly either the main reason or a significant reason why participation and involvement have not proved easy to introduce into our society. For example, there is considerable evidence to suggest that management resistance is one of the principal reasons for failure in Quality Circle programmes. Not only is it important to remove this resistance; we must go further. Somehow, we must create an environment where managers actually want their people to become involved.

One approach is to use the merit rating system. Upper management can become a major influence in the introduction of participative management by making sure that line managers are in no doubt that they are being judged, not only on their ability to get results in terms of quality and output, but also on their ability to create a participative environment. In the longer term this can be supported through the selection process. New appointees will be selected, not only on their technical ability, but on their attitudes towards participation and on their previous track record in this aspect.

It is important to emphasize to such managers that managers get results through people. With people there are three principal elements to consider:

1 attitudes;
2 motivation;
3 working environment based upon management style.

Management controls neither the attitudes nor the motivation of the workforce. The only aspect actually in management control is the working environment. In this respect, managers can opt for a participative style at one extreme or an authoritarian style at the other. Most are somewhere within the spectrum.

The authoritarian manager tends to be Taylor-oriented. He or she interprets poor performance as evidence of hostility to work itself and responds through the use of incentives and penalties: the carrot and stick approach. The participative manager on the other hand is distinctly non-Taylor-oriented. He or she interprets poor performance as evidence not of hostility but of poor job design, and will naturally attempt to find ways of making work itself more interesting, more rewarding and more enjoyable so that people will adopt more positive attitudes to work and to becoming motivated. The theories are debatable but there can be no debate about the fact that people work better when they enjoy what they are doing.

The lesson is that upper management must make clear to middle management its collective desire that the middle managers must adopt the participative approach. This will not be easy. Many managers fear participation, because they think they may be losing control. They also fear the possible consequences which may arise from subordinates highlighting problems which managers think they should themselves have solved.

Again, upper management has a responsibility in this respect. The only way to convince the middle manager that there is nothing to fear from such an approach is to assure him or her that there will be no recriminations. One way is to make a positive statement along the lines of:

> Of course you have problems in your department. There are problems in every department, right through the company. We know that yours are not likely to be any greater than anyone else's. We also know that JIT cannot be achieved without having solved these problems and we know that you cannot

possibly solve them on your own. The fact that they exist is not your fault, it is the fault of the system of management based upon Taylorism. We intend to change that system and we need your help. To achieve this, we are supporting you in the introduction of involvement. Those managers who are most successful in the involvement of their workpeople in improvement activities will be congratulated.

Some managers will respond readily to such an approach, others will not. This is only to be expected, but many of them will become supportive when they realize they are being left behind; particularly when better results appear in the other departments.

The third aspect of middle management motivation relates to its own participation. Taylorism has also affected the role of the direct employee and the supervisor who, under the craft regime, were the main specialists on the payroll. Following the introduction of Taylorism, the role of the foreman has diminished since many of its responsibilities were devolved to off-line specialist functions such as work study, production engineering, quality control, personnel and the like. Consequently, the manager became reliant on these services over which he or she had no direct authority.

A more participative style puts demands upon the manager to develop a closer relationship with his or her people and to evolve a teamwork style. This may not be easy for many managers. A colleague of mine spent a day in the company of a finance director and his subordinates. The director confided afterwards that he found the experience extremely stressful because he had never spent a whole day in the company of one of his subordinates before, let alone many of them.

The lesson apparent from these comments is that a considerable amount of remedial work is necessary to gain the wholehearted support of middle management. Real success with JIT is totally dependent on the effectiveness of this support.

Technical specialists

Much of the discussion relating to middle managers also relates to technical specialists, particularly the aspects concerned with lifetime employment. But in relation to this problem there is an added dimension regarding the specialist. Movement from company to company usually results in the specialist developing a loyalty to his or her professional speciality far in excess of loyalty to the organization in which he or she is currently employed. A production engineer, for example, would tend to regard himself or herself as a 'production engineer' first, and a company employee second. This priority is even greater in the case of the professionally trained chartered engineer. This duality of loyalty does not necessarily conflict, but the loyalty to the company and to its goals can be considerably weaker than for an equivalent person doing the same job in Japan.

In extreme cases, the specialist might take the view that he or she does not care what happens to the company since employment can always be obtained elsewhere. If the specialist is treated less well than he or she would like, such a tendency would be quite likely. Some would argue that such an attitude is 'unprofessional' but the sad fact is that it is true.

A Japanese reader would probably be astonished at such a prospect. The reason is that 'professionalism' is much less in evidence in Japanese society than in ours. Japanese graduates might join a company with a view to specializing in specific aspects of management, for example finance, production engineering, design and so on, but they would not usually be allowed to do so in the initial years of their development.

It is quite common in Japanese companies for graduates on management development programmes to experience job rotation right up to the age of forty. During this time they would serve for long periods in design, sales, marketing, production, finance and so on before finally settling into a specific area of responsibility. There are many advantages to be gained from such an approach:

1 The individuals develop a spirit of company-mindedness rather than 'profession'-mindedness.
2 They will develop strong links and friendships with colleagues across the entire spectrum of the company's functional activities.
3 The internal customer/supplier interrelationship is strengthened and a common language assured.
4 The problem of sub-optimizing, that is, the situation where the solution to a problem in one department may well create a bigger one elsewhere, is greatly reduced. It is more likely that solutions will be found which optimize on a company basis.

The belief is that long-serving specialists will be more highly motivated to tackle long-term problems, particularly if they know that they will be present when the fruits of their labours are to be gained.

A second aspect of motivation of the specialist is also related to the Taylor concept. Under this concept, management is highly dependent upon the specialist as a consultant and a problem-solver. When JIT and improvement activities are commenced without thorough preparation, it is easy to overlook the implications of such a change as seen through the eyes of the specialists.

They are likely to think 'My job is solving problems, why are managers now doing my job?' When the concept is also extended to the workforce, such fears are further strengthened by the belief that they (the specialists) will soon be put out of work.

Nothing could be further from the truth. The demands of JIT are such that more such resources are likely to be required rather than less.

In fact, the introduction of JIT can overcome some of the problems created by Taylorism, particularly when applied at the lower levels. In a Taylor regime, where workpeople are required to do nothing more than their jobs according to instructions, specialists are viewed with deep suspicion. They are seen as people who spend their life trying to find ways of putting people out of work. When they are not doing that they are finding ways of making people work harder, faster, and on ever-tighter rates of pay. They are also seen as people who have descended from another planet, do not speak the language of the shop and are insensitive to workers' needs. Consequently, workers can be extremely unco-operative when such specialists are involved directly with the work of operatives. However, when the operatives have been trained in problem-solving techniques, and have themselves begun to tackle projects, they soon find that the specialist can be quite helpful, and a good source of information. Consequently they adopt a different attitude towards such personnel.

As this change develops, it soon becomes apparent that the specialists are tending to do more work in the areas where this concept is developing because they are able to do their own jobs more effectively. In such cases, the specialists become the strongest advocates for continuation of the change process.

Foremen and supervisors

The spectrum of ability and suitability of personnel in this category is so broad that it is difficult to be specific as to the motivational needs.

The reason is that, once again, due to the use of the Taylor System, the relevance of this category of persons, as seen by upper and middle management, varies widely from company to company.

Prior to the introduction of the Taylor System, there would have been little argument as to the role or qualities required of such personnel. In those days their role was to provide leadership, transfer skills, develop their subordinates, organize the work, liaise with management, be involved in the selection process and so forth. Additionally, they would be expected to have developed social skills, since it was widely recognized that in the eyes of the workers the foreman *was* the company. Good foremen knew instinctively that their performance was judged by the performance of their team, and results were achieved through unity of purpose and mutual respect.

This understanding has not entirely disappeared since the introduction of Taylorism; there are many examples to be found where such a relationship has survived, particularly in the traditional craft industries such as the potteries. But it is also true to say that, as a broad generalization, the modern foreman or supervisor plays a very different role from his or her counterpart of yesteryear.

The 'de-skilling' of work and the transfer of responsibilities to specialists have left modern supervisors denuded of the responsibilities which had been vested in their predecessors. This has in turn led to a broadening of their span of control, from perhaps seven to ten subordinates to around twenty to twenty-five. In some cases, the span of control has reached the sixties and seventies and, in such situations, the supervisors clearly have no personal relationship with the workpeople at all.

Training and personal development of supervisors is also patchy. In a few far-sighted companies the development of future management, starting at supervisor level, is customary practice. In such cases supervisors are selected on the basis of future management potential. They would be encouraged to study and be given the opportunity to attend courses intended to develop their managerial skills. At the other extreme (and the distribution is heavily skewed towards this end of the spectrum) there are many cases where foremen and supervisors receive no training whatsoever. They will have been selected not on their ability to manage but for a variety of reasons including:

1 being longest-serving in the department;
2 being a tough character;
3 being highly skilled in the job (but not necessarily a good manager of people);
4 because no one else can be found to do the job.

In such cases the supervisors will have received no formal training whatever. Neither will they have received any guidance on how to do the job properly. 'Just get on and do it!' is a common instruction from managers who in some cases may even be illiterate or semi-literate. I have personally experienced many such cases, among managers across a wide range of industries. Added to this, many are quite inarticulate.

The reader may well be shocked at these claims but they are true and nothing is to be gained by hiding from the truth. I have no idea what the situation is like in the reader's own company, but any reader who is seriously intending to move his or her organization wholeheartedly into the JIT approach must take account of these claims. The fortunate reader will find that his or her company's back record in this respect is good. If so, motivation and the development of active support for JIT will present few problems. If, however, the facts are otherwise, considerable work will be required to create the best environment for JIT.

Managers will have to face up to the fact that some foremen and supervisors who may have been selected on a haphazard basis may not be capable of self-development in the skills required. Others may be quite capable, but will require a considerable amount of training, both in people skills and in the qualitative and quantitative techniques essential for effective JIT progress to be made.

To assist the reader to identify these skills, the following list of activities with which supervisors will need to become involved should prove helpful:

1 *Improvement activities*

- problem identification
- theorizing on causes of problems
- testing theories through the collection and analysis of data
- identification of possible remedies
- implementation of remedies
- overcoming resistance to change
- holding the gains through control

2 *Control activities*

- Process Capability Study and analysis
- Statistical Process Control activities

3 *JIT-related teamwork*

- project team leadership
- team building and team development
- job design
- people building and development
- motivational skills
- communication skills
- enthusiasm

The typical foreman or supervisor faced with the opportunity to participate in a JIT programme might react in several ways:

1 Enthusiastically grasp an opportunity to demonstrate creative ability, and express a desire to work closely with management and subordinates to achieve the goals.

In my experience, such personnel are by no means rare, even in the worst of environments. In fact, on a subjective assessment, at least 50 per cent of supervisors would react this way, provided that their role is clearly stated and they know what is to be expected of them. A good presentation of the concepts prior to the commencement of a programme will pay considerable dividends later on.

2 An apparently passive reaction and a marked unwillingness to give any

indication as to whether the concept is approved or disapproved. Such a reaction can hide many true feelings.

In some cases it later turns out that such personnel have in the past allowed themselves to become guinea pigs for some management initiative which has either failed or not been properly supported by management. In such cases the supervisors may have felt that a hot potato had been thrown in their lap, and they were left to get on with it. The current reaction (or lack of it) would be caused by a reluctance to suffer a similar experience. This reaction is by no means uncommon, and in some companies may well be the biggest problem to overcome prior to a successful start to JIT. The problem is by no means confined to supervisory levels either. It can be experienced at all levels up to the top, particularly in multiple-location organizations.

The passive reaction may also be due to fears of personal inadequacy and a corresponding fear of change. The worry being that the individual concerned might not be able to meet the challenges of the new demands. The fear might be well founded in some individuals. In the majority of cases, however, the reaction is probably the result of a severe lack of self-confidence brought about by a Taylor-style society and not because of any real lack of ability.

Once such a reason is suspected, some form of confidence-building training is essential to unlock the energy and positive thinking of which such personnel might be capable. There are many good courses on the market to achieve this.

3 An extremely hostile or negative reaction may sometimes come from a number of individuals. However, this is quite rare. Actually, it is to be preferred to the passive reaction, since it is clear where people stand and they make their views known. With the passive reaction, much digging has to be done to get to the roots of the problem. With the actively negative or hostile person no such digging is necessary. Paradoxically, such negativity is usually to be welcomed. While there may be a tendency to produce a defensive response to such a reaction, it usually transpires that there are extremely good reasons why the person has reacted that way. If these reasons are taken seriously and analysed, an opportunity may well surface to solve a problem previously unknown to managers. Managers sometimes respond: 'Why didn't you tell us before?' The answer is frequently 'You never asked!'

Another virtue to be gained from negative responders is that in many cases they may be articulating the very problems which have resulted in the passive response from some others. Frequently, the negative responder becomes a spokesperson for such people, and they then cease to be passive.

The resulting interest shown by management and its concern to tackle the problem usually results in an extremely positive reaction from the supervisors. Here is a clear demonstration of management's intention to work together with them.

Experience suggests that the supervisors (or managers) who fit into this category become the strongest allies once they have been convinced of the validity of the concepts and the sincerity of management. Rather than to suppress, ignore or dismiss the reactions of this group, there is much to be gained from the accommodation and serious consideration of their objections.

Direct employees

Companies who have gained recent experience with Quality Circles would generally agree that this aspect is likely to be the least of their worries.

In most organizations the payroll personnel are ready, willing and able to participate, just as soon as they are given the opportunity. Sadly, the problems associated with the motivation of middle management and supervisors are more likely to be the cause of a lacklustre programme than any shortcomings of the payroll department.

Where resistance has been experienced, it is rarely due to a collective decision from groups of employees not to participate. More usually, it is due to the resistance of an individual with a strong personality. This rarely affects more than an isolated group, and tends to be short-lived. Most companies overcome the problem most easily by avoiding confrontation. Since it is unlikely that JIT will be commenced on a company-wide basis initially, it is better to start in areas where there is no resistance. If JIT is introduced correctly, it is likely that those involved will become very enthusiastic about their achievements. This enthusiasm tends to be infectious. Eventually, it will reach the departments which initially demonstrated a negative response. In most cases, the workers who were not resisting will themselves overcome the resistance of other individuals through peer pressure. To those readers who have yet to experience such a development, this part of the text will probably seem naive and unrealistic. There are many who would be prepared to bear witness to its validity.

A key point in this discussion is the importance of starting small. A small-scale tryout will tend to avoid raising fears in the sceptics and, equally important, will also avoid the danger of overstretching the available resources. At the commencement of a JIT programme, it is impossible to predict with any degree of accuracy the resource required to implement, develop and sustain it. It should be regarded like a newborn baby: it cannot survive on its own; it will need care and nursing. Too ambitious a start may well founder due to lack of support at crucial times. This is particularly true when involving supervisors and direct employees for the first time.

Trade union response to JIT

One thing, however, is clear. Good collaboration with the leaders of organized labour is essential if JIT is to be achieved. There are virtually no aspects of JIT which will not affect the legitimate interests of trade unions in one way or another. Properly implemented, JIT can have a phenomenal effect on productivity, efficiency generally, and the profitability of the company.

People will be required to work in very different ways from the past, and their co-operation is essential.

For JIT to be achieved effectively requires collaboration right through the supply chain. Customers are not only concerned with their own internal union relationships, but with their suppliers as well. The Austin Rover case, mentioned earlier, was a case in point. A major supplier, Lucas, experienced a lengthy industrial dispute which quickly affected Austin Rover. The usual strategy for avoidance of such difficulties has been multiple sourcing and the retention of high stock levels. Since JIT concerns the reduction of both of these, that is, a tendency towards zero inventory and single sourcing, it is obvious that the supplier's industrial relations become of critical importance.

Not only do we need to consider 'no strike' agreements with our own organization, we need to work closely with our suppliers to help them achieve the best possible relationships themselves.

Agreement with the unions involves a broad range of issues, for example:

1 participation of direct employees in Quality Circle-type activities;
2 profit sharing from improvement activities;
3 job rotation, job enlargement, job enrichment;
4 communication processes such as team briefing;
5 changes in job design;
6 'no strike' arrangements;
7 discussions on matters relating to inter-union relationships both internally and from customer to supplier. This may be novel to many.

Many of these factors would be discussed as a matter of routine anyway, but there is a changed emphasis when they are related to JIT.

In companies where labour is highly organized, there may well be a case for setting up some form of joint management/union committee to agree objectives and so monitor improvement towards JIT.

Summary

1 Motivation for JIT is a broad and complex issue. The biggest and single most important factor which will distinguish those companies which have been successful in the application of JIT from those which have not is likely

to prove to be motivation. Those who are able to motivate all their operating sources will be stunningly more successful than those who cannot, irrespective of the application of technique.

2 The secret lies in the ability to obtain the *Gestalt* effect where everyone from the top to bottom works collectively to make 'their' company the best in its business; to take advantage of the pride which comes from being a member of a winning team; always striving to do better, and achieve even more challenging goals.

3 In the true JIT company, nothing should be regarded as impossible. All problems should be viewed as opportunities.

4 This is true for other organizations as well. If they can survive now, without JIT and with all the problems which can be easily identified, just consider their potential when the problems have been overcome. *But* it requires the motivation to do so. JIT is exciting. Failure is not. We have to produce winners.

Recommended further reading

Belbin, Dr R. Meredith (1981) *Management Teams – Why they Succeed or Fail*, Heinemann.

Juran, Dr J. M. and Gryna, Dr F. M. (1980) *Quality Planning and Analysis*, McGraw-Hill – particularly Chapter 6, 'Quality improvement – operator controllable defects; motivation for quality'.

8 ADVANCE PLANNING

This chapter should help the reader to decide how to organize for Just in Time.

The first prerequisite for the successful achievement of JIT is preplanning. Pre-planning features right through JIT. The eight-minute injection mould tool changeover referred to in Chapter 1 did not require any special techniques, but it did require meticulous planning, and probably considerable practice. This is equally true for the disassembly and assembly of the gun carriages at the Royal Tournament in London.

Some nationalities appear to take more readily than others to the idea of planning.

Planning for JIT can be extremely effective through the selection of a key individual, or preferably small group, to conduct a detailed study of the concept prior to start-up. A team is preferable for four principal reasons:

1 As is apparent from the text, the subject is very broad and covers many disciplines, some of which must be appreciated in depth.
2 The study will benefit enormously from the distillation of shared experiences.
3 The proposals to upper management will be far-reaching and will probably require considerable resourcing. The credibility of a well-chosen team is usually higher than that of an individual no matter how well selected.
4 It is probably better to share the work than to assign a key person totally to a single task for a long period.

The study team would be required to make proposals for three principal considerations:

1 to evaluate alternative approaches;
2 to prepare cost estimates for each preferred alternative;
3 to produce an outline plan for the implementation and development of the programme.

Evaluation of alternative approaches

Although the Japanese are two to three decades ahead of the rest of the world in the application of JIT-related activities, considerable progress is now being made in the leading industrial countries.

JIT is a concept which can be approached from many different directions, and it would be wrong to suggest that any one approach is better than another. Every company must make up its own mind how it intends to progress. Every company has its strengths and weaknesses, its own unique culture, history and markets. These will all influence the choice of path to follow.

It would obviously be beneficial, therefore, to study what other organizations have done, identify the pitfalls they have found and make comparisons with others. This fact-finding activity should ideally include three key elements:

1 Visits to other companies known to be actively pursuing the JIT objective, including as many companies as possible in the same industry. It is also worth while visiting a selection of others in different fields to gain a broader perspective.

2 The study of as wide a range of literature on the subject as possible. Compare the suggestions in the reading matter with the views of practitioners in the field. Some surprising differences may emerge which will indicate the importance of broad-based research.

3 Inviting proposals for assistance from as many different consultants as possible, but this aspect should be left until at least three user companies have been studied. This will make it easier to judge the real experience of the consultants. Before meeting them, obtain the views of their clients as to their experiences with the consultants. Different consultants will present very different approaches to the subject and will vary markedly on the level of support they can offer, or propose. Relate the personality of the consultant to the culture of the company, and above all attempt to judge the consultants on the rate at which their support is designed to transfer dependency from consultant to company. Some consultancies will attempt to maintain consultant dependency for far too long. Others will attempt to hand over too quickly. Obviously consultants can be an expensive consideration but, as with anything else, the correct balance must be achieved, and will require judgement by the study team.

Do not overlook the value of obtaining a greater breadth of knowledge from the experiences of consultants during this phase. It is also an excellent way of assessing their credibility.

Evaluation of other organizations can be invaluable, not only as a means of answering the question 'Should we or should we not embark on a JIT programme?' It can also result in long-term benefits. Many companies have been so pleased with the assistance they have been given in the early stages by other friendly organizations, that they have been keen to reciprocate later on when they have achieved some successes. This reciprocation leads to an informal networking which is clearly beneficial for all, particularly from the point of view of sharing experiences and helping overcome difficulties.

Although it may appear costly, it is also recommended that study team members should be given the opportunity to see for themselves how JIT is developing in other countries. There can be no substitute for first-hand experience, and the credibility of study team members will be increased enormously as a result.

The unquestionable leaders in the achievement of JIT are the Japanese, but some impressive progress has been made in the USA. A study of the Japanese will indicate the state of the art, but they have probably forgotten many of the problems they faced in the early stages. Even if this were not the case, their experiences might well not be relevant.

JIT is now developing rapidly in West European countries, particularly in the automobile and electronics industries.

Report from study team

It is both usual and desirable for the study team to present its report to the company's board of directors or management team. By this time the study team should be quite knowledgeable on the topic, and will be more convincing and make more impact in a live presentation as opposed to submitting a formal report. Ideally, all study team members should participate in this presentation, which should include:

1 Overview of the state of the art

- potential of JIT
- what has been and is being achieved
- how competitors are doing – what pressure we are under
- perceptions of our customers and suppliers
- what we think we can achieve in the long and short term

2 How the programme should be structured

- programme design overview – distilled from outside experience
- functional/inter-functional activities
- reporting
- monitoring
- development

3 Role of outside consultants (if proposed)

- comparison of alternatives – strengths and weaknesses
- *modus operandi*
- suggest presentations by short-listed consultants

4 Cost comparisons if alternative approaches offered

- consultant costs
- internal costs

5 Proposed timetable

- implementation
- development

Planning the system

'We have tried it before and it didn't work' is probably one of the biggest deterrents to progress in industry today. Every minute spent in the preparation for JIT will be repaid many times over at a later date and, as with most other concepts, it is usually best to start from first principles.

The principles of the organization set up to achieve the JIT objectives should include the following:

1 Establishing a 'Quality Council' to co-ordinate the JIT-related responsibilities of all the functions in the organization. This structure is discussed in Chapter 9.
2 Taking responsibility for only those functions which cannot reasonably be carried out by some other function.
3 Ensuring that JIT-related action taken by any function is consistent with the general plan.
4 Designing the system so that it is self-auditing and self-improving.
5 Above all, generating the attitude that JIT is everybody's business, including hourly-paid personnel.
6 Ensuring the establishment of the 'no blame' concept and the development of internal customer/supplier relationships.

The major responsibilities of the Quality Council in relation to JIT are:

1 to plan the JIT-related system for the entire company for the achievement of the stated objectives;
2 to construct a feedback system from all points in the organization that have a bearing on JIT, and to conduct a continuous audit and review of JIT-related improvements and activities to ensure holding the gains;
3 to ensure that all responsibilities are so organized that the needs of JIT are not subordinated to the needs of production;
4 to identify the JIT training requirements for all personnel in design, production and service operations;
5 to monitor the effectiveness of the programme by means of quality cost analysis, customer complaint data and work-in-progress;

6 to provide adequate and appropriate publicity to JIT so that everyone understands the concept and has a clear role;

7 to design and implement schemes for the surveillance of suppliers and potential suppliers, and to monitor the quality of incoming material;

8 to monitor and develop the programme on a continuous year-by-year basis;

9 to formulate and publish a clear policy statement so that it is clear to everyone what JIT means to the company and to them.

It is important to realize that the application of the suggested objectives and principles in one firm will not necessarily produce anything like the system that might be appropriate to another company. There will also be differences in organizational requirements owing to the size of the company, the nature of its products, its market outlets and the existing internal organization structure.

As with other fields of management science, no textbook can offer a system which has universal application. A text can only guide management along a path towards a solution to its problems, a solution which will in the event be tailor-made to suit its particular requirements and probably unique. This point should also be appreciated by those reading this section of the book with the object of assessing the organizations of others. It is a matter of some concern to those who have taken part in the development of vendor appraisal schemes that the assessor should not develop preconceived ideas as to the proper structure of the systems to be studied. The Ministry of Defence emphasizes this point in its instructions to its assessment teams. The test of any company's organization structure, however unusual, must always be whether the assessor has confidence that this aspect of the system will produce the targeted results.

Planning for internal customer/supplier relationships

Figure 8.1 shows a typical structure from marketing to after-sales service. For the achievement of customer satisfaction the customer's requirements must first of all be determined. This is clearly the function of market research. However, properly organized market research does not always exist in a company, or it might not always be compiling information from a product quality point of view. Even when the information is obtained, it does not always follow that it will find its way to the design department, or be in the form that will be of most use. Market research departments are often set up for the purpose of obtaining sales data and market trends, and are not intended as a link with product design. The function of the Quality Council at this point would be to create an organization which draws attention to these deficiencies and suggests how they may be overcome.

The design department can only provide customer satisfaction from its

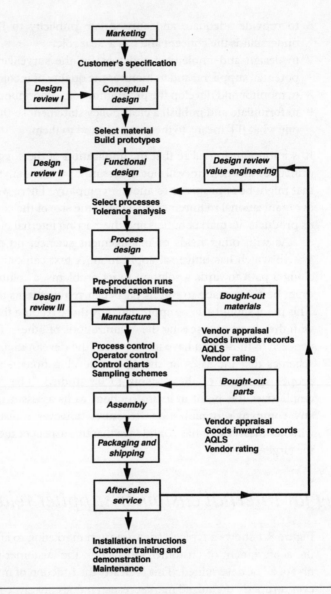

Figure 8.1 Basic structure of an organization

designs if they have been properly thought out and properly tried and tested throughout the whole range of environmental conditions. The design life of the product should match the requirements of the customer. It should be safe, and designed for ease of manufacture, assembly and maintenance. To ensure that each of these aspects has been carefully considered, it is necessary to take an extremely well-disciplined and well-organized approach to each phase of the process. It is the Quality Council's task to organize audits of the system in operation, highlight weaknesses and suggest the means by which improvements can be made. It should then carefully monitor all feedback information from production through to after-sales service to ensure that these objectives continue to be achieved.

At the production phase, quality assurance must ensure that the procedures adopted by production are unlikely to produce quality-loss problems. This area covers the entire production cycle, starting with pre-production planning, continuing with production and incoming materials control, and ending with assembly and packaging. Quality assurance is concerned mainly with the procedures adopted by the production function for ordering long-delivery items, design and maintenance, jigs, tools and fixtures. Production personnel need training in conformity with specification, the effectiveness of quality control procedures, the organization of inspections, and the calibration and care of all inspection, measuring and test equipment.

Packaging of products is an area where quality assurance must always take a keen interest. The customer will have little satisfaction if the product has been broken or has suffered from the elements in transit, however carefully it has been designed and manufactured. New export markets in countries with different climatic conditions, long periods of storage or rough handling will always create problems. Recent regulations for the packaging of dangerous products, and the product liability implications of contamination from packaging materials or dirty containers, only increase the importance of quality at this stage of manufacture.

On delivery of the product to the customer, little satisfaction will be derived if the product proves difficult to assemble or to operate. A large manufacturer of domestic electrical products recently conducted an analysis of customer-complaint data on one of its products where the customer was required to assemble the handle on an otherwise complete product. The survey showed that 28 per cent of the complaints were due to the customer not being able to carry out the assembly. A simple change to the instruction sheet, with one or two diagrams, reduced this problem to a mere 3 per cent of the total, giving increased customer satisfaction and considerable reduction in costs.

Quality assurance should monitor all data obtainable from the customer to ensure that these problems are minimized and that adequate customer training and after-sales service are given. It is also important that customer data are retrieved to ensure the effectiveness of subsequent design reviews, and to compare the customer's opinion of the company's products with the marketing specification. These data should be analysed and presented to the Quality Council, thus completing the cycle of the closed feedback loop.

It can be seen from the beginning how the Quality Council is responsible for planning the system within which the other functions operate.

The designer obviously knows more about the design requirements than a quality assurance engineer, and it is right that he or she should, but quality assurance personnel are better placed to have a perspective of design and other functions in relation to the general objectives, and to ensure that all departments are working towards the same objectives. Quality assurance is not therefore entirely responsible for product quality as such but it is responsible for coordinating the activities of those who are.

The quality manual

The quality manual is an essential document in a properly organized establishment, because JIT can only be developed effectively if the aims, objectives and procedures of all functions are clearly understood by all concerned. The quality manual should be written with several objectives in mind:

1 as a means to communicate the official quality-related objectives of the company to all functional groups in the organization and to identify the interrelationship between each of these groups;
2 to provide a basis for training of personnel, and others in those aspects of their work which affect product quality and JIT;
3 to formalize the organizational plan in relation to each function so that the organization may be kept under continuous review;
4 to give assessment teams the opportunity to compare the company's organization and attitude towards product quality with their own requirements.

The value of a quality manual, like most other documents circulating in industry, is generally inversely proportional to the number of words. It is therefore vitally important that each section of the document should be short and to the point, and long-winded explanations avoided. It should also be so designed and edited that the contents may be reviewed and amended as necessary.

The manual should preferably include the following:

1 A statement of the company's quality and JIT objectives, signed by the managing director.
2 A section describing the administration of the quality management functions, giving an organization chart showing the Quality Council and its relationship with the board of directors, other managers and heads of departments. The section should state in general terms the relevant responsibilities allocated to the various managers and department heads.
3 A section describing in detail the quality-related functions during design and development, and stating the group or person(s) responsible for each. This also includes design review, value engineering, value analysis and product review.
4 A section describing in detail the quality control methods and procedures, both before and during manufacture, and stating the group or person(s) responsible for each.

5 A section describing in detail the organization, staffing, methods and procedures for quality achievement.

6 A section describing in detail the procedure for control of documentation, including drawings and specifications. This should also include drawing change control procedures.

7 A section describing in detail the procedure for collecting, monitoring and presenting quality cost information. This should include all failure, appraisal and prevention costs incurred during the review period.

8 A section describing administration of vendor surveillance, including appraisal, rating, goods inwards control. Collaborative arrangements and process control requirements should be included.

9 A section describing in detail the quality-related functions in assembly, packaging, delivery and after-sales. This should include a description of the means by which used information is fed back to and used by design.

10 A section describing the procedure for the construction of quality plans.

11 A section that includes all the documents in the quality function and referred to in the text.

The quality plan

A quality plan is normally a requirement for all contracts and orders negotiated under Ministry of Defence 05-21 and 05-24 conditions. These plans are often also required by companies other than those concerned with MOD contracts, and the technique described below provides a useful graphical way of representing a complete production process. From this it is easy to determine the appropriate stages where quality control points should be considered and where JIT problems may develop. The technique allows a 'bird's-eye view' of even the most complex product to be produced on a single sheet of paper.

GUIDE TO THE PREPARATION OF QUALITY PLANS

Quality plans may be constructed by means of the 'flow process chart' technique, developed and used by work study engineers. These represent a procedure or process symbolically, so that subsequent analysis may take place.

The following symbols are normally used. These were originally developed by the American Society of Mechanical Engineers, and are known as ASME symbols. They are also described in BS3138. There are basically two principal activities:

1 *Operations*, denoted by the symbol ○.
2 *Inspection*, denoted by the symbol □.

An operation occurs when an object is intentionally changed in any of its physical or chemical characteristics, or prepared for another operation, for transport, inspection or storage. An operation also takes place when information is given or received, or when planning or calculating takes place.

An inspection does not take the material any nearer becoming a completed product. It merely verifies that an operation has been carried out as to quantity or quality. Were it not for human shortcomings, many inspections could be done away with!

Often a more detailed picture will be required than can be obtained by the use of these two symbols alone. To achieve this, four more symbols may be used:

3   *Transport*, denoted by the symbol ⇨.
4   *Delay*, denoted by the symbol D.
5   *Storage*, denoted by the symbol ∇.
6   *Combined activity*, denoted by the symbol ◯.

To determine when to use the symbol for either delay or storage, the latter is generally used when paperwork is required for further movement to take place.

Each activity should be briefly described and the method of quality control should be detailed, for example 100 per cent examination or sampling schemes to an appropriate specification, such as BS6000. Preparation of the chart should be in the form of a line drawing, working from top to bottom, and showing each process in sequence, together with quality control stations and frequency or mode of control. Where desirable, non-manufacturing operations, for example quality or process controls, may be superimposed on a manufacturing process and the two shown as a combined activity.

Each point or stage should be numbered consecutively. The procedure for numbering, the method of layout of a chart, and use of abbreviations are shown in Figure 8.2. The usual convention for the construction of such a chart is as follows:

1   Start with a component to which all the other components and sub-assemblies will eventually be attached.
2   Starting in the top right-hand corner of the page, draw the symbol which describes the first event. This will probably be requisition from stores and will be denoted by the symbol ∇.
3   Continue down the page, using the appropriate symbols for each event in the sequence.
4   For assemblies, a point will be reached when another component or sub-assembly must be attached. A study of Figure 8.2 will show how to proceed from this stage.

Provided the above procedure is carefully followed, and each new item introduced from the left, the preparation of these charts is quite simple, and skill in

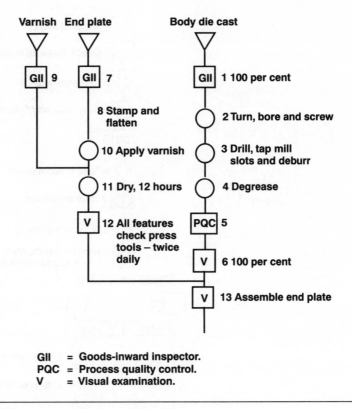

Figure 8.2 'Flow process chart' technique

their preparation can be acquired surprisingly quickly. See also Figures 8.3 and 8.4, showing complete charts for a component and an assembly respectively. These charts were based on QAD(w) leaflet *Guide to the Preparation of Production/Quality Control Plans*.

DOCUMENTATION PROCEDURES

An almost unbelievable number of JIT loss problems can be related to this aspect of organization. The problems that arise can take any of the following forms:

1 clerical errors;
2 lack of co-ordination between specifications and other documents;
3 inadequate control of document circulation lists.

Clerical errors

A booklet entitled *Clerical Quality Control*, published by the Institute of Administrative Management, lists ten different forms of clerical error:

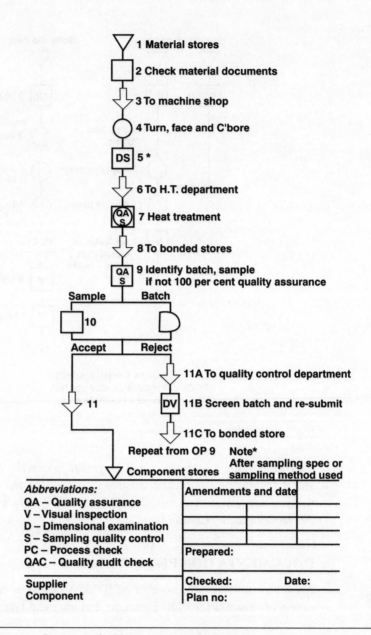

Figure 8.3 Production/quality control plan for component

1 Errors of *principle* include errors due to lack of training or lack of job instruction and also inefficient organization, methods and procedures.
2 Errors of *omission* generally concern the basic design of a form, and usually occur when departments lack an understanding of each other's requirements.
3 Errors of *carelessness*: the errors attributable to this cause are markedly

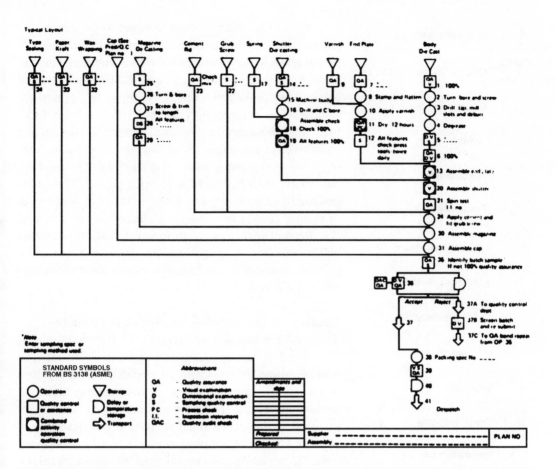

Figure 8.4 Production/quality control plan for an assembly

similar to the problems discussed in the section entitled 'Human reliability' in Chapter 5. They are frequently caused by fatigue, boredom, distractions, office lighting, and other environmental factors.

4 Errors of *illegibility*: the causes include bad handwriting, inability to read the lower sheets of multiple-copy documents, and previous errors corrected by writing over the mistake.

5 Errors due to *lack of knowledge*.

6 Errors due to *bad dictation*.

7 Errors of *spelling*.

8 Erasure.

9 Faulty layout.

10 Machine error.

Lack of co-ordination between specifications and other documents

The lack of co-ordination between related documents can often be the source

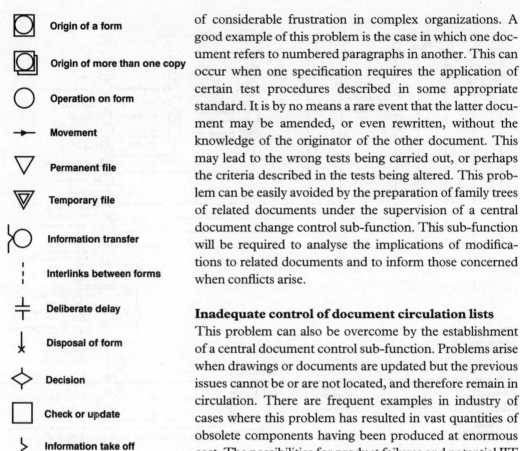

	Origin of a form
	Origin of more than one copy
	Operation on form
	Movement
	Permanent file
	Temporary file
	Information transfer
	Interlinks between forms
	Deliberate delay
	Disposal of form
	Decision
	Check or update
	Information take off

Figure 8.5 Procedural analysis flow chart key

of considerable frustration in complex organizations. A good example of this problem is the case in which one document refers to numbered paragraphs in another. This can occur when one specification requires the application of certain test procedures described in some appropriate standard. It is by no means a rare event that the latter document may be amended, or even rewritten, without the knowledge of the originator of the other document. This may lead to the wrong tests being carried out, or perhaps the criteria described in the tests being altered. This problem can be easily avoided by the preparation of family trees of related documents under the supervision of a central document change control sub-function. This sub-function will be required to analyse the implications of modifications to related documents and to inform those concerned when conflicts arise.

Inadequate control of document circulation lists

This problem can also be overcome by the establishment of a central document control sub-function. Problems arise when drawings or documents are updated but the previous issues cannot be or are not located, and therefore remain in circulation. There are frequent examples in industry of cases where this problem has resulted in vast quantities of obsolete components having been produced at enormous cost. The possibilities for product failures and potential JIT situations are considerable if proper procedures are not evolved.

PROCEDURAL ANALYSIS OF DOCUMENTATION

The study of documentation systems can often be a complex task, but essential JIT-related situations are to be avoided. In many organizations the documentation procedures were designed for the company when first formed. As the company grew, the documentation system also grew, but not in a co-ordinated way. Consequently many documents carrying inadequate information may exist. Important instructions may be passed on pieces of paper, or sometimes only by word of mouth, with no record of the decisions made. Many documents may be meticulously filed for no apparent reason, and copies circulated unnecessarily.

Figures 8.5 and 8.6 have been included to enable interested readers to apply the technique of procedural analysis to quality documentation. As with the 'flow process chart' (Figure 8.2), described earlier in this chapter, the

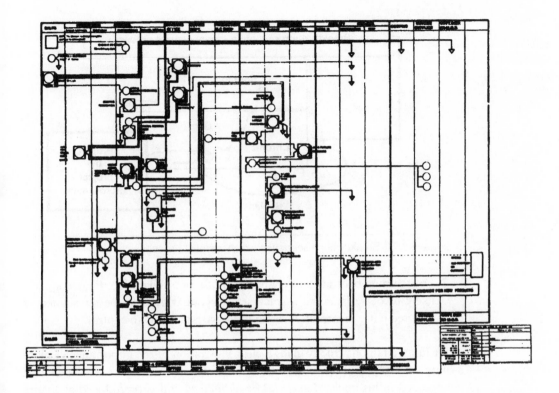

Figure 8.6 Procedural analysis flow chart

technique enables the investigator to obtain a bird's-eye view of the documentation procedures and portray them in a form which may be readily understood by all concerned, and the resulting procedures will make a valuable contribution to the value of the quality manual.

Planning and replanning

However carefully or meticulously the plan has been prepared, no plan is ever perfect. There are bound to be deficiencies which will not surface until the implementation process begins. For this reason, it is not advisable to commence a JIT programme on a company-wide basis. A small-scale tryout has many benefits over the company-wide launch. For example:

1 A pilot scheme will not stretch the resources and will ensure that the first efforts can be well supported to guarantee success.

Remember, with anything new there are always going to be sceptics waiting in the wings for failure. Also, it is not possible to guess with certainty exactly how much resource will be needed until some experience has been gained.

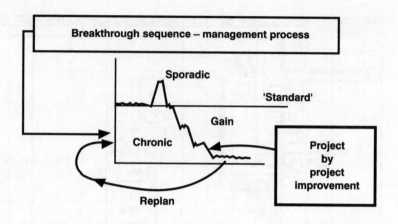

Figure 8.7 Breakthrough sequence – management process

2 Overcoming resistance to change is another consideration. People are less likely to be resistant to a small-scale tryout which can be terminated or adapted if it is incorrect. A major initiative is less easy to control.

Dr Juran's famous trilogy gives a clear illustration of the importance of planning and replanning, and is best illustrated by the diagram which first appeared in his book *Managerial Breakthrough*, and is reproduced as Figure 8.7.

This model shows the typical cycle of breakthrough when new levels of achievement are reached.

We start with a plan. At this point it is the best we can do, based on the knowledge acquired to get started. Following start-up, there are occasional unexpected deviations from the plan which occur sporadically. This level of performance, together with the occasional sporadic peaks, will continue indefinitely unless a formalized improvement process is introduced. In the case of the complete programme, this improvement process will be initiated by the Quality Council. Its job will be to identify weaknesses in the plan, find remedies and apply them to the programme. As time passes, this acquired knowledge can be transferred to new initiatives in other parts of the organization, which will enable them to commence their plan at an improved level to the original and so on.

This planning and replanning is a continuous process in JIT organization and applies both to the programme as a whole and to the specific elements of JIT, for example materials handling and stock levels, and to the essence of project by project improvement.

Summary

1 Pre-planning is essential if JIT is to be effectively achieved.
2 JIT involves many disciplines and considerable reading should be done with the aid of the recommendations included in this text.
3 A study team should be appointed to evaluate the needs.
4 Activities of the study team should include visits to companies, discussions with consultants and, if possible, visits to both Japan and the United States.
5 A Quality Council formed of upper managers is proving to be an effective mechanism to co-ordinate and develop JIT-related activities.
6 Planning for JIT should include an analysis of all functional boundaries throughout the company.
7 A quality manual is a very effective means of describing all quality-related systematic aspects.
8 The production of a quality plan enables the process to be formulated and defined. Flow diagram techniques are an effective means of producing such plans.
9 JIT planning should also include the quality of documentation.

Recommended further reading

All texts mentioned in the 'Recommended further reading' sections of earlier chapters are relevant at this stage and should not be overlooked if a serious attempt to achieve JIT is to be made.

9 ORGANIZATION

Following the initial planning and preparation, the study team mentioned in Chapter 8 will typically present its recommendations to the board of directors who would make the decision to go ahead.

While the organizational requirements for a JIT programme will be more structured and formalized in a large company than in a smaller company, the same activities require to be carried out. In the very small company of less than 100 employees, these activities might well be carried out entirely by the general manager or his assistant. In the larger company, many have found the need for a formal structure to implement, guide and develop the process on a permanent basis. In this chapter the typical elements of such formal organizations are reviewed. The reader from the smaller company might not find the elements to be relevant, but the work content will be.

Process design team

In many organizations a design team has been formed. This will frequently comprise members of the original study team and an outside consultant when this has been considered desirable.

The role of the design team is to carry out the detailed design of the whole programme. The value of using members of the original study team lies mainly in the fact that they will have acquired considerable knowledge on the topic. The principal activities of the design team will be to:

1 design the structure for the programme as a whole;
2 design the structure for the Quality Council (or company strategic team);
3 design and lead the first company strategic team workshop;
4 design the structure for regional strategic teams in multi-location organizations;
5 lead the initial regional strategic team workshops;
6 design the structure for site strategic teams on a site by site basis;
7 lead the initial site strategic team workshops;
8 design the structure for functional strategic teams where these are thought to be relevant, for example finance, operations, and so on;
9 design team leader/facilitator training courses;
10 conduct the initial team leader/facilitator training courses;

11 conduct counselling sessions for all levels of groups as the programme develops;

12 assist team leaders and others to develop projects.

COMPANY STRATEGIC TEAM (TOP TEAM) OR QUALITY COUNCIL

This team is permanent and will usually be headed by the chief executive, but should contain executive directors or senior executives from all key functions such as marketing, distribution, commercial, finance, research and development, production and personnel. The team will be responsible for the programme as a whole. In a small to medium-size company, operating on a single site, this may be the only formal organization necessary. At the other extreme, a large company with multiple locations and with different product lines will need a further support organization. The important criterion is to ensure that responsibility for key aspects of the programme should devolve to the lowest level of organization possible.

The Quality Council usually accepts several responsibilities, for example to:

1   construct and publicize the general publicity statement;
2   construct and publicize specific policies;
3   set clear general objectives;
4   plan the programme as a whole;
5   identify major JIT projects, for example establishing new forms of supplier policies and so on;
6   tackle high-level projects relevant to top team members;
7   create project teams to tackle other key projects;
8   screen nominations for projects from lower levels;
9   provide in larger organizations a link to other permanent teams in sub-elements of the organization;
10 authorize publicity training budgets and programmes;
11 authorize expenditure on key resource requirements;
12 set budgets and goals;
13 provide support and encouragement;
14 audit and review the programme.

REGIONAL STRATEGIC TEAMS

With larger, multi-location organizations, the top team will not be sufficient to provide day-to-day support for the programme. In such programmes there will usually be a need for some form of devolution to a regional level (see Figure 9.1).

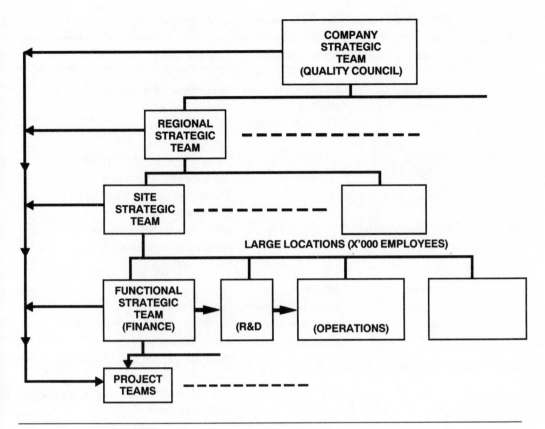

Figure 9.1 Formal structure for implementing a JIT programme

The regional directors would normally be members of the top team, but each will also be the head of a regional team normally comprising general managers from the operating units.

This form of organization has the advantage of providing general leadership from the top team, but at the same time providing maximum opportunity for participation in planning and development at each level of organization. It also provides backward linkage through the process of making each team leader a member of the team at the next higher level.

A further advantage of this type of organization is the opportunity afforded to the regional teams for cross-fertilization of ideas and experiences through their mutual involvement in the top team. This type of organization is becoming widely used in Company-wide Quality Improvement programmes and is therefore a key feature in JIT.

Table 9.1 Composition and responsibilities of permanent teams

Team	Membership	Responsibilities
Company strategic team	Chairman Main board Regional directors	Overall policy and objectives Identify key projects Set up project teams Tackle major projects Screen nomination from lower levels Steer the programme as a whole Allocate resources for systems improvement and process control and supplier controls Audit and review resource programme
Regional strategic team	Regional director Factory or location general managers	Regional policy Regional objectives Identify key regional project teams Tackle major projects Steer nominations from lower levels Steer regional programme Keep in contact with other regional teams Audit and review
Factory/ plant/location strategic team	Factory or general managers Functional heads, key specialists	Plant-level policy Plant-level objectives Identify key projects Set up project teams Tackle major projects Screen nominations from lower levels Steer plant programme Keep in contact with other plant teams Audit and review

SITE STRATEGIC TEAMS

A further distinctive feature of the larger programme is the establishment of the site strategic team. The object is to drive responsibility down from the regional level into each specific location.

This type of organization is also useful to ensure that JIT projects can be identified by the people who are most likely to be aware of specific problems, rather than deal in generalities. If this structure is used, the information in Table 9.1 will be helpful to understand the responsibilities at each level.

It will be noted that membership at this level includes functional heads. This will depend to some extent upon the size of the operation. In some small establishments the general manager may well take personal responsibility for the programme.

FUNCTIONAL STRATEGIC TEAMS

The structure described above is satisfactory when each location is virtually independent of the others. For example, they may have totally different product lines. More frequently, however, there are varying degrees of interdependency either of operations or of services.

To illustrate, let us consider a typical white goods manufacturer. Electronics assembly may take place at one location, sheet metal work, painting and final assembly at another, and research and development, commercial, distribution and sales at yet another, but with some involvement at each.

Many companies with this type of organization have found it useful to include a further group of permanent teams organized on a functional basis. Their responsibilities are similar to those previously described, but their main attention will be focused upon inter-functional problems. It is also a useful medium for collaboration on inter-functional problems as well, irrespective of the site or location where the problems exist.

At this point the reader may have become concerned at the prospect of all this apparently elaborate organization. Actually it is not as complex as it may appear, since there is probably an existing structure within the organization similar to that described, but established for a different purpose. Most, if not all, large companies would have a main board, regional board and the on-site management team. Except in the more autocratic organizations, the functions would also usually have a formal or informal decision-making group. In some cases there would be no point in setting up a parallel group to any of these.

What must not happen is the relegation of the JIT programme to the status of an agenda item. In such cases it is inevitable that JIT will 'fall off the bottom' of a busy agenda at some time or other. Once this has occurred, the priority given to JIT may diminish and eventually disappear altogether.

If an existing team is to be used, it should be made very clear indeed that JIT should have a separate agenda, and the meetings should preferably be held on a separate occasion from other meetings of the group.

WHY ALL THIS SUPERSTRUCTURE?

In some respects, the goal of JIT could be regarded as 'just another business objective', and as such simply be treated as another item on the agenda of day-to-day business meetings. This would be fine were it not for the fact that JIT represents as much a massive change in organizational culture and style as it does the apparently simple objective of inventory reduction. The topics within that agenda item will be so numerous that JIT would grossly outbalance the other items of the agenda. On such agendas, JIT may not always appear to be the most burning issue, and it is highly likely that there will be many occasions when JIT is deferred to the next meeting, with possibly serious consequences for the programme.

For one thing, it will be a visible demonstration of lack of commitment to JIT. For another, the deferral may not have immediately apparent consequences. Therefore, having postponed discussion once, it will be easier to do so again, with the result that decay in the JIT programme will have set in at the top. This will be unlikely to have gone unnoticed at lower levels, with the effect that the decay will be progressive.

The main value of the structure described will be to ensure that the topic gets the attention it deserves, and that meetings will be more likely to take place. It will also ensure that JIT permanently retains its level of importance.

JIT policy

LEVEL OF PROFILE

The level of exposure which upper management chooses to give JIT will vary from company to company. At one extreme, no publicity at all will be given, at the other, every attempt will be made to give the programme the highest profile possible.

There can be no clear guidelines as to the 'correct' approach other than to point out a number of considerations to take into account. A plan should then be constructed which will suit the culture and history of that company. The considerations are:

1 possible cultural resistance from upper management, middle management, supervisors, trade unions and the workforce;
2 avoiding the arousal of suspicions;
3 need to obtain collaboration and willing support, and sense of being trusted and involved;
4 demonstrated commitment of upper management;
5 difficulty in achieving some objectives if awareness is too low.

Each of these is considered below.

Cultural resistance
This is born mainly out of fear and the prospect of losing whatever comforts may be experienced in the current situation. People will want to feel assured that the changes will be for the better so far as they personally are concerned.

Fear will usually relate to concern about the permanence of their jobs and their personal ability to meet the demands of the new arrangements. Resistance to change will normally relate to perceptions gained from the information available as to how the proposed changes will affect these important considerations.

The policy statement, its wording, and the means by which it is to be conveyed to employees will obviously be critical to the smooth introduction of JIT-related policies, concepts and techniques. Experience acquired in the introduction of JIT-related programmes indicates the following guidelines:

1 The programme should be initiated by the preparation and publication of a comprehensive policy statement.
2 As much opportunity as possible should be given for discussion of this statement at all levels of organization.
3 Wherever possible, backward linkage should be used to achieve this goal. For example, the presentation to senior executives should be given by a director, that to middle executives by the appropriate senior executive and so on right down through the hierarchy. The presentation is usually supported by a key person nominated to ensure that no dilution of the message takes place.

Care should be taken to ensure that people will not be pushed into anything and that one of the objects is to achieve the goals through collaboration and teamwork.

In many organizations trade union representatives may wish to discuss the programme in detail with management representatives, and this should be encouraged. Detailed aspects of JIT will have many implications for trade unions and their relationships with companies, and some of these will involve negotiation. It is therefore imperative that trade unions are given the maximum opportunity to be kept fully informed of all aspects of JIT.

Arousal of suspicions and lack of trust
These are more likely to be born of secrecy than of openness. It would be impossible to implement a successful programme of JIT in secret, since collaboration and teamwork are essential ingredients.

Experience indicates that it is better to be fully open right from the beginning than to feed the programme out in bits and pieces. People are extremely sensitive about the degree to which they are being trusted and respected. This usually leads to suspicions regarding management motives when information is believed to have been concealed.

Commitment by upper management
This is essential to any initiative and none more so than JIT. 'Nailing one's flag to the mast' may require a great deal of courage at the outset, particularly if

other initiatives have failed in the past. However, one can hardly expect the troops to become enthusiastic and take risks if management is not prepared to do the same.

A high-profile implementation may be risky, but it is also a dramatic demonstration of initial commitment. On the downside, too high a profile may cause people to fear being pushed faster than they are willing to go.

Level of awareness

This may also be critical to the achievement of goals related to the teamwork aspects of JIT. Some companies have been disappointed with the levels of enthusiasm generated in the first year or two. In many such cases there has been no publicity whatsoever, either related to the programme as a whole, or to the achievements of groups or individuals. The explanation for this low-profile approach was that the company hoped that the programme would be carried forward by the enthusiasm of those involved. Experience suggests that this is not sufficient except in the most exceptional cases.

In summary, careful consideration must be given during the planning phase to:

1 the amount of pre-publicity;
2 the form of pre-publicity;
3 who should be informed, how and when;
4 the opportunities for discussion of the proposals to be afforded to trade unions and other key interests.

The policy statement

The policy statement should be brief, but should contain sufficient detail to convey both the philosophy and an indication as to how individuals might be involved. It usually also includes a number of specific objectives for clarification.

Because the JIT objective is so intrinsically interwoven in the concepts and goals of Company-wide Quality Improvement, this would normally be stressed in the statement.

A typical policy statement is given opposite. It represents a distillation of the many I have studied in collecting the material contained in this book.

It must be stressed that the programme is continuous and depends to a large extent on annual, project by project improvement. That improvement involves everybody from the top to the bottom of the operation.

In many organizations, this policy statement forms the basis of the initial awareness programme, and subsequently for induction training of new employees.

Quality Policy Statement

It is the policy of ————————, and any subsidiaries which may from time to time be established, to become and to remain world leaders in all aspects of their respective fields. This includes ————————, ————————, ————————, ———————— and our own administration through the process of continuous annual improvement.

We aim to achieve this policy by ourselves practising the concepts we preach to others and through the development of a sense of corporate pride, identity and loyalty in all our employees through the recognition of their efforts and the continuous development of their skills.

Specific objectives affecting all DHA personnel

- Continuous quality improvement is the responsibility of every individual.
- Everyone must be given the opportunity to participate in the preparation, implementation and evaluation of improvement activities.
- Quality improvement must be planned, carried out, audited and reviewed in a systematic manner.
- Quality improvement must be a *continuous* process.
- Our organization must concentrate more than ever on the needs of its customers and users.
- Every function must consider the next upstream operation to be its supplier, and each downstream operation to be its customer.
- The performance of our competitors must be made known to all relevant personnel.
- Important suppliers must become closely involved in the achievements of our Quality Policy. This relates to both external and internal suppliers of goods as well as of resources and services.
- Widespread attention will be given to education and training and assessed with regard to their contribution to the Quality Policy.
- Publicity must be given to the Quality Policy in every part of the company in such a way that it can be understood by everyone.
- The Quality Council, which includes members from all functions, will provide support and co-ordination and report on the progress of the implementation of this policy as a permanent feature of the agenda of all meetings.

Signed _____ Date _____

An impressive demonstration of commitment to the policy is often obtained by the display of such statements framed on the walls of offices in the organization and in the reception area.

In small to medium organizations one such policy statement may be sufficient. However, in larger multi-site organizations, particularly those where products, technologies and markets differ from site to site, it is often necessary for local strategic teams to produce a further policy statement related specifically to that operation. This also has the advantage of giving local identity to the programme.

Project team facilitator

Most organizations which are developing the project by project approach have found the need to appoint one or more persons to the role of facilitator. In the case of Quality Circles such an appointment is essential.

The term 'facilitate' means 'to make easy or to make possible', and this adequately describes the role of a facilitator.

The task of facilitation of management project teams differs somewhat from that for the facilitation of groups of direct employees. The main reason is that in general the managers are usually in a position to do their own facilitating; they are more mobile than the other types of group, and can make higher-level decisions without the need for authorization. Project team facilitators are usually part-time appointments and they are there to help the groups to become properly established, and to form a link between groups, strategic teams and specialist help when required.

The facilitator is not usually a member of any specific team, but has close links with them all. Ideally, he or she will be a member of the company strategic team, and will be the main source of detailed information regarding the health and vitality of the groups, the state of their projects and so on.

Facilitating for teams of direct employees is often more demanding than for project teams. In the early stages, the teams will usually require a great deal of support from the facilitator, and great care should be taken to ensure the selection of the best possible person. Facilitating at this level is also more demanding in terms of time and, as a rough guide, it can be assumed that a facilitator will spend approximately three hours a week in support of each group. In other words, fifteen teams will require one full-time facilitator. Many companies are wary of the cost of full-time facilitators, but the potential for improvement through this process is such that even with this additional cost, very attractive returns on investment should be achieved.

The need for facilitators should be identified at an early stage in the pre-planning. Ideally, they should be appointed as early as possible, and preferably before the implementation of the process has begun. The best facilitators usually have great in-depth knowledge of all aspects of the process within the company, and this is usually the result of having been involved from the beginning.

Project sponsor

A further supportive element found to be popular in some companies is the concept of the project sponsor.

This person is not a member of a project team, but may be a member of a company, regional or functional strategic team. The object is to ensure that each official project is seen to have formal legitimacy and is clearly supported from a high level.

The project sponsor will normally be a senior executive, and will maintain a close relationship in a supportive role to the project team leader.

Team leaders

MANAGEMENT PROJECT TEAMS

These leaders can be selected from those who, by the nature of their job or responsibilities, have been chosen to lead a nominated improvement project.

The team leader usually participates in the subsequent selection of the team members. This is preferable to the alternative of building a team without the collaboration of the leader, and then to expect him or her to be successful – personalities may clash.

Figure 9.2 indicates how projects are usually identified, leaders and teams selected and projects undertaken through to holding the gains.

DIRECT EMPLOYEE GROUPS

Because these teams are normally formed from within a single department, and team members concerned with direct work-related problems, it is normal and preferable for the team leader to be the foreman or supervisor of their group.

This approach avoids problems of the supervisor feeling bypassed, and it also helps to ensure that projects selected are genuinely work-related, and that the process has formal legitimacy.

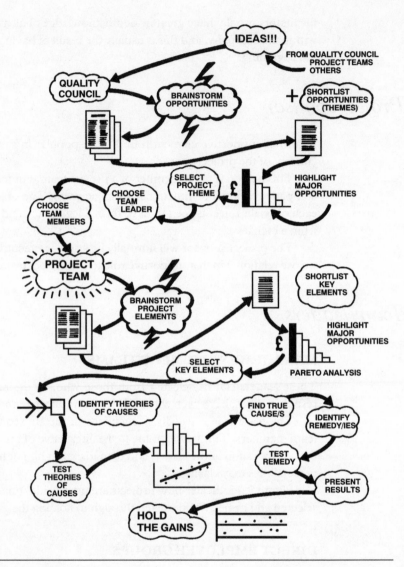

Figure 9.2 Project by project improvement

Conclusion

So far we have considered the involvement of employees from a conceptual viewpoint. In recent years more and more organizations are beginning to realize the value of highly focused employee participation. This has led to the introduction of a concept known as Total Productive Maintenance or 'autonomous self-managing workgroups'. This is an extremely forceful concept and is therefore covered in detail in the next chapter.

10 TOTAL PRODUCTIVE MAINTENANCE

The previous chapter dealt with participation in general. In this chapter participation will be considered as it applies specifically to the goal of JIT.

Total Productive Maintenance (TPM) challenges the view that maintenance is no more than a function that operates in the background and only appears when needed. The objective of TPM is to engender a sense of joint responsibility between supervision, operators and maintenance workers, not simply to keep machines running smoothly, but also to extend and optimize their performance overall. The results are proving to be remarkable.

Overall Equipment Effectiveness

The goals of TPM are measured using an Overall Equipment Effectiveness (OEE) ratio:

OEE $\quad=\quad$ availability × performance × quality rate

$$\text{Availability} \quad = \quad \frac{\text{available time} - \text{downtime} \times 100}{\text{available time}}$$

Downtime can be calculated by adding together the amounts of time lost due to equipment failures, set-up and adjustment, and idling and minor stoppages.

$$\text{Performance rate} = \frac{\text{ideal cycle time} \times \text{processed quantity} \times 100}{\text{operating time}}$$

Speed losses are calculated by combining time lost due to idling and minor stoppages and time lost due to reductions in speed.

$$\text{Quality rate} = \frac{\text{processed quantity} - \text{defective quantity} \times 100}{\text{processed quantity}}$$

Defective quantity is calculated by combining defects in process start-up and reduced yield.

Typical calculations for OEE prior to implementation of JIT-related strategies usually range between 40 per cent and 60 per cent with the former being the more normal. Experience indicates that it is possible to raise this to between 80 per cent and 90 per cent in a period of some two to three years from start-up. However, the improvement will usually follow an exponential upward curve with the bulk of the gains being in the latter part of the period.

The 'six big losses'

Total Productive Maintenance was developed in Japan in 1971 by the Japanese Institute of Plant Maintenance (JIPM). TPM involves everyone in the company. The JIPM also identified what they refer to as the 'six big losses'. According to the JIPM, 'The goal of TPM is to increase the productivity of plant and equipment'. Consequently, maximized output will be achieved through the effort of minimizing input – improving and maintaining equipment at optimum levels to reduce its life cycle cost. Cost-effectiveness is a result of an organization's ability to eliminate the causes of the 'six big losses' that reduce equipment effectiveness:

● reduced yield (from start-up to stable production)
● process defects
● reduced speed
● idling and minor stoppages
● set-up and adjustment
● equipment failure.

The JIPM also states that:

> Both operations and maintenance departments should accept the responsibility of keeping equipment in good condition. To eliminate the waste and losses hidden in a typical factory environment, we must acknowledge the central role of workers in managing the production process. No matter how thoroughly plants are automated or how many robots are installed, people are ultimately responsible for equipment operation and maintenance. Every aspect of a machine's performance, whether good or bad, can be traced back to a human act or omission. Therefore, no matter how advanced the technology is, people play a key role in maintaining the optimum performance of the equipment.

Whilst in the early stages the workforce involvement will usually be limited to membership of multi-layer teams, in the longer term, usually in around two to three years, the operator involvement will have developed into fully autonomous self-managing maintenance group activities.

Typically, in the early stages, a pioneer team of managers, technical specialists (including maintenance department personnel) and operators work on one problem production line. Using the project by project disciplines the team select specific problems from amongst the so-called 'six big losses' that they believe can be solved quickly and easily but which produce tangible and measurable improvements.

At this stage, the programme is then given a high profile and extended to include everyone in the plant. The initial teams of workers will be trained in the problem-solving tools and taught how to select process-related problems as projects. Managers and specialists will act as consultants to the newly formed teams and guide them in the best use of problem-solving methods.

5S housekeeping programmes

At this point the workers will be encouraged to carry out simple plant-cleaning activities using the 5S housekeeping concept referred to later in this chapter. This can be likened to steam cleaning the engine of an automobile. When dirty, it is impossible to tell if there are any screws missing or loose, or if there are any oil leaks. However, after cleaning, missing screws can be easily identified, and after a few days, any possible oil leaks can be seen indicating worn oil seals or potential bearing failures. At the same time, the operator can begin to understand better how his or her machine actually works.

Even at this early stage it is not unusual to achieve a reduction of stoppages in the order of some 50 per cent. However, do not forget that this is a long process and that experience indicates it takes approximately three years to achieve the main benefits.

In parallel with this, the team leaders and supervisors will be trained in simple plant maintenance and the relevant technology. This will free up the time of the maintenance engineers to do more complex work and develop their own skills. Later, this training will be extended to the operators themselves.

As the teams begin to mature, they will soon be able to look after the machines themselves. As they become more confident there is a marked change in attitude and a will to take wider responsibility for the performance of their operations.

Some organizations around the world have used the Japanese Institute of Plant Maintenance's Plant Maintenance Excellence Award criteria to judge the quality of their productive maintenance efforts. The award includes the following 10 elements:

1 policy and objectives of TPM;
2 organization and operation;
3 small-group activities and autonomous maintenance;
4 training;
5 equipment maintenance;
6 planning and management;
7 equipment investment plans and maintenance prevention;
8 production volumes, scheduling, quality and cost;
9 safety, sanitization and environmental conservation;
10 results and assessments.

Full details of the award criteria can be obtained from:

Japanese Institute of Plant Maintenance,
Shuwa Shiba-Koen,
3-Chome Bldg,
3-1-38, Shiba-Koen,
Minato-ku,
Tokyo 105.

Other details may be obtained from their web site at:

http://www.jipm.or.jp/en/05/paddress.html

Getting started with TPM

Whilst the ultimate goal of TPM is the mature development and involvement of the workforce in autonomous maintenance self-management activities, it is not usually advisable to start at that level unless the organization is already heavily committed to the support of Quality Circle-style activities and these have been operating for probably a year or more.

Many organizations in the West have ignored this advice only to achieve disappointing results. In an environment in which the workforce have not been encouraged to voice their opinions or to participate in organized project by project improvement activities, the probability is that their initial reaction to management's suggestion that they participate in such activities is likely to be one of cynicism and mistrust. They will also rightly point out that there are many problems that should be tackled by management as well.

This is almost certain to be the case. In all work-related situations problems follow the Pareto principle. The Pareto principle will suggest that 80 per cent of the cost of maintenance-related activities will be accounted for by just 20 per cent of the problems. Conversely, 20 per cent of the cost is shared by 80 per cent of the problems. If we study this further, we will find that the majority of the vital 20 per cent of the problems are management solvable not worker controllable. These problems will include those related to the following:

- overall maintenance policy
- housekeeping
- yield losses
- set-up cycle times
- equipment failures.

The workforce will be very aware of this. Any suggestion that they are responsible will usually be met with stiff resistance and accusations that the big problems are caused by management not by the workforce. Unfortunately for management these observations will almost always be correct. Maintenance often will have been neglected, mostly relying on swift action following breakdowns rather than using preventive measures. Overall housekeeping may be poor with work areas badly lit and in a poor state of decoration. Walkways may be uneven and covered with grease and dirt. Machines may be filthy and caked with years of dirt. Set-up processes may be poorly defined and badly organized.

Management would be well advised to make a visible start on these problems before attempting to approach the workforce. Then the managers will be coming with clean hands and will almost certainly meet with a better reception. Such an approach also provides the strongest possible indication of management commitment, which is a vital element in obtaining the support of the workforce.

As a leading Japanese consultant once observed, 'In the West you think that continuous process improvement is like lighting a fire. In this case it is better to start at the bottom. Unfortunately, it is more like sweeping the stairs in which case it is better to start from the top!'

Ideally, commencing TPM should be an outcome of the Hoshin Kanri (Management by Policy) process. Hoshin Kanri is a term used in Japan, but which does not translate easily into English. It indicates a system through which strategy is determined at the top of the organization, translated into goals and then cascaded down through the organization. Concepts such as the 'balanced score card' described by Caplan and Norden, Harvard Business School, in which individual goals are determined, work well in conjunction with this concept.

These policies will include all of the features to be found in the criteria for the European and US National Quality Awards. (See Chapter 11 for these.) Those related to TPM can be seen on the following tree diagram:

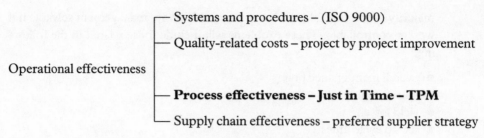

Operational effectiveness
— Systems and procedures – (ISO 9000)

— Quality-related costs – project by project improvement

— **Process effectiveness – Just in Time – TPM**

— Supply chain effectiveness – preferred supplier strategy

This policy should set out the goals, budgets, resources, responsibilities and timetable for the TPM programme.

The TPM Steering Committee

A steering committee should be formed which ideally should link back to the overall Company-wide Steering Team if this is in existence. Otherwise it should link to the top Performance Improvement Management team. Membership should include representatives from the central maintenance department, line maintenance if it exists, technical specialists, line management, personnel and training, finance, the union if applicable, supervision and the TPM Facilitator (see below).

The committee should be both visible and accessible to all of the workforce. Its responsibilities include:

- interpretation of the overall policies of the Company-wide Committee as they relate to TPM
- clarification of its own terms of reference
- creation of the implementation and roll-out plan
- selection of initial management-led projects (maximum four projects, minimum two projects)
- selection of management team leaders
- provision of training for the initial teams (typically, three days by qualified expert)
- identification of first departments to commence worker involvement activities
- training of workers in problem-solving skills
- development of training plan for supervisors in simple maintenance routines
- development of plan for extending training to the workforce
- creation of awareness training materials and development of awareness training plan
- design of publicity materials including answers to the most frequently asked questions
- design of employee handbook

- selection of TPM Facilitators if not already selected (see below for selection criteria and role of Facilitator)
- monitoring results and dealing with matters arising.

The TPM Facilitator

It is now widely recognized that all forms of small-group activities require the services of someone who has both the time and ability to provide continuous support for the activities of such groups. It is often those organizations that have been poorly advised in this respect that run into trouble. Careful selection of such personnel is therefore critical if success is to be achieved.

ROLE OF THE FACILITATOR

The Facilitator is the main link between the autonomous maintenance teams and the Steering Committee. He or she will be the committee's main source of information about the activities of the group and the means by which the activities of the committee are communicated to the teams. The Facilitator will ensure that teams are properly trained and that they have the necessary resources to carry out their work. During improvement projects, the Facilitator will be available to ensure that the teams are following the methods they have been taught and will coach them and help increase their self-confidence as they begin to mature. Good Facilitators will also take it upon themselves to ensure that they themselves are at the forefront of knowledge in the field of TPM and its related sciences and disciplines.

SELECTION OF THE FACILITATOR

Whilst it is desirable that the Facilitator should have a good background in the maintenance sciences, this is secondary to their personal qualities. If these are excellent, then the initial knowledge of TPM-related disciplines is not critical. Requisite personal qualities are:

1 First and foremost, the candidate should be an enthusiast for this type of work.
2 They should also be someone who is trusted and respected at all levels of the organization and who has credibility with key managers and other influential personnel.
3 They should be quick to learn, have a warm personality and considerable self-confidence.
4 A good Facilitator is someone who is happy to let others take the credit when they are following his or her advice.

5 Ideally the Facilitator should have training skills although in some cases this may be devolved to others such as the training department.

Initial projects

Initial projects for the TPM process should be selected using the following criteria:

1 Those which have a positive impact on the work environment, for example housekeeping. This is in order to gain the appreciation of the workforce.
2 Those which are relatively simple but with a tangible payback. This is to gain credibility for the project process as a way of achieving results and as a motivator for team members. Everyone likes to think that they have done something useful.
3 If possible, choose projects in which the advice of members of the workforce can be of value. When this is forthcoming make sure to offer thanks and give recognition.
4 Make sure that the projects selected can predictably be completed and the results implemented in around three months from the beginning or less. People will lose interest if the projects go on for too long.
5 Be very careful not to take on anything too challenging in the early days. A failure at this stage would be a major upset in the implementation process. Remember, Rome was not built in a day. TPM is a long-term process and a little care at the outset will reap huge rewards later.
6 Projects selected should be either measurable or countable and stated in a negative form. For example, loss of yield from process X would be measurable and stated in its negative form. 'Too many breakdowns on Line X' is countable and also in the negative form. The reason for the use of the negative is that the next question will be 'What causes ...?'. Usually there will be many theories offered by the team members. If properly trained, the team will use such techniques as process mapping and analysis, the fishbone diagram or other language data techniques in order to identify and analyse these possible causes in a scientific manner. Always remember that if you cannot quantify the problem then you will not be able to verify its severity and you will not be able to demonstrate an improvement.

Improvement project management

1 Before attempting to find the possible causes, it is also important to record the current state of the problem. Collect and organize data to show its severity, and use graphical techniques such as the Pareto diagram in order to dramatize the situation. Frequently, with housekeeping-related problems

or in cases where there may be severe wear or catastrophic breakdown, photographs or video can be ideal methods for recording the current state. They will also be useful historical evidence years later. For example, at Short Bros. Ltd, the Belfast-based aerospace company, they have an exhibition showing the internal condition of all of the departments before they began the improvement process and then, subsequently, the various stages of progress over the following years. It makes an impressive display.

2 When the possible causes have been identified, before going on to the next stage, it would be as well to seek the opinions of the relevant members of the workforce and anyone else who may have valid opinions. In one such situation in the early days at Short Bros. Ltd, a worker was asked why he thought leakages occurred around the small rivets which joined adjacent parts of an aircraft wing. He explained that he believed the shape of the tool fixture was incorrect and suggested an improvement. His idea was implemented and proved successful. One of the more cynical of the managers asked 'Why did you not tell us before?'. The response was 'You never asked.'! The more the opinions of the workforce are solicited, the more enthusiastic they will become and the easier it will be to gain volunteers for autonomous workgroup activities when these first management-level projects have been completed.

3 Typical problems and possible causes include:

Loss	Possible cause
Breakdown losses	Checking and cleaning
Equipment failure losses	ditto
Set-up losses	Waiting instructions
Jig and tool losses	ditto
Start-up losses	Waiting materials
Other downtime losses	Waiting personnel
Minor stoppage and idling losses	ditto
Reduced speed losses	Quality instructions, measurement and calibration
Defect and rework losses	ditto
Waiting instructions	Management planning
Waiting materials	ditto
Equipment downtime	Management organization
Equipment performance	ditto
Methods and procedures	ditto
Skills and loss of morale	Management environment
Line organization losses	Management training
Measurement and setting losses	Resource planning

4 Finding the true causes from amongst the many theoretical causes requires the collection and analysis of data. Usually the data for the type of projects

selected for TPM activities are easily recovered and do not normally demand the use of sophisticated techniques such as designed experiments and so on. These tools will be more appropriate for the more complex problems to be tackled by specialists and engineers.

5 In almost all cases the data will provide convincing evidence as to the true causes. When these have been determined, the team will then turn their attention to the selection of appropriate remedies. Depending on the nature of the causes, these may be many and varied and will therefore require evaluation. Remedies are evaluated in respect of cost of implementation, difficulty to implement, resistance to change, further problems that may arise from the solution, and reversibility. Wherever possible, the most popular remedies will be from amongst those which are irreversible, in other words those which are foolproof. If non-foolproof solutions are to be implemented they will need to be included in periodic audits to ensure that the improvement is continuing to be applied.

Following the completion of the early projects, a full TPM awareness programme can be implemented. The initial projects should be used to demonstrate management commitment and the methodology involved.

It is recommended that the training of direct employees takes place on a voluntary basis and initially in those areas where the greatest enthusiasm is detected. It is possible, depending upon the history of the organization, that there may be suspicion and even hostility in some areas despite the proven commitment of the managers. Provided that there are areas where a start can be made, this resistance should not prove to be a problem. As soon as the initial teams begin to show achievements and appear enthusiastic about this work, others will very soon come forward to participate from other sections of the organization. In many respects, this early reluctance on the part of some may prove to be an advantage. It is important to start off with a number of small-scale tryouts. Remember, not only are the teams going through a learning experience but the managers and specialists are doing so as well. Therefore it is important not to be too ambitious. Only start as many teams as can be safely supported through their early learning experience. If there is too high a level of initial enthusiasm from too many people, there is the possibility of disappointment when some of them discover that it may be some time before they can become involved. The only solution to this is either to increase the amount of support to be given in these early stages or to simplify the initial activities and restrict them to those which can be more easily handled by the teams and which are less demanding on the facilitation resources.

As the teams develop their capabilities, it then becomes possible to increase their range of problem-solving skills. They can also be encouraged to tackle more difficult problems and to introduce a degree of self-management. This can best be achieved by encouraging the teams to set themselves annual targets for process performance improvements. Initially, they should be taught to collect data to determine the overall operating efficiency of their unit of operations. To do so will require data on set-up times, start-up times, delays, yield from basic materials, inventory in their section, break-down losses, running processes at less than full speed, and so on. This information can then be used to set targets and enable the selection of appropriate projects.

Work groups can also be encouraged to participate in what in Japan are referred to as 5S campaigns. Whilst the exact translation of each of the five S's does not transfer directly into a convenient set of 'S' words in English, the following can be safely regarded as being very near equivalents:

SEIRI – Systemizing and Standardization
Utilization of equipment:
Classification, tool selection, material and suitable equipment for each task or activity, information selection and recording of that required to perform the task.

SEITON – Sorting
Tidying up:
Finding the right place to save objects and general organization of the place of work.

SEISOU – Sweeping
Cleaning:
Keeping the work area clean.
Retaining only the information and items needed to work on the specific tasks.

SEIKETSU – Sanitizing
Health, hygiene:
Creating good conditions of hygiene, checking, illumination, atmospheric pollution, sound and temperature, and so on.
Keeping visible records providing easy evaluation and comprehension.

SHITSUKE – Self-discipline
Self-discipline:
Developing the habit of looking at procedures and rules. Self-control and self-direction.

Typical TPM implementation plan

The following is a summary of a typical development programme for the establishment of autonomous maintenance teams as recommended by the Japanese Institute of Plant Maintenance:

1 Elimination of the 'six big losses' based on project teams organized by the TPM Steering Committee.
2 Planned maintenance to be carried out by the maintenance department.
3 Autonomous maintenance to be carried out by the production department in seven steps as follows:

- initial cleaning
- actions to address the causes of problems identified when removing dust and dirt
- establishing cleaning and lubrication standards
- general inspection training
- autonomous inspection
- establishment of general workplace standards
- full implementation of autonomous maintenance

4 Preventive engineering carried out mainly by the plant engineering department.
5 Easy-to-manufacture product design carried out mainly by the product design department.
6 Education and training to support the above activities.

In parallel to the above, training can begin in simple maintenance procedures. Operators can be made aware of the differences between Improvement Maintenance (IM), Preventive Maintenance (PM), Breakdown or Corrective Maintenance (CM) and Planned Maintenance (Pl.M).

Table 10.1 Simple test for training in TPM

Activities	IM	PM	CM	Pl.M
Process modification				
Planned maintenance				
Unscheduled maintenance				
Process redesign				
Change set-up procedures				
Emergency repairs				
Diagnostic fault detection				
Implementation of remedial action				
Foolproofing				
Time to time trend analysis				
Diagnostic fault detection				
Process Capability Studies				
Failure mode and effects analysis				
Fault tree analysis				

To check on understanding simple tests can be used such as the one shown in Table 10.1. Here the trainee is required to mark the appropriate column that he or she thinks is appropriate for the particular maintenance-related activity.

Multi-skilling

Some of the training can be given in the company using employees from the central maintenance department. More detailed training can be given using the services of the Engineering Department from the local College of Further Education. The syllabi should include such subjects as basic mechanics. hydraulics, electrical technology, lubrication, fitting, disassembly and assembly of basic mechanisms, the product life cycle – wear-in, normal useful life and wear-out modes – preventive maintenance policies and the conditions applicable to failure replacement, block replacement, the concept of whole-life cost of ownership, and so on.

Incentives to participate in this form of training can be both financial and through recognition. The use of recognition can be based on an adaptation of the Nissan Multi-Skill Monitoring method. At each process line a large squared matrix board can be erected, as shown in Figure 10.1. On the left-hand side of the vertical axis, each of the employees in the department or

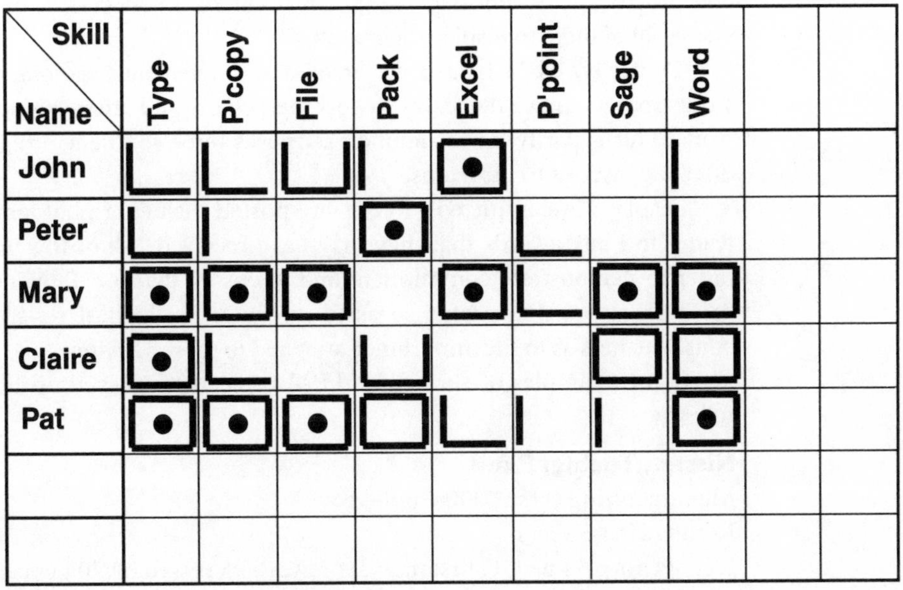

Skill / Name	Type	P'copy	File	Pack	Excel	P'point	Sage	Word		
John	⌐	⌐	⊔	ǀ	◉			ǀ		
Peter	⌐	ǀ		◉	⌐			ǀ		
Mary	◉	◉	◉		◉	⌐	◉	◉		
Claire	◉	⌐		⊔			▢	▢		
Pat	◉	◉	◉	▢	⌐	ǀ	ǀ	◉		

Figure 10.1   Typical multi-skill board

section is listed. On the top of the horizontal axis, each of the relevant skills is described.

For each skill, against the appropriate operator, the boxes are filled in the following manner:

1 If the operator has been trained to perform the task and can do so with supervision but only in three times or less than standard time, a thick dark vertical line is drawn down the left-hand side of the box. It will look like a letter I.

2 When the operator can perform the task under supervision in standard time, a further line is drawn along the bottom of the box. It will now appear as an L.

3 When the operation can be performed without supervision in standard time or better then a further line is drawn down the right-hand side of the box. It will now appear as a squared-off letter U.

4 When the operator is sufficiently skilled to be able to train others then the line is extended across the top of the box making a complete rectangle.

5 If the operator becomes sufficiently skilled to be able to make improvements to the process a heavy dot is put in the centre of the box.

Recognition

In all organizations where success is known to have been achieved, considerable efforts have been made to give recognition to successful teams and to enable all of them to display their work.

Typically, TPM boards are erected at convenient locations near to the work areas to enable the teams to post their charts and other examples of their work. This is partly for recognition purposes but also to encourage others to offer suggestions to the teams.

Displays of completed projects are posted including photographs of the teams and any awards that they may have received. All of this activity is in order to demonstrate commitment and to ensure that the TPM concept has the highest possible profile so as to maintain the highest possible level of consciousness as to the importance attached to these activities.

Some examples of successful TPM projects, displayed on the Internet, follow:

Nissan, Tochigi Plant
Manufacturing cars, 7 000 employees.
Results after 3 years.
No. of cars passing QC first time, no rework increased by 70 per cent.
No. of breakdowns reduced by 80 per cent.
Overall equipment efficiency increased by 30 per cent.
Comment from company: 'We cannot manage our plant without TPM.'

Nippon Lever, Utsunomiya Plant

Manufacturing Lux soap, household cleaners.

Results after 2 years.

Reduction in operating costs – £2.8 million.

Cost of introducing TPM £90 000!

Production efficiency:

⇒ Domestic filling line – up from 76 per cent to 95 per cent.

⇒ High-speed soap line – up from 54 per cent to 85 per cent.

Comment from company: 'The ideal status of a machine is to have no defects, no breakdowns. You may think that's impossible. But when you see the Nippon Lever plant, you realize it is possible.'

11 JIT ASSESSMENT

US National and European Quality Awards

Whilst the US National Quality Award and the European Quality Award have now been in existence for several years, for some reason Americans have been far more active in using the criteria of their award for the enhancement of their industries. As a consequence, American organizations have in many cases managed to close the gap between their business performance and that of their leading Japanese rivals. In contrast, whilst the award criteria for the European model are at least as well thought out and structured, there is a noticeable reluctance by most companies to pay much attention to it and to avail themselves of its self-assessment criteria. In fact it has been claimed that fewer than 3 per cent of British companies were making any use of the concept in 1997. The probability is that this reluctance derives from the gross over-attention paid to ISO 9000, the exaggerated claims made for its benefits and therefore disillusionment due to its lack of any real impact on business results. This may in turn have led to suspicion that the European Excellence Model criteria may be more of the same. If this is the case then it is a tragedy. Whilst the achievement of ISO 9001 or 9002 may help in gaining a few points in the 'Processes' section of the European Excellence Model, the structure, purpose and content of the two are significantly different.

When first published, the European Excellence Model differed from both the US National Quality Award and the Japanese Deming Prize mainly by being focused on business results, the rationale being that unless the actions taken by a company resulted in improved business results, they would have doubtful validity. More recently, the American award criteria have also moved towards this advantage of the European award criteria with the consequence that whilst the two awards are structured differently, the content of both is largely similar at least in so far as they relate to the application of Just In Time strategies.

This chapter has been included for two main reasons. First, in order to enable the reader to evaluate the impact that JIT should make on their organization's performance against the European Quality Award self-assessment criteria, and second, hopefully to stimulate interest in the award itself. It should be noted, however, that the principle of continuous improvement is adopted in each of the Deming, Baldrige and the European awards. Therefore, the criteria may change slightly from year to year. To evaluate a programme precisely, it is recommended that the appropriate award documentation is obtained from the relevant source. A further point to note is the fact that most countries also have their own national awards. In the case of European countries, the majority are based precisely on the European Excellence Model with the notable exception of Sweden, which uses the Baldrige model.

In the following text, references are from a recent version of the European Excellence Model. Due to the similarity of thinking between this and the Baldrige Award criteria, although the structure of the various categories of questions is different, it would not be difficult to transfer from one to the other in the case of relevance to JIT.

The European Excellence Model

As can be seen from Figure 11.1, the European Excellence Model is divided into nine separate categories: Leadership, People Management, Policy and Strategy, Resources, Processes, People Satisfaction, Customer Satisfaction, Impact on Society and Business Results.

With the possible exception of 'Impact on Society', a properly conceived JIT programme will impact on each of these in varying degrees. Note that each of the elements of the self-assessment criteria has a weighting. Each element contains a number of key questions which should be answered using a rating from 0–4. For any evaluation other than zero, objective evidence must be available to support the scoring.

The nine categories, and how JIT impacts on each of them, are described in the remainder of this section.

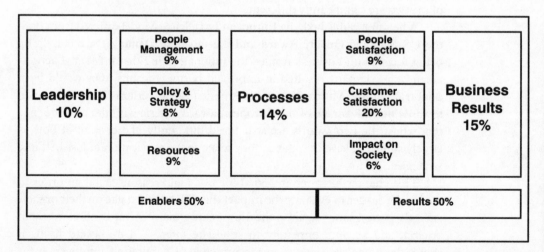

Figure 11.1 The European Excellence Model

LEADERSHIP

In this category the objective is to determine how well the the executive team and all of the other managers lead the Company-wide Business Performance Improvement Programme (referred to in the model as Total Quality) as being the fundamental means for continuous improvement.

The issues most affected by a serious JIT programme in this category include:

'Executives and managers take positive steps to:
⇨ *demonstrate commitment to Total Quality*
⇨ *make themselves accessible and listen to employees*
⇨ *act as role models leading by example (e.g. taking part in improvement projects)*
⇨ *give and receive training (e.g. in improvement tools)*
⇨ *communicate with employees (e.g. briefing groups).'*

⇨ Score 0–4

Considerations

There may be positive evidence of the chief executive and his senior managers leading the Total Quality programme. If JIT is a major part of the business programme, then the existence of the JIT Steering Committee led by the chief executive would be a key consideration here.

There may be quality improvement teams which demonstrate that managers and staff members are committed to Total Quality. A Total Productive Maintenance initiative organized in the manner described in Chapter 10 would be a clear demonstration of this feature.

Senior managers giving training to all the employees would also be satisfied by the appropriate training given for the development of TPM.

Since both JIT and TPM should be part of the company's vision and mission derived from the business plan, if this is the case, then this issue would also be satisfied.

The next relevant statement suggests:

'Executives and managers provide timely recognition and appreciation of the effort and successes of individuals and teams at local and divisional levels and at customers and suppliers.'

Score 0–4

Considerations

TPM notice-boards with pictures of team members, descriptions of completed projects, team targets and performance monitoring, and charts showing the extent of multi-skilling, as described in Chapter 10, would be impressive at the local level. Internal conventions, newsletters and awards for performance improvement would also be relevant.

Training in simple maintenance and use of local colleges would also be influential.

Supplier involvement in JIT activities together with supplier participation in training programmes and approved supplier status could contribute significantly to this.

'Executives and managers provide support in the form of resources and assistance to their employees in:
⇒ *funding learning, facilitation, improvement activities, those taking initiatives and championing a cause*
⇒ *helping to define priorities in improvement activity.'*

Considerations

Costs of relevant training should be related to the results. This can be achieved in part through monitoring the effect on the Overall Equipment Effectiveness ratio described in Chapter 10. The more progressive companies tend to spend around 4 per cent of sales revenue on training but most of this is linked to results monitoring.

Again, the facilitation requirement for autonomous maintenance teams will influence scoring in this section.

'Executives and managers take positive steps to:
⇒ *meet customers and suppliers and anticipate problems*
⇒ *set up "partnerships" with customers and suppliers*
⇒ *participate in joint improvement.'*

Considerations

The 'Toyota family' concept is a good example of this. Just in Time can only be effective when it is applied along the entire supply chain starting with the primary producers and working through to the ultimate user.

JIT requires the preferred supplier approach where customer and supplier are each aware of the value of their mutual dependence. This is in contrast with the more familiar 'multiple sourcing' method using threats and penalties. The typical penalty is to give the next order to a competitor. Under this system there is no mutual aid and the relationship usually includes considerable mistrust between the parties.

In a JIT regime, the ultimate producer usually provides expert assistance and training for the upstream suppliers in order to facilitate continuous improvement.

POLICY AND STRATEGY

In this category the objective is to determine the extent of development of the organization's vision, mission, strategic direction and how well these are deployed down into the organization.

Whilst there are implications in all of the questions, the most relevant which deserve separate treatment are as follows:

'*The concept of Total Quality is reflected in the organization's values, vision, mission statements and strategy statements, e.g. customer first, empowerment, teamwork and continuous improvement.*'

Considerations

JIT could appear in a mission statement related to processes in which it is clearly stated that the organization will be quick to respond to customer requests through the development of highly responsive processes that operate throughout the supply chain, with negligible inventory or interruptions to the smooth flow of materials or instructions and other relevant documentation.

It will require evidence that a 'pull' process is in operation at the customer end of the chain in which the customer requirements determine what is to be produced and by when.

There must be an employee involvement programme similar to that described in Chapter 10, with the development of autonomous self-managing groups involving teamworking and continuous improvement activities.

The next element advises that:

'*Policy and Strategy are formed with inputs from:*
⇒ *feedback from customers and suppliers*
⇒ *feedback from the organization's people*
⇒ *data gained through benchmarking competitors and "best in class" organizations and processes.*'

Considerations

The biggest most likely impact of JIT on customers will be the difference between making for stock and making to order. One might imagine that the customer would prefer to buy from stock as the product will be immediately available. However, if the product can be made to order very quickly, as it should with Just in Time, then there will be a perceived advantage if this results in the opportunity for a degree of customization. Clearly, there are opportunities here to make an impression on the customer of a very high level of efficiency. There is also the advantage with some degradable products that making to order will result in the elimination of shelf-time losses.

The supplier's reaction to a Just in Time policy will be very dependent upon the likelihood of a long-term relationship, and also on-line technical support. If these do not appear to be forthcoming and the supplier is being expected to perform without knowing how, he or she will more than likely take a very jaundiced view of the whole approach. It is critically important if JIT is to be achieved to maintain the closest possible relationship with suppliers.

JIT cannot be achieved without the intensive involvement of the line people in the autonomous self-management activities of TPM and the intensive application of on-line Statistical Process Control, particularly as a diagnostic tool. Any really serious Total Quality programme would be able to demonstrate involvement of the workforce beyond the expectations of most 'empowerment' programmes. This is perhaps the most significant difference between the European and US Quality Awards as compared with the Japanese Deming Prize. In the case of the latter, more tangible evidence of highly developed employee development and involvement would be expected.

Knowledge of competitors' capabilities is critical when developing JIT. As Dr Juran observed, it is not the fact of improving but the rate of improvement that is important. If the competitors are improving at a faster rate we will still be left behind eventually even if we are in front now. To be in front it is useful to observe 'parallel industries' as well as competitors. Competitors often do the same thing as we do. This is because people move around in industries, and also, providers of plant and equipment, industry-based consultants and trade magazines circulate information. Equally, people in different industries often do the same things by different means and sometimes we can learn from them. This is particularly applicable to such challenges as cycle and set-up time reduction strategies.

The next relevant point in the Policy and Strategy category is:

'*The organization regularly evaluates the effectiveness and relevance of its policy and strategy and systematically reviews and improves it.*'

Considerations

The closed feedback loop of management control (PDCA cycle) if applied should provide continuous feedback on process-related performance data, then weekly, monthly and half-yearly summaries and reviews at each ascending level of hierarchy. At the highest level there would be an annual audit and review at two levels: 1) how much of the JIT plan is in place and working, and 2) the tangible results achieved against the plan, for example lead time reduction, inventory reduction, and so on.

PEOPLE MANAGEMENT

This category considers how the organization makes use of the potential of its employees in order to achieve continuous performance improvement.

All of the questions raised in this category are impacted by the TPM element of JIT if the advice given in Chapter 10 is followed; therefore it is not necessary to deal with each one separately other than the following:

'There are specific methods of promoting employee improvement contributions such as an effective employee suggestion scheme.'

Considerations

Suggestion schemes in the West usually do not produce particularly impressive results. This is generally due to the fact that there is no policy deployment programme in place. For this reason the workers do not know the goals and therefore do not know what is important. However, when TPM has been introduced as part of a JIT programme, then the workers are motivated to make suggestions for improvement. Improvement suggestions in Japanese companies operating TPM are often in the order of 10–40 per month per employee with an implementation rate of around 96 per cent.

'Employees are rewarded for innovation.'

Considerations

Reward can take varied forms and it is not advisable to make too much of the idea of giving financial rewards. Where these are given it is advisable to make them as nominal as possible and not to relate them directly as a ratio of what may have been saved as a result of any group-based performance improvement project. Rewards can include recognition using various forms of media or by making improvements to the work environment. If there is to be any direct reward it should be to the workforce generally in response to the overall effect of the achievements.

RESOURCES

It is worth checking through the 'Financial', 'Information' and 'Application of Technology' sections of this category because there are some minor effects related to Just in Time. The main impact here is under the sub-section 'Material'. This is specifically related to JIT and says so as follows:

'All purchasing wherever possible is on a "just in time" basis.'

This means supplier JIT. Do not forget that JIT is not JIT unless it runs right through your organization as well. This is picked up in 'Processes', below:

'Out of stock situations do not occur.'

OK for the award criteria but overstock situations should not occur either!

'Fixed assets are utilized to optimum effect.'

This is a case for TPM if ever there was one!

'*Effective and efficient material inventory systems are used.*'

For this to have any real value, it should emphasize that to have the inventory system documented is not enough. Inventory at all points in the process must be subject to the PDCA concept and in a continuous state of improvement if JIT is to be realistically achieved.

The total points in this sub-section are worth 16/72 of the total × 9%.

PROCESSES

This category covers the core of JIT and TPM. With the exception of the question on ISO 9000 (the only place that it is specifically mentioned in the self-assessment method), the remainder of the 16 questions account for 60 × 14% of the total points.

Typically these are:

'*Critical business processes are clearly defined.*'
'*The impact on the business of critical processes has been evaluated.*'
'*Interface issues between business processes and elements of processes are resolved quickly and systematically.*'
'*The concept of process ownership is established.*'
'*Performance measures relative to process management have been identified, e.g. improvement goals and operating standards.*'
'*Feedback from customers and suppliers is used as a basis for setting operational standards.*'
'*Benchmarking is used when setting operational standards.*'
'*The performance of key business processes is regularly and systematically reviewed.*'
'*The organization stimulates innovation and creativity in business process improvement.*'
'*The creative talents of employees are brought to bear on process improvement.*'
'*A procedure exists for piloting new or changed processes.*'
'*Process changes are effectively communicated to all those affected.*'
'*Employee training where appropriate is always undertaken before process changes.*'
'*Processes are verified as being capable of operating to specified requirements.*'
'*There is a procedure for the audit and review of process changes.*'

CUSTOMER SATISFACTION, PEOPLE SATISFACTION, IMPACT ON SOCIETY, AND BUSINESS RESULTS

These are outcomes to be measured whereas the previous categories are 'inputs'. Therefore, where relevant it is possible to determine the effect of the

JIT programme. There should be a noticeable improvement in 'Customer Satisfaction' as a result of shorter lead times, more consistent quality and reliable deliveries. A substantial effect on 'People Satisfaction,' some effect on 'Impact on Society' and a very significant impact on financial 'Business Results' should also be observable.

Note: One of the key principles of both the US National Award and the European Award and its national derivatives is the continuous development of the award criteria themselves. Therefore, they are subject to possible annual change. If you have an out-of-date copy it would be as well to obtain the current version for a serious evaluation of your organization's health in this respect.

Conclusion

Many concepts and techniques have been explored in this book. None of them is simple, and none of them stands alone. The real power lies in total interpretation, one of the outcomes of which is JIT through the positive application of these concepts, and there will then be nothing to stop any organization becoming one of the most powerful companies on earth. If all companies apply the concepts, the likelihood is that society in general will be changed, and the entire work ethic altered.

Work is not something we have to whip ourselves with. Work should be one of the most rewarding and fulfilling aspects of our lives. It is through our work that we gain self-respect and the respect of others. Each of us has a duty not only to develop our own lives but to assist in the development of others. Promotion should not be seen as an opportunity to manipulate and manoeuvre others. Through promotion we have a greater opportunity to make the lives of subordinates more interesting, more rewarding and more enjoyable. The winning team is the one where everyone knows their place and there is a place for everyone. Nothing succeeds like success, and the pursuit of JIT is a goal worthy of any organization. All the concepts contained in this book are relevant whether JIT is the goal or not, because we are talking mainly about the best way to run a business.

Good luck!

INDEX